BADGER BARS & TAVERN TALES
An Illustrated History of Wisconsin Saloons

ISBN 1-930596-20-0

Published by THE GUEST COTTAGE, INC.
PO Box 848
Woodruff, WI 54568
1-800-333-8122
www.theguestcottage.com

Printed in Canada

The
Guest
Cottage Inc.
dba Amherst Press

HIGHLIGHTS

Welcome to... **WISCONSIN**

The Badger Bars State

INTRODUCTION

In 1987 the Authors of this book were given a tour of the still functioning, but slowly sinking, Walter's Brewery in Eau Claire, Wisconsin. This was not a tightly scripted multimedia tour that you might expect at Miller, Anheuser-Busch or Coors. It was ad-libbed, for the most part, by a high school age girl who took an hour or so off from her not exactly hectic front office duties. She led us through the warehouse, past the brew vats and around the canning and bottling lines. On the wall of the bottling house was an advertising clock above the workers at the labeling machine, it probably had been returned from a closed tavern. The clock had a lighted glass panel that once advertised Bub's Beer, from nearby Winona, but now had a Walter's Beer sticker pasted crookedly over the Bub's lettering. In the late eighties, times were tough as the small brewer competed against the major breweries. Money was very tight and they certainly did not have any extra for new clocks. But it did the job, and would have to do until better economic times arrived.

Unfortunately those times never did arrive. The brewery closed its doors in 1988 after over 100 years of brewing beer to stock tavern coolers, tap lines and customers' refrigerators throughout west-central Wisconsin. In the spring of 1998 we returned for a postmortem tour of the facility. The new owner of the property was considerate enough to escort us throughout the grounds and buildings. The years since the closing had not been kind to the old structures. Nearly every window had been broken and this allowed pigeons and bats to take up residence, pipes were lying bent and twisted, and there were hundreds of rotten cardboard cartons and paper bottle labels scattered nearly everywhere. In one of the buildings was a large dark room that was nearly empty. The concrete floor was covered by sheets of ice and dirty pools of water. We saw an object lying next to the far wall and walked carefully over to inspect it more closely. It turned out to be the advertising clock we saw on our previous tour, broken and rusted, lying face down in the water. It was the only piece of equipment left in the once busy bottling room.

OK, so it is not as sad as the death of Ol' Yeller, or more relevantly, the passing of Vince Lombardi, but with the loss of Walter's a little bit of the distinctiveness of Wisconsin was gone. It is noted when a business as large and historic as Walter's ceases operations. Less noticed has been the closings of many much smaller businesses throughout the state that are an even larger component in whatever makes Wisconsin, Wisconsin. Without beer and taverns, Wisconsin is just a colder and slightly more hilly and woodsy version of Nebraska. The neighborhood tavern is as much a part of the identity of Wisconsin as sunshine is to Florida or cold to Alaska. A variety of factors has led to many Wisconsin towns seeing the number of taverns fall by half or more in the past 30 years. The decline started with the advent of television which allowed people to stay at home and have entertainment brought to them, rather than going out and about on an evening of congenial good times. The downturn continued with both overall changes in attitudes and demographics as the World War II generation and the Baby Boomers moved past their prime time drinking years. Those changes and others could be extensively documented and precisely analyzed, but that would be about now and this book is about then. Let's just say that the significance of taverns and the associated drinking culture, integral components of the societal history of Wisconsin, is a topic that lacks a comprehensive and intelligent study. Until someone does that, this book will have to do. In the meantime, pour yourself a cold one and look through this chronicle of places filled with smoke, jokes, the music of jukeboxes, and of times less stressful, more casual and less sober. We hope you enjoy your time spent here, in the words of Buttsy and Evie, *"Your Pleasure, Our Success."*

OLD TIMES

Hops Upon The Brain

We've come from Lake Superior, where they raise their copper crops
But all the way a-down the road, there's nothing else but hops
The farmers give up corn and wheat, all other tilling stops
And all you hoe, or sow, or smell, is Hops, Hops, Hops!

You ask a man the time of day, "It's forty-five a pound"
Or, forty if you take them, as they lay upon the ground
We asked a man the other day, the right road to Berlin
He answered, "Seven acres now, and three more coming in."

But some there are, who are bound to keep, their conscience bright and clear
They go against your raising hops because they're used for beer
While others wished that they could raise the crop the whole year round
They do not care, they only want their sixty cents a pound.

We saw a landlord, down the road, a-scrubbing up the floor
We laughed, he sat and grumbled, And we rather think he swore
He says "Oh laugh if you liv'd here, you'd get enough of hops
My rats have left confound them all, a gone to picking hops.

On the road up from Waupaca, a chap sat on a rail
We though he was consumptive, he looked so wan and pale
He asked his girl to marry him, she said you blubber chops
Go home and put your head to soak, I'm going to picking hops.

They'll be a famine by and by, if this thing does not stop
For all the land is being used, to cultivate the hops
There'll be no corn, or wheat, or rye, nor any other crops
The only thing we'll get to eat will be Hops, Hops, Hops.

For it's Hops, Hops, Hops - Away with corn and grain
Wisconsin folks are running wild, with hops upon the brain
For it's Hops, Hops, Hops - Away with corn and grain
Wisconsin folks are running wild, with hops upon the brain.

H.S Thompson
Dubuque, Iowa 1868

–Transcribed from Civil War Era Sheet Music

Old Times & Ancient Age ⎯⎯⎯⎯●

The drinking history of Wisconsin probably started in 1634 when a canoe riding, beaver-seeking, French fur trader named Jean Nicolet might have taken a long pull out of a travel flask, a few paddle strokes into the Fox River near the area that would become the city of Green Bay. The story of Wisconsin taverns began much later, but still long ago, when the area was only about 30 years beyond being ruled by the British, a great forest formed a nearly unbroken canopy of leaves and branches which sheltered buffalo, grizzly bears, wolves and elk. The tiny settlement of Prairie du Chien was a small clearing in that vast shroud of nature. There and then a new species appeared, the Badger Bar Fly. For in 1823, the first licensed drinking establishment opened for business with the roll of several coins across a roughly hewn bar in exchange for a portion of spirits.

As early as 1840 the first house was built on the site by a man named Lamb, who conducted it as a Tavern, enjoying considerable patronage from the rough class of fisherman and hunters who passed this way. It is said that Lamb was an old soldier, doubtless of the War of 1812-1815 with Great Britain, also that he was so dissipated as to be unfit to conduct business. He married Margaret Demarie, an adopted daughter of Louis Demarie, a resident of what was then know as French town. In a former history of this county was printed a story of a murder that was committed at Lamb's place… as there are probably many people of Dunn County now living who have never heard of it, and also because in a work which aims to chiefly present the better side of human nature and of record worthy actions, it raises the veil for a moment by way of contrast, of scenes and actions of a different kind, which were not uncommon in pioneer days in this region, when the conditions of life were rough, and whiskey was cheap and almost universally consumed, often to excess. "In 1848 Lamb disposed of his business to his brother-in-law, Arthur McCann, who had come to the Chippewa River in the previous year with his brothers Stephen and Dan McCann, and had recently married Rosalie Demarie, a sister of Mrs. H.S. Allen. He had in partnership with J.C. Thomas commenced in 1843, and nearly completed, the "Blue Mill," now (1892) known as Badger State Mills. They had

continued…

employed on the work a man named Sawyer, who, when his time was up, came to McCann for a settlement. The business part of the meeting disposed of, Sawyer was invited by the former to a game of cards. The play went on until evening, the men drinking freely, when a dispute arose and hot words ensued. McCann threw a scale weight at Sawyer, when the latter at once repaired to the cabin of Philo Stone nearby, loaded a rifle, returned to the door of McCann's house and called him. When he came to the door, Sawyer took deliberate aim and shot him dead. The murderer made good his escape and was never afterwards heard of, though a large reward was offered for his apprehension. The young widow returned to her parents and afterwards married George P. Warren, the first County Clerk of Chippewa County. Philo Stone took possession of the tavern. His wife was a full blooded squaw and proved to be a good housekeeper.

–A History of Dunn County, Wisconsin 1925

The amusements of the early settlers were dancing, card-playing, hunting and fishing; in the latter of which the women were often as expert as the men; and so great was the love of dancing, that parties have been known to go from Eau Claire to Chippewa Falls, breaking the way through deep snow, to attend a dance. The fiddle was about all the kind of musical instrument known for many years. The first piano was brought by Phineas Branch and wife, in 1855, to the company's hotel, then kept by Mrs. Bullard. While keeping the hotel, which she did in the absence of her husband who was in California, Mrs. Bullard received an offer of marriage from an old Indian Chief, who admired her and pitied her lonely condition. The hotel was destroyed by fire in 1859, and this proved to be a great loss to the traveling public, and the seekers of amusement who had made it their headquarters for many years. It was also in this hotel that the live men of what is now Dunn County, resolved no longer to countenance the evils of drunkenness and gambling by the sale of liquor, or by indulging in the amusement of card playing. This occurred in 1854. A party had gathered one evening in the hotel bar-room to play for amusement. But they played for oysters, wine and finally money; and the whole resulted in something which they had not played for, a quarrel, or a row of some kind. The unlooked for result of that one evening's amusement set them to thinking, and being truly thinking men, they saw their error, and resolved thenceforth to make amends for it.

–The American Sketch Book, A Collection of Historical Incidents, 1874-5

The first recorded license for a tavern in Wisconsin was issued May 13, 1823, at Prairie du Chien, to John Brunet, by County Clerk L.L. Findly… In the decades prior to the Civil War, whoever liked might make liquor and so plentiful was Whiskey that it was sold for 12-1/2¢ a gallon, or 3¢ a drink over the tavern bar, often indeed being dispensed in pleasing schooners. People drank socially, not in the manner of a moonshiner with jug secreted in barn or cellar. A distillery existed in almost every neighborhood and a bushel of corn or rye would purchase a gallon of intoxicants. Whiskey was easily the favorite beverage and it was freely provided at Taverns, at homes, at barn raisings, and all social gatherings. Even women would take a little sweetened and diluted with water… an announcement that appeared in the Western Elkhorn June 10, 1852 was characteristic of the time:

Planter's House
Hales Corners, Greenfield,
Milwaukee County
By William Hale
"A Little of the Critter to be had if Desired"

–Stage Coach and Tavern Tales of the Old Northwest, 1930

The Baraboo Whiskey War ——●

"The Baraboo Whiskey War," the only war that Baraboo ever experienced, began in the barroom operated by Michael Kornel in the Wisconsin House, which stood at 136 Fourth Avenue, at the present time [1930] the location of the Al. Ringling Theater. During the spring of 1854 a great temperance wave engulfed the village, the leading spirits in the movement being the Reverend W. Cochrang, pastor of the Congregational Church, and the Reverend W.H. Thompson, Methodist minister.

At the time there lived in Baraboo a hard drinker who was a good citizen when not in his cups. He was a habitual patron of Kornels' bar in the Brick Tavern as the Wisconsin House was then called, to the sad neglect of his family; and at a desperate moment he made an attempt to take the life of his wife. The proprietor of the bar was besought to refrain from selling rum to this individual, but the appeal was unheeded. At last death intervened and the grave closed over the inebriate. The following Sabbath the Reverend Mr. Thompson became savagely eloquent over the sale of liquor in the village, then numbering about one thousand persons, and he wished "to God the thunderbolts of heaven would shiver the Brick Tavern and its contents, animate and inanimate." Attorney Pratt a few days later said that he would be happy to see "all the liquor in the village poured into the streets." Indignation gathered momentum as the days went by. An impromptu meeting was held and a few zealous women decided to attack with berserker fury. A writer describing the scene says:

"Hark! There's a sound of devastation—a sudden unloosing of liquid devils. The barroom of the Brick Tavern is in the process of female invasion. Fumes of liquor infect the air. Rye, Bourbon, and Fine Old Tom meet a common fate, and are rapidly absorbed by the parched earth in front of the hotel. The whilom dispenser of these evil spirits is wrapped in slumber; for it is early morn and none but sober citizens are aboard. The righteous work of destruction proceeds so quietly that his repose is not disturbed. In disposing of the empty bottles a corrugated schnapps is deposited in an ancient drygoods box in which a reveler of the previous evening has taken lodging. The breaking of the fallen bottles does not

At a point in time after the Whiskey War, but before Prohibition, a stylishly dressed fellow stops in a local saloon for a cold schooner of the product of Baraboo's City Brewery.

Bill Heifnider Collection

molest him, but there is a familiar smell about it which brings him to his feet with all the alacrity of a toper invited to drink; and he looks upon the strange scene and weeps."

After the visitation at the Brick Tavern, the band of women marched to a place nearby where they found the proprietor had sensed trouble and prudently locked the door. The visiting women made a proposition to purchase his wares, but while he hesitated to set a price an entrance was affected at the rear, and there was a quiet turning of faucets which soon flooded the floor. By the time they reached French Pete's the news of the revolution had spread throughout the village and a crowd gathered upon the scene. As one of the women attempted to gain entrance to Van Wendell's saloon she found her way blocked by a patron, who was caught by the waistband and rudely jerked aside, the suddenness of the attack causing some of the fastenings to give way. Deputy Sheriff Chapman advanced and began to read the riot act, calling upon the crowd to disperse. Addressing one of the ministers, he said, "Mr.

continued…

Cochrang you disperse!" The man of cloth calmly informed him he did not know how. ...Some days later a number of the ladies were escorted to Sauk City by Sheriff Munson that an impartial trail might be held. However, the case was remanded to circuit court, the women returning to Baraboo under protection of the officer. When the case was called by Judge Wheller the damage was fixed at one hundred and fifty dollars which was immediately paid, thus ending the Baraboo County War.

–Stage Coach and Tavern Tales
of the Old Northwest, 1930

50 years or so after the turmoil of the Great Whiskey War, Baraboo is home to "America's Finest Beer," if you can believe the rooftop advertising of the Ruhland Brewing Company.

Terry Post Collection

A Fiddler with an appreciative audience, from the Hayward area, about 60 years after the heyday of Uncle Ab's.

Uncle Ab's Mineral Point Tavern
"Liquor in the front and Poker in the rear"

Telling of their experiences at Uncle Ab Nichols' celebrated tavern at Mineral Point, Alexander F. Pratt says: "There were all kinds of fun, sports and music going on in the room… Such a sight as presented itself to our view we never saw before or since. It seemed that the miners were in the habit of assembling there on Saturday nights to drink, gamble, and frolic until Monday morning. The house was composed of three or four log cabins put together, with passage-ways cut from one to another. This was the only public house in the place. The barroom in which we were sitting contained a large bar, well supplied with all kinds of liquors. In one corner of the room was a faro bank discounting to a crowd around it; in another a roulette; and in another sat a party engaged in playing cards. One man sat back in a corner playing a fiddle, to whose music two others were dancing in the middle of the floor. Hundreds of dollars were lying upon the tables; and among the crowd were the principal men of the territory - men who held high and responsible office then and now… The landlord showed us through a dark room and opened the door on another, in which two men were also playing cards and a third lay drunk upon the floor. The landlord set down his light, seized the drunken man by the collar and dragged him into the next room."

–Stage Coach and Tavern Tales of the Old Northwest, 1930

The Liquor War

In the year 1874, a few of the go-ahead women of Menomonie resolved to put a stop to liquor traffic, and their influence at the polls was such that a law forbidding its sale was passed. The practicability of such a law in a single town is questioned by many; but having caused its adoption, the women were determined that those who broke it should be punished. It was like one man fighting an army, but women who could show such heroism when their country was needing aid, would not likely to falter themselves, or fail to instill in their daughters' minds some of their own heroism, at a time when the law was being transgressed. A caustic old settler, in a note, says: "The last great social spasm in Menomonie was the anti-liquor vote of last spring; and the anties, or, as some wags put it, the "aunties," carried the day. The ladies are now prosecuting the saloon-men, with unflagging zeal, and average success. But the end is not yet. The coming election promises to be ardent, spirits or no spirits."

Since the commencement of the liquor war, the vexed problem of whether or not lager-beer is intoxicating, has been decided in the negative. A brewer was arrested for selling a keg of beer to one of the citizens. He was fined, but appealed his case to a higher court. Great excitement prevailed when it was brought before Judge Humphrey. Several men swore that beer can intoxicate, and several men that it cannot. The judge seemed to be slightly prejudiced in favor of the beer, for he demanded to know of the temperance men how they knew beer to be intoxicating, and if it ever intoxicated them. They, of course, did not like to own to such a weakness, and cited what they had seen. But he waived such evidence, telling them that they must be able to speak from experience or not at all. He said, moreover, that he had nothing to do with any beer except the contents of that particular keg in question, which had been seized and brought to the court as evidence. What he wished to decide was whether the keg contained any intoxicating beverage. By an order given, the contents were tasted, but as it had been two days tapped, and the beer was really "flat," the decision was that that particular keg contained nothing that could intoxicate anyone; and a verdict was rendered in accordance with the facts. Since then, it is said, the brewer pursues his regular vocation unmolested by the law.

Another case was equally as remarkable. While Justice Hull was in the act of fining a saloon-keeper for breaking the liquor law, a man fresh from the dentist's hands, came into Hull's drug store to get some whiskey to rinse his bleeding mouth. A Mr. Johnson, a school teacher, with no thought except to be kind, asked Justice Hull if he should get the desired article. Hull, whether thinking of the question or not, nodded assent; at least, so thought the questioner, and he poured a small amount in a glass. This was used for the purpose mentioned, after which the patient laid down a ten-cent script in payment, and the teacher put it in the money drawer. The saloon keeper who had been fined, saw the whole proceedings, and he immediately had the teacher arrested for selling liquor. Johnson called on Hull to witness his innocence; but, Hull disclaiming any knowledge of the affair, the former was fined ten dollars and costs for violating the liquor law. He will probably harden his heart in the future when suffering humanity wants whiskey, especially if he is in a town where no licenses are granted.

–The American Sketch Book, A Collection of Historical Incidents 1874-5

SALOONISTS AFTER CHURCHES

Waukesha- Arguing that clergymen work for salaries, and collections are taken up at services, and that therefore Sunday services are a violation of the closing law, the saloonkeepers of the city declare that they will have them abolished in retaliation for the action of the clergymen in securing the closing of the saloons. The movement has not yet taken definite shape. Expert legal opinion has been consulted to see if there is a possibility of having the churches closed on these grounds; and if the reply is in the affirmative, proceedings will at once be instituted to compel the cessation of Sunday services. The ministers are aware of the intentions of the liquor dealers, but are not alarmed by them. They look upon the affair as a joke and say that both their Sunday services and their agitation against the saloons will continue.

–Tomah Journal, January 24, 1908

The Exchange House in the 1920s
60 years after the exploits of Wisconsin's Rosa Parks of Happy Hour

Suds for the Senegambian

Nigger Dick, a character at Baraboo prior to the Civil War, once performed a daring trick at the Exchange House on Water Street, conducted for a number of years by Volney Moore and others. The central figure in this episode was on his way to Sauk City for the June picnic, expecting to make the journey over the bluff astride a horse. The day was hot and the Senegambian decided to have a cooling draught before departing on his long ride. When Dick thrust his dark countenance into the room and made known his wants, he was refused. Wheeling about, he strode to the horse tied to a post, untied the strap, swung himself into the saddle, and rode daringly into the office, to the serious detriment of the furniture. With this bold act he apparently had the individual in charge of the bar completely buffaloed, for the desired potation was immediately forthcoming.

–Stagecoach and Tavern Tales of the Old Northwest, 1930

Ridgeway Ghost

Wisconsin contains, if yarns are an indication, more ghosts per square mile than any other state in the union. Apparently the fabrication or perception of haunts has been an important pastime of the Wisconsin people, for there is seldom a community that does not have a haunted house or its favorite ghost story. The famous Ghost of Ridgeway in Iowa County was the most notorious. Some think the ghost was originated by wags who were hopeful of ridding the district of an undesirable element which frequented the taverns. In any case practical jokers spread the growing belief in the ghost, whose presence and pranks soon became more or less feared by nearly all the settlers. There are many stories about the spirit, the following is one of them.

"One night three men sat down to a game of cards in a saloon in old Pokerville. It is said that they had been doing some really serious tipping of the jug and were ready for anything.

There was a fourth seat vacant at the poker table. They played several hands, and had considerable money on one hand of "Stud." The miner with a full house won the pot and was about to reach for his spoils. Suddenly an unseen hand seized the deck and began to deal the cards. They appeared to fly from the ghostly hand to the table in front of the men. They then noticed the fourth seat was occupied by a stranger they had never before seen. His hat was partly pulled over his face. The stranger began to play and the cards performed all sorts of peculiar tricks as he cast them down. When a player would try to pick up a card it would instantly leave his grasp and fly around the room. Soon cards of every suit were circling the table. The poker players couldn't stand the strain, they rushed the door, stumbling over each other, and in their hurry carried the door right off its hinges as they went out. The money on the table disappeared, and so of course, did the mysterious stranger.

Obviously, the Ridgeway Ghost had come to the tavern. Seeing a vacant seat, he took a hand in the game. The tavern keeper dropped to the floor behind the bar when he recognized the Ghost and remained there for sometime. While there, it is said, he consumed several bottles of his stock-in-trade."

–Wisconsin Lore

Incident at a Saloon in Stratford, late 1800s

"Dad had to go to Marshfield on business, an all day trip with a good team of horses. He left Frank Pagel, a young man, in charge of the saloon. Frank did not know that it was illegal to sell liquor to Indians. The log drive had just finished and the Indians came to town to shop. They went in our saloon and Frank did a landlord business. When the six o'clock whistle blew and our regular customers came in from work in the mill, they took one look and kept right on going to the next place. The place was full of Indians, shooting pool, throwing dice, dancing and raising hell. When Dad came in, he got rid of them in short order. Several Indian ponies, loaded down with provisions, were tied up in front of the place. Dad simply untied the ponies and chased them down the street. He then opened the door and hollered that the ponies had gotten away. The ponies were running down the street, with canned goods, etc. flying everywhere, and the Indians were after them. Dad locked the doors and put out the lights, and none too soon, because the boys were trying to get back in."

–Len Sargent, Stratford

Old Castle Rock Brewery and Roadhouse, Active in Civil War Days

One of the oldest brewery buildings in Western Wisconsin, little changed in appearance since it was built three-quarters of a century ago, stands in a little valley above the Winona dam near highway 35, a limestone and timber monument to John Schuler, early Trempealeau valley settler who hewed his logs, quarried stone and put them together. He called it the Castle Rock Brewery and in the post Civil War days operated a roadhouse in conjunction which was patronized by settlers, rivermen, stagecoach travelers, and —when he could not help himself— John and his family served brew to Indians. A son of John Schuler, Charles, who died recently in Winona, recalled that his father on those occasions put into practice what is now called the "off-sale" beer business. The Indians, he said, learned that here was a place to get that "deliciously damaging drink made by the white man," and would come in bands of four or more and squat patiently on the floor till their request for beer was granted. Schuler would have to give them beer, but "made it perfectly clear that they were not to drink it on the premises —a rather early use of the modern "off-sale regulation."

Once, this son said, Indians living on a nearby Mississippi island got very drunk and with "murderous whoops surrounded the place demanding more fire water. Fearful of what they might do if they had some more, Schuler refused their demands and barricaded himself and family in the building, arming everyone with whatever weapon could be found." Charles and a brother sat grimly by a window holding a common hatchet, and all wondered what would happen should the crazed Indians break down the door. Soon the effects of the beer wore off and the Indians became less belligerent. When Schuler ventured out carrying a gun in his hand he was able to persuade them to go home and "sleep it off."

Downriver from the Castle Rock Brewery and Tavern was La Crosse and the Gund Brewery. According to this 1914 newspaper advertisement, the Gund Brewery had a humble origin and similar construction as well. The similarities ended there, for the Gund Brewery grew into one of Wisconsin's largest brewers and operated until Prohibition in 1920.

continued…

There was another incident well remembered by the Schuler family, when early one morning two young men "dressed at the height of fashion" came to the tavern on foot and got breakfast. They sat where they could watch the road, and when they left they tossed a gold coin to Mrs. Schuler and announced, "We're the Williams Brothers." They were feared bandits in this section at the time. Later in the morning Mr. Schuler found they had made their way down river in his skiff...

[The Brewery and Tavern] was quite a building when he completed it, with a large cellar for aging the beer far back in the hillside, and a second floor reached by an outside stairway that would serve as living quarters and a tavern room. Logs were used for rafters as well as walls, so that floor boards and windows, and a pair of sturdy doors were all he bought. Shingles were the kind that were split from a short length of log, called clapboards, when the place was built, although these were later replaced with factory made shingles. As time went on and business improved, Schuler was not satisfied with the trade that came to his door, although the stage line connecting La Crosse and St. Paul passed by the tavern and many travelers lodged there and stopped for refreshments. When there was a good supply of beer on hand he would load up his wagon and, climbing the narrow road that wound up the valley, peddled his product to the farmers that lived on the ridge farms. Or another time he might go down to the river, about the present site of the Winona Dam, where he would take a ferry named appropriately "the Turtle," which would carry him to the village of Minnesota City, where he would call on farmers until his supply would be exhausted. The brewery was not in operation for many years. The large breweries in Fountain City five miles up the river and also in Winona downstream on the Minnesota side gave the owner of the Castle Rock Brewery too much competition. Although Schuler would never admit they could make a better beer.

–1951 Article, Fountain City Historical Society

FARMINGTON CENTER

During a recent Temperance Meeting in Farmington Center, Polk County, several of the fresh bloods of the town, prompted by a desire to distinguish themselves by something sublimely funny, brought a keg of beer into the meeting, tapped it, and deliberately proceeded to put themselves outside of its contents. Sheriff Ufford, of that city, unbeknownst to the "Boys" was in the audience, descended suddenly on the gang, sent the keg flying into the outer atmosphere like a comet, and the boys following on the rear, like the tail of that heavenly body. Of course they wanted him to come out and let them thrash him, contrary to their expectations he came out. They decided not to punish them then, and since the Temperance Movement has proceeded in that town without rupture.

–Hudson True Republican, February 12, 1879

The Farmington Center "Hoodlums" who tried to breakup the Temperance Meeting at that place, were arrested and taken to St. Croix Falls last week, tried and compelled to deposit in the county's coffers the sum of $25 and costs apiece. Nowadays a person can't indulge in an innocent pastime without some fastidious individuals taking exceptions.

–Hudson True Republican, February 19, 1879

Diamond Town

In 1886, just two years after Prentice had been surveyed, platted, and recorded, Louis Hallstrand surveyed an area between the two railroads. Intentions were made to create an adjoining town but nothing more was done about it. This area, separated from the village by a thin strip of woods, was given the name of Diamond Town.

There were no roads leading into Diamond Town. It was accessible only from the Soo Line Railway or by a narrow path that trailed across a large swampy area. Possibly because it was so well isolated it became a breeding ground for gamblers and out and out "toughs." These individuals moved in, put up a number of buildings and proceeded to make themselves known to others of their kind.

Whispers and rumors floated over to Prentice from Diamond Town. There were about thirty professional gamblers who lived there. There were whispers about a murder, but there was no investigation. No one dared to investigate. As soon as darkness fell, swinging lights were seen making their way across the swampy expanse, and watchers knew that a big night of gambling was on.

One gambler "Slippery Sullivan" was apprehended by the law. His trial came up on the day of a raging forest fire. Judge Wascott's office was surrounded by all the inhabitants of Diamond Town. They threatened the Judge with dire destruction to the town if Slippery

Sullivan was not released. Judge Wascott was not going to take any chances. He was old and his heart had a way of acting up. While the lawyers were arguing over some technicality, he jumped to his feet and loudly proclaimed, "The lawyers can't agree so I herewith discharge the prisoner." Diamond Town was jubilant, the Village of Prentice was furious.

–Prentice Centennial Album

Fighting Fifield ●

Fifield needs a bard to sing the saga of "the fighten'est town in the world" in its heyday—to recite the feats of the Chochranes and the Kennedys, of Michigan Smith and Pat Kelly, and the boss of them all, Leo Kaliski.

Fifield is a sleepy little village now. All summer long the tourists stream through, for it is at the crossroads of Northern Wisconsin, the junction of highways 70 and 13. Sportsmen know it as a headquarters for fishing and hunting, but to most of those who come and go it is just another little village.

The main street, so empty now, had 27 saloons in its four blocks back in the eighties. The woods for miles around were full of lumberjacks. Three or four big logging operations were in progress and Fifield was the center of action for 10,000 or 15,000 men. It never was a lumbering town of Escanaba or Hurley in Wisconsin, with a "Hell's Half Mile" of dives and harlots. Fifield was just rough and tough. The "jacks" were seldom "rolled" or knocked on the head. Knife and gun play was almost unknown, except when a gun sometimes flashed to make sure that no one interfered when two fighters rolled around in the muddy street, biting and gouging, to see who was the better man.

The fame of the bullies of Fifield spread the country over. The Chochranes probably were the most famous fighting family. George, Miles, Sam and Tom No. 1 and Tom No. 2, brothers and cousins,

came from the lumber camps of Maine. Pat Kelly also came from Maine and went back, but George Cochrane sent for him to return to Fifield.

In those days men fought for the love of battle. Most of the time ill feeling was wholly lacking, they fought to see which was the better man. A bully from some other town, itching to see if he could best the famous men of Fifield, would come to town, hunt up the man he wanted to fight, and line up at the bar beside him. After buying the Fifield bully a drink, the visitor usually would follow the standard formula:

"I hear you're a pretty good man"
"Yeah? What about it?"
"Well, I'd like to take you on"

Dan Menzie, now a guide at Fifield, recalls the old days vividly. "They usually got action," he said, "and most of the time they got licked. We had some great fighters here in those days. Why, back in the eighties it used to keep us kids busy running up and down the street to see which was the best scrap. Sometimes there was a dozen fights going at once in the four blocks.

"I remember one time, McDonald and Finney - they were ring fighters- were standing on the street when a teamster named Harvey came along. One of them called Harvey a big hayshaker and the other one made some wisecrack.

continued... **11**

"'You fellows are going to run into a snag' says Harvey. One word led to another and Harvey collared those two fellows and before he got through with them he dragged them over to the pump and doused their heads good." "Michigan Smith" heard about Harvey beating the two prize fighters and there was nothing to it but he had to find out if he could handle Harvey. Harvey was out teaming in the woods and Smith went out to see if he could get a job loading. Whenever he loaded for Harvey he would bungle the job and beef about everything that Harvey did.

That went on for a day or two and Harvey didn't take long to see what Smith was up to, so one trip he told a couple of fellows to watch. Then he got the team into a bad position and cussed Smith out for the way he loaded.

"Smith got down and went for Harvey and the teamster gave him about the sweetest trimming he ever got."

One of the legends of Fifield is that Leo Kaliski went down to Milwaukee when John O. Sullivan was barnstorming. He lined up with some other huskies who had stripped to the waist for the champions inspection, and Sullivan, after passing along the line, returned to the Fifield bully and said, "This is the best looking man, I'll box with him."

"No," replied Kaliski, "I won't get into the ring with you, but if you'll come out back of the theater I'll fight you rough and tumble." "I'll fight you in the ring," said Sullivan, "but not in the alley."

One of the memorable battles of Fifield was between Pat Kennedy, now a Park Falls rooming house keeper, and Charlie Wilson, when Wilson arrived from Park Falls to avenge his brother, who had been worsted by Kennedy. Another famous fight, between Michigan Smith and Pat Kelly, is recalled by F.G. Traenkle, one of the oldest men of Fifield. "They went to it hammer and tongs," he said. "It was a fight and they were both good men. Finally they lay in the street, too exhausted to fight anymore. Kelly was chewing Smith's finger and Smith was chewing Kelly's ear and once in awhile one of them would get enough gumption to reach over and make a weak pass at the other one. Well, it was a standoff and the boys called it enough. Kelly was a State O' Mainer and while he and Smith were standing at the curb, washing up, 10-15 State O' Mainers —the Cochranes and the rest of them— gathered around and began to pick on Smith. It looked as though they were going to jump him. Leo Kaliski was crippled up by rheumatism by then and walked with a cane, but he forgot his rheumatism and stood on the sidewalk over Michigan Smith waving his cane to keep them back. "I can lick any State O' Mainer," he roared, "I'll take you one at a time! Leave him alone! And when they didn't get aback from Smith he rapped a couple of them over the head with his cane. He bent their knees for them too."

The bartenders of Fifield were fighting men. Sometimes a visiting bully would challenge and they'd put everyone out and lock the doors and go to it. Once in awhile when the visitor licked the bartender, he'd unlock the door and let in the crowd. "Come in fellows! Let's clean up." Then the victor and the crowd would get gloriously "lickered" on the beaten man's stock.

–Milwaukee Journal, December 28, 1930

DOOR COUNTY

John Wester reports a narrow escape from having his nasal appendage disfigured, if nothing more serious resulted in the end. A week ago Saturday while at a saloon near his place he met a neighbor who owed him a dollar. Having waited for it as long as he thought he ought, Mr. Wester quietly requested payment of the debt. This so angered the debtor that he instantly flared up and calling him harsh names seized Mr. Wester's nose between his teeth. The latter succeeded in freeing himself before anything serious had been done, but the mark is still there.

–Door County Advocate
January 11, 1902

IRON RIVER

"We hear that in Iron River, Wisconsin, they had an old horse hitched to a livery wagon that would make trips from the saloons to the whorehouse without a driver. The saloonkeepers would load the jacks into wagons and head the horse toward the whorehouse that was about a mile from town, give him a slap on the rear, and he was off. When the "queens" at the whorehouse wanted to get rid of the lumberjacks, they would load them up and the horse would take them back to town. They tell me that the horse would make many trips a day back and forth... "I had heard for many years of the famous "crib houses" of Superior. When I first came to Duluth in 1922, a friend of mine, Paul Perrault of Blackduck who was clerking in one of those camps, and I made a special trip to Superior to view the "crib houses." These "crib houses" were about three blocks of small buildings along 3rd Street, with one girl in each house. The police were walking back and forth in front of the "cribs" to be on hand in the event one of the girls wanted to get rid of an unwelcome visitor. We walked the full length of street and back, and as we walked past each "crib," the girls would ask us in. It was soon after this that 3rd Street was closed up, and the girls moved to the hotels and rooming houses."

–The Lumberjack Queens, J.C. Ryan

Norway House

"I know it was in 1895—my father and mother bought the Norway House from Alexander Wiley and they ran it until 1915. Then they rented it out and they owned the building until it was tore down in 1938. The Norway House was located on Grand Avenue, 23 West Grand Avenue... then was McGuires' livery barn and on the other side of the Norway House on the west side was Henry Powers and McCormack's livery barn... I'll never forget this either... there was a saloon on the corner... It belonged to, that whole corner belonged to Theriault's daughter... and big Andrew Hanson had a saloon on that corner. McCarthy had a liquor store for many years afterward. Well this was in the spring. I don't know if they were going up on drive or comin' off the drive, but anyway during the winter Mr. Hanson had his bar fixtures taken out and taken up to the brewery and refinished. He had all the varnish taken off and new varnish put on.

Local Advertisement 1933

Sanded, dressed down nice and smooth. [He] had that all in there. Well, that invited some trouble. You know, when those River Pigs (lumberjacks) come to town with those calk shoes. They wanted to put their bark mark on his bar. Nice, new bar he had there. So Andrew Hanson he was a tremendous big man. Great big man. And I was on my way to high school when all of a sudden he came out of that little door on that corner with these two men, you know, and he was tryin' to push 'em out, or pull 'em out. He was trying to pull 'em out and they were hanging on to the door. And all of the sudden he gave a yank, and what do you suppose happened? The whole door jamb, the whole thing fell right on the sidewalk—everybody fell. Pulled everything right off the building... Well, one thing about a lumberjack, or a River Pig, if you don't cross 'em up or try to pull something on 'em, by golly, they were as true as steel. But if you cross them up, my Lord, look out. If he gets a few drinks he may not say nothing, but just like a bolt of lightning somewhere you'll get a jolt that will knock you to kingdom come!... No, I learned be honest with 'em, don't try to pull any shenanigans, you got a friend for life. He'll go half the way with you."

–The Flavor of the Times, John Myhre of Chippewa Falls

BLACK RIVER FALLS

"The beer garden recently started on this side of the river, by permission of our town board, continues to grow more offensive. The rabble from the city and the county meet there and sometimes form nothing but drunken mobs. It is not safe for women to pass along the road near this place. Bloody fights are of a daily occurrence and drunken men may be found lying around the bushes on all sides. Wife whipping has come into vogue since the new institution was forced upon us... What it may end in need hardly be conjectured."

–Black River Newspaper, July 1915

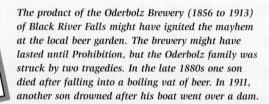

The product of the Oderbolz Brewery (1856 to 1913) of Black River Falls might have ignited the mayhem at the local beer garden. The brewery might have lasted until Prohibition, but the Oderbolz family was struck by two tragedies. In the late 1880s one son died after falling into a boiling vat of beer. In 1911, another son drowned after his boat went over a dam.

EAU CLAIRE

A semi-riot and "big fight" occurred at the Beer Garden of John Ollinger last Sunday evening, in which stones, clubs, bottles, and other weapons were freely used, and a number of persons were badly injured. The house was badly damaged by having the windows smashed in, furniture broken, & c. Taken together it was a very disgraceful affair, and certain parties who roam our streets and pride themselves on their "nius" promiscuously punching everyone who does not move to suit them, deserve having the stern hand of justice laid upon their shoulders, with a demand to "come up to the Captain's office and settle..." As usual, whiskey was at the bottom of the affair.

–Eau Claire Free Press, June 20, 1867

One of many beer gardens was Ray's Resort & Beer Garden on Lake Wissota as shown in the 1940's.

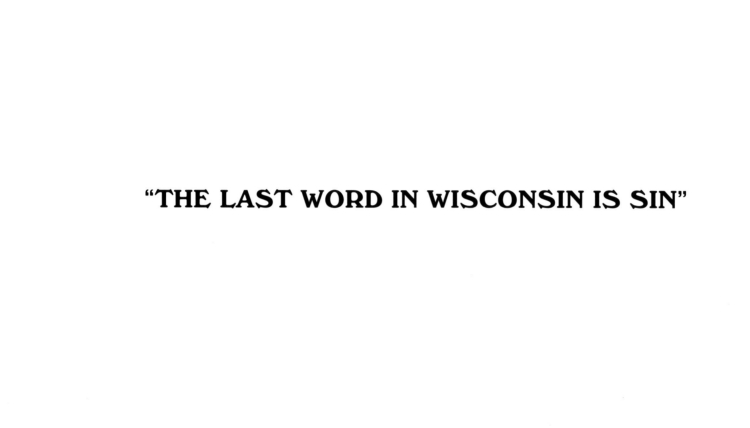

"THE LAST WORD IN WISCONSIN IS SIN"

The Teasdale Report of 1913

"Moonlight Outing Club" of Muskego Lake in 1913

Report and Recommendations of the Wisconsin Legislative Committee to Investigate White Slave Traffic and Kindred Subjects

Because of concerns throughout the Badger State regarding alcohol, prostitution, and related social ills, the 1913 Wisconsin Legislature established a committee to investigate the extent of this bad behavior and report back with the results. The committee held town meetings, contacted local police departments, and even hired five undercover detectives. The dicks visited dance halls, saloons, cigar stores, road houses, and brothels in 35 Wisconsin towns and cities (and got paid for it as well!). They interviewed johns, bartenders, madams, pimps and prostitutes. The result of this research yielded photos, letters, testimonials, arrest records, interviews, and other documentation by the box load. All in all, revealing enough drinking, carousing, gambling, sex, sins, and lechery to make a sailor blush. Enough of the preliminaries, let us take a look at the highlights of the low life.

The following pages are excerpts from that report…

Nelson ⏤⏤⏤⏤⏤⏤●

I was informed Saturday of a joint that is running in Wisconsin, directly opposite to the City of Wabasha, in the State of Minnesota. This is a saloon and roadhouse, and girls are brought over every night from Wabasha for immoral purposes, and I understand some are kept at the roadhouse. This is about 3 miles from any village in Wisconsin, down on the bottoms of the river, and I am informed it is one of the worst dives, in western Wisconsin. The present owner and running it is Joe Stafford, who recently bought it from some man who became afraid of trouble, so traded it to this man and transferred to him his license which under the law of Wisconsin he could not even do with consent of the town or city. As the main traffic is from Minnesota, so not in our jurisdiction except as to the case, I send it to you. It is in the Town of Nelson, but best reached by Wabasha.

In Sheboygan they have four or five houses; one is Rose Parker, 227 South Water Street; Bayview House, 420 Pennsylvania Avenue; Red House, 2127 Calumet Road (Lizzie Rice, Keeper); there was one on North 8th Street. Now it is claimed these are the only places in the city, and that they think they have no hotels or rooming houses where immorality is allowed. Now, as to Manitowoc, the suspected places are the College Inn Palm Garden, 418 North 7th Street; Stahl Laundry (Snow Flake), 901 York Street; there is one place near the water tower; also the Glen Hotel is supposed to be wide open for prostitution. ...Also look up Mary Wilson, 8th Street, across the river; she keeps sort of a candy store which is more of a blind than anything else; who is supposed to be a regular procuress. This woman has recently been arrested and may be out of business. She is the owner of what is called the Silver Lake Resort... I also understand the girls in the Williams Hotel have separate rooms in which they stay; find out what the facts are and what their morals are. If you have the opportunity I wish you see Mary Mitchell of the pea canning company; she may be able to tell you of the morals of the girls working in that establishment.

—Letter from Teasdale Committee to an Operative

"Sheboygan is a very bad place as far as the morals of girls and married men are concerned. According to size, there is no worse place in the state."

Ashland - November 3, 1913

"This girl was above the average found in these houses. She was bright and could carry on a good conversation. She said her home was in La Crosse. The girls here seemed to think that it was smart to drink. The girls all wore short dresses which reached just below their knees, but did not have anything on underneath those dresses. Asked this girl if there were any other house of ill fame in the city and she said this was the only house in town. Of the 11 men in the parlor, all of them foreigners except myself. They appeared to be lumberjacks... Girls names: Anna, Gertrude, McDonald, Tutts and Pearl... Walter was the name of the piano player."

James Sokolik Roadhouse and Saloon about 3½ or 4 miles from town on French Island. Mr. Sokolik, Polish, about 45 years old. This is the largest and toughest place on the island. It has a good size neatly furnished bar in which there are slot gambling machines and a turkey raffling machine. At the rear is a large dance hall, at the left of the bar is a dining room which is used as a wine room for those desiring a little privacy. It is said to be a hangout for crooks and gamblers from town, also that Mr. Sokolik has a penitentiary record. Men to the city come out here frequently to have a game, Mr. Sokolik says, away from police interference. Among the games played is "Chuck Luck," a dice game which is said to be one in which the house seldom loses. Until very recently they had two inmates out here but they left. Mrs. Sokolik says they are trying to get others and asked me to send her some if I came across any good looking girls downtown that really want to make money. Sokolik's has been in business here several years, some say over 3 years. Gund's Brewery holds a mortgage on the place and controls it. Mr. Elsen's Saloon and Roadhouse on French Island about 3 miles from the city and a short distance from Cushner's… Has a plainly furnished bar in which there are several slot gambling machines, at the rear of the bar is a small dance hall. An electric piano furnishes the music for dancing. The private rooms and living apartments are on the 2nd floor. Two young women named Ella, age about 22 years, and Fannie, age 25 years, don't live on the island but come here to solicit men, whom they take to the rooms above, price $2.00. The girls and Mrs. Elsen hustle drinks in the bar. There is a table in the dance hall at which to drink but few use it, all stand around the bar. As soon as a man appears these women take him by the arm and lead him to the bar and surround him as long as he will treat them. This place is a tough class of trade, and others who are just rough. Mr. Elsen, only having the saloon since July and new in the business, doesn't seem to know how to handle them. The toughest sort of dancing, ragging, and the tango are allowed in the dance hall, saw three couples doing this vulgar dancing during my stay.

ART'S TAVERN
1322
La Crescent St.
French Island
La Crosse,
Wis.

Terry Post Collection

19

Beer Keg Parade

1st: Did you not allow a blind pig to run full blast up at the Old Depot?

2nd: Did you not allow an Assignation House with four inmates to run up at the Old Depot, without interference?

3rd: Is it not a fact that last Sunday when Father Zuecher gave his lecture in the armory the people going to hear him were met by a beer keg parade composed of 20 or 30 hoodlums with beer kegs over their shoulders, shouting and yelling, crowding people off the sidewalk, scoffing and jeering at the people because they were going to hear Father Zuecher lecture on temperance and that you did nothing to stop or prevent this beer keg parade?

We make no war on the respectable saloon, but we pledge ourselves if elected to office to put the low dive out of existence. And in this movement we should get the support of every voter that has manhood enough to stand by and protect his son, his daughter, or his sister from danger.

–Charges leveled in a local newspaper advertisement by C.W. Schlaebitz on March 21, 1914 against Mayor Mirlach

These charges were all refuted by Mayor Mirlach in a letter to Senator Teasdale on April 4, 1914. The Mayor's opponent, Mr. Schlaebitz, might have been outspent, the charges could have been false, or maybe the men of the town cared more about keeping the dives open and the taps running than they did securing the safety of the womenfolk and the young-uns. Whatever was the case, Mayor Mirlach was reelected in this pre-female suffrage election. He served as Mayor from 1911 to 1922 and again from 1924 to 1926.

The atmosphere seemed to have lightened up by the 40s, at least at the "Hotel Beaver"

Beaver Dam

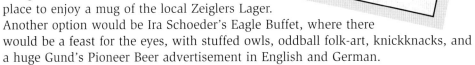

The sporting crowd in Beaver Dam had some appealing options: A "Blind Pig" at the Old Depot or C.W. Erickson's "Princess Buffet & Cafe." Despite the effeminate name, the establishment had mainly manly features, such as pre-prohibition Pabst and Miller advertising as well as a nice assortment of girly pictures. Note the extra-capacity spittoons, probably polished to their bright shine by an energetic town drunk. All in all, a fine place to enjoy a mug of the local Zeiglers Lager.

Another option would be Ira Schoeder's Eagle Buffet, where there would be a feast for the eyes, with stuffed owls, oddball folk-art, knickknacks, and a huge Gund's Pioneer Beer advertisement in English and German.

JOYOUS NEW YEAR

Celebrate NEW YEAR'S EVE At The HOTEL BEAVER PALM GARDEN Dancing Favors Fun From 8:00 'Till ? ? HOTEL BEAVER

The letter below was in response to a questionnaire the County Attorney returned to the committee that denied any vice in Bayfield County.

Dear Sir:

In reply to my question as to whether or not there are any reputed houses of prostitution in your county and you answer, NO. Now, I would ask you in regard to the Lake View Saloon, John Donahue, Proprietor, in the City of Washburn, which on November 4th had two girls there as prostitutes, as reported to us, named Emma Mischler and Etta Olin, whose charge for services was stated to be $1.

I would also ask in regard to the house which is located out about a mile and a half or two miles from Washburn, and also to the house two miles and a half out from Bayfield, run by Lydia Merchy, which on November 6th, 1913 had four inmates present, and whose charge for service was stated to be $2 each. Anna and Bessie are two of the inmates. I understand one of these houses is owned by a fellow at Iron River who makes daily trips out there to collect his pay from the women. Please inform me of what you know about the conditions there.

Very Truly Yours,

Chairman Commission of White Slavery

*November 1913,
Washburn Times*

Washburn - November 14, 1913

I met John Donahue in his saloon (the Lakeview). He was showing some dirty pictures in the bar room and I asked him to show them to me which he did. I asked him if he knew where I could get some... he said we could get some at the Why Not Saloon. But he was out so we went into Bennett's Saloon and had several drinks. We then went back to the Lakeview and a little later on our way back to the Saloon we met John Donahue and he introduced us to ----- and told him that I wanted to buy some of those dirty pictures. He said all right and we went into his store and he sold me exhibit A at 45¢, exhibit B at 25¢, exhibit C at 25¢. Then John Donahue and myself started back to the Lakeview and we met two girls that John Donahue said were upstairs drinking in the Lakeview. We took the two girls, Emma Mischle and Etta Olin back to the Lakeview and had several drinks. One girl agreed to go upstairs with me and we went up. In the rooms were tables and chairs and beds, there was one bed made up with dirty bed clothes on it and she says it was pretty dirty but would have to do. I says don't John Donahue charge anything for the room, she says no, just buy some drinks. I decided I did not want to stay. Her price was $1.00. She says she is married and has one girl six years of age and her husband is living and is a woodsman.

Mary's Monkey

MARY HAS A LITTLE MONKEY JUST AS CUTE AS IT CAN BE. IT WAS COVERED WITH THE SOFTEST HAIR THAT EVER YOU DID SEE

①

TO KEEP IT NICE AND CLEAN WAS MARY'S GREATEST HOPE. SO SHE WASHED HER LITTLE MONKEY WITH THE BEST KIND OF SOAP.

②

THE BOYS ALL LIKE MARY AND LIKE HER MONKEY TOO. AND WHEN THEY PLAY SO NICE WITH IT, WHAT CAN MARY DO?

③

ONCE MARY'S MONKEY GOT REAL COLD THAT FILLED HER WITH ALARM. SO SHE BOUGHT SOME WOOLEN PANTS FOR TO KEEP HER MONKEY WARM.

④

MARY WENT IN SWIMMING AND SHE TOOK HER LITTLE PET. WAVE HIT HER IN THE "GOOD OLD SUMMER TIME" AND SHE GOT HER MONKEY WET.

⑤

⑥

MARY NOW IS MARRIED AND IT KEEPS HER ON THE JUMP. AND BETWEEN THE MAN AND MARY, HER MONKEY HAS TO HUMP.

These are the exhibit C postcards purchased at the Lakeview Tavern. The report on file with the Historical Society also includes exhibits A and B. Because they are photographs that show actual "monkeys," they are not included with this book.

Watertown
November 29, 1913

Saloon at 121 West Main Street... On the first floor is a plainly furnished barroom, having inside connection from a hall at the rear with two wine rooms... on the second floor are plainly furnished rooms that are let for assignation purposes... rooms are let to couples at $1 each, the place is open all night, and this seems to be the only class of trade upstairs, very young girls with men are accommodated here, by common reputation it is a tough sporting resort... Hartig's local brewery furnishes the beer here... This is the worst small town I have ever visited, though its population is only about 10,000. Most of the girls of working age are employed but live at home, in spite of this they go out with men and just get home the next morning in time to get back to work. Even girls still in short dresses, school girls, make dates with boys and accompany them to wine rooms

William Biessner's Saloon at 121 West Main Street

William Jannke Collection

St. Mary's Hospital in Watertown, circa 1909. A few years later, the town pin-cushion, Dorothy, the Chief of Police and the Newspaper Editor could very well have spent some uncomfortable days here in that pre-penicillin era.

where they drink beer and other liquors and then go to any of the assignation resorts. Some of the parents are as bad as the daughters as in the Skellerman family, two daughters and the mother gave birth to illegitimate children about the same time. Mr. and Mrs. Jahrling are said to be as tough as Francis, Mrs. (name withheld) the mother of two bad girls is their boon company, and there are others. The parents who would have their children be decent seemingly have lost control of their acts, and do nothing as they are not heeded... The boys are just as bad, though underage the Saloons still serve them liquors, they run around with girls and are often seen in their company, intoxicated in the wine rooms... Venereal disease was spread pretty thoroughly among boys and men, even the married men by Dorothy, a young girl who worked at the N.W. Hotel and the ---- for Mrs. Heon, last summer who has since died from its effects. Even (the) Chief of Police and the Editor of the local paper had it so bad that they were cripples. This became common knowledge among a certain class. Mrs. Buckly and Mrs. Heon told the investigator that the Chief was unable to walk except with a crutch and has only recently laid aside a cane. While he was so bad last summer he sent his wife to California. His son William is one of the worst young men in the town. If there is a curfew law or any other way to curb the actions of minors they are certainly not enforced, even the small children curse as do some men.

23

Green Bay - December 20, 1913

Minnie Carrington, located in what is called the swamp, corner of Jackson and Reber Streets, the Town of Prebble. Has a very nicely furnished two story frame dwelling house, it is a regular parlor house sporting resort, with ballroom and parlors. Called a $2.00 house, landlady relieves half of inmates earnings, there is no board charges, the girls pay $2 a week for lights. There are seven inmates, names of five are as follows, Dottie Wells, Belle, Marion, May, and Catherine… they are dressed plainly in loose apron dresses and caps as in $1 dollar resorts, the landlady is dressed the same… Sells local beer at 50¢ a bottle. Keeps two day maids and a beer maid at night, the beer maid is one of her former girls who is now resting up… went to the Saturday night dance that has been held regularly at Music Hall, corner of Maple and Walnut Streets, found the hall closed and in darkness. Waited around for more than an hour, during that time counted 40 girls ages apparently from 14-17 years who came to the dance unescorted, some bold girls, others quiet in manner. The boys came together in bunches, most of them were of the pool hall type. No one seemed to know why the dance was not being held, many waited a good while hoping the hall would be opened, finally some said it might be on account of this being Advent. From a talk investigator had with a man in Gamm's Seed Store, across the street, learned that this is a rough neck dance and that no sensible, decent girl attends them. He says there is no bar in the hall, that they go to nearby Broadway Saloons for liquors, further says he thinks the protests of pastors of the city has last caused the authorities to close it. Said there had been considerable talk of closing it on account of bad characters because there were so many young girls attending it, that everything was danced there: bear dance, tango, hesitation and all other sin in their most vile manner.

Unidentified Music Hall, somewhere in Wisconsin, Circa 1915

Brice's Saloon of Green Bay, 1890s

Superior

Douglas Hotel
314 Tower Avenue - Proprietor: Paul Maltry

This is an assignation hotel resort with bar and cheap restaurant. It also has men lodgers of the laboring class. Rooms are very plainly furnished. The house has a reputation as a gambling resort. A poker game is a frequent occurrence in one of the rooms upstairs. On a previous visit, I saw a man apparently putting away the poker chips. He counted them as he did so. This time could hear men talking in subdued tones but could not get into the room. To my knock a man came, answered, stepped into the hall and closed the door quickly.

Mystic Hotel
622 Tower Avenue - Proprietress: Hazel Long

This is a very neatly furnished sporting house, or hotel. Upstairs over Naughtous Saloon. Hazel, the landlady here, is said to have had a house at one time in the restricted district on Cummings Avenue; there she found a man friend, a wealthy Iowa farmer, and it is said he bought out the Mystic Hotel, paying $4,000 for it. She still claims him as her friend, but also has Mr. J.R. Nix of the Reno Hotel, Duluth, Minnesota, as her real lover. Hazel often phones Annie Sunstrom for girls when she runs short. Price of rooms $1-2, price for use of girls $2.00-5.00, Beer sold: Fitger's - per quart bottle 50¢.

Badger Bars Collection

Some of the boys on the town in circa 1915 Superior

Delmonico Cafe
720 Tower Avenue
Proprietor: Mr. Sommers

This is a restaurant having lunch counter, dining room and private dining rooms. Northern Beer is sold to those who are known at 25 cents a bottle with a lunch. The rooms above are let for assignation purposes - price $1.00. Trade is sent up from the restaurant, because the manager lives upstairs and is on very friendly terms with the old lady running the house and it is said he has a money interest in the place.

House at 1315 Tower Avenue
Proprietress: Mrs. Potter

This is a high class sporting flat resort. The landlady is also the proprietress of a milliner store. Those frequenting her flat are shop girls, nice women, and the better class of sporting. All cater to the better class of men. As they claim to lend an air of decency to a good assignation business carried on at night, only keeps a few men roomers. Miller's beer is kept.

Golden Key Club
1211 North Third Street
Proprietor: Wade Leek, alias Hicks (Colored)

This is a negro gaming club. On second floor in large room are pool tables and card table. In other room is a small bar, a piano furnishes entertainment. Liquors are sold at all hours and Sundays without a saloon license, although anyone can quench their thirst here. Women rounders, prostitutes, and pimps frequent; also a few others out for a good time. Poker, craps, and blackjack games are in progress whenever enough men with money get together and desire a game.

Kehtel Family Collection

The Elcora Cigar Company of Duluth supplied fine tobacco products to businesses in Superior and Duluth.

Club at 1216 North Third Street (Colored)
Proprietor: Henry Graham, better known as "Rab"

On the first floor at this address there is a pool hall, this is connected by inside stairway to a large room above, in which there is a small bar, piano, and other furnishing as any cafe. Toward the front there is a small room partitioned off for a card room. This is a gambling house resort of the lowest order. Craps, blackjack and poker are played here. Its patrons are sporting women, pimps and rounders. The races often mingle here on the quiet.

European Hotel
1912 Broadway
Proprietress: Mrs. Pallard

This hotel has a bar with small drinking rooms and dining rooms at the rear. Patrons seem to be men of the rough and boisterous laboring class. Upstairs the rooms are plainly furnished. There is a drinking parlor upstairs and inside rooms where I learn that liquors are served at any hour. The maid tells me that she has the privilege of entertaining men in her room… This is the lowest appearing place I have yet visited. The landlady was lying ill in a dirty bed with a drunken man lay across it at her feet, so drunk he could not be awakened.

Cummings Avenue (No Address Given)
Proprietress: Lottie Brown

Very little beer is sold since the order was given against it. Great care is taken that no one except old patrons of the house are served. This a regular parlor house resort. The landlady and the inmates are colored. They cater to white men only. Here the girls do the nude dances called the "Oochie Macuch." …Price of girls $1,2,3, and $5.

Sporting House at 101 Cummings Avenue
Proprietress: Lina Mills

Sam Garfield is the consort of Lina Mills, is a bartender and a gambler, and a great friend of Kid Taylor's [the ex-ball player]. Miss Mills and Flo Davenport seem to be the boldest in selling liquor since the order was given to cut it out. The inmates here do not blame the officials, but denounce Reverend Milford for interfering with their business… Sam Garfield runs his money (protection money) to Police Headquarters by the "Drug Boy." The "Drug Boy" is a young man about 21 years of age, who has been taking orders for drugs in these houses for the past six or seven years. He was pointed out to me as the "Drug Boy."

House at 105 Cummings Avenue
Proprietress: Flo Davenport

Beer and Whiskey: both sold, apparently without fear of arrest, even though order has been given that no liquor be sold in the house. It is said the Mayor and Phil Gannon are close friends of Kid Taylor the ex-ball-player, consort of Flo Davenport. This is regular harlot house resort… The girls here say they cannot make any money on account of Old Milford. When I asked who he was, they said that Crazy Minister at the Mission; he is trying to turn the whole town into a church.

Sporting House at 131 Cummings Avenue
Proprietress: Bessie Johnson (alias Hunter)

This is a regular parlor house resort; the landlady and inmates are colored, but they cater to white men for trade, exclusively. Owing to ill health, Miss Bessie leaves the running of the house to Miss Sadie, another colored woman. Briscoe Hunter is the consort of Miss Bessie. Weiss beer is sold here. The inmates do a nude dance called the Hootchi-ma-kootch. They use this as a means of enticing men in to spend money. After hours colored pimps are allowed to go to bed here with their women inmates.

Arlington Hotel
1710 Winter Street
Proprietress: Mrs. Anna Sunstrom

This is a 21 room neatly furnished hotel, on the second floor at this address. Anna Sunstrom bought this hotel from a Mrs. Stephenson, about two months ago. She was before this an inmate at the Mystic Hotel. Her consort is Edward Nelson, who has a saloon at 605 Tower

Unidentified saloon, Superior area, circa 1915. Is the fellow getting ready to slug down a shot of Rye, in the checkered pants and boxing gloves, the long forgotten, boxer and whore-mongering Curley Aldrich? Unlikely.

Avenue. She was also an inmate at a Hibbing, Minnesota resort. Anna claims to have been here five years and says Sweden is her native land. Bessie, one of the inmates, claims Hibbing as her home. She lays her pregnant condition to one Burt Conklin, whom she says boards at the corner of Ogden Avenue and Broadway. She says he don't want her to hustle, but her physician says it doesn't hurt her. Instead it will help her later on. She expects to be confined in January… Beer sold: Fitger's Beer - per quart bottle - 50¢ …price of girls $2.00 - $5.00.

Sporting House at 102 Hammond Avenue
Proprietress: Julia Wilson

This is a regular harlot house, having dancing hall with slot pianos for entertainment. Curley Aldrich, the Ex-Prize Fighter, has been the consort of Julia Wilson for six years. Five Girls. Prices: $1,2,3, and $5.00. Beer sold: Miller's High Life at 50¢ per quart bottle.

Rhinelander - January 14, 1914 •

Operative saw the Bartender at O'Malley's Saloon, presumably Mr. O'Malley himself, sell liquor to a boy who was at the most 15 years of age and who looked to be only 13 or 14 years old. The boy came in and asked for a pint of whiskey and it was given to him without the asking of any questions whatsoever. Operative spoke to Mr. O'Malley and expressed himself as desirous of getting a girl for immoral purposes. He was told that he could probably pick one up on the street. O'Malley then went into the other room and started to hammer on the stove. The operative took the hint and went in the other room and was told in a whisper to go to the Model Restaurant and he would be able to get a girl there, but if they were busy that he should get a date with a Mrs. Liddlefeld, a widow woman in the town who did business for five dollars a time. She was described as being a good looking woman and she lives in a respectable part of town. She did not let fellows come up to the house as she was afraid that the neighbors might catch on, but she had a place to take them so he said. Operative then went to the Model Restaurant but there was a man there and the girls had gone out so there was nothing doing that night. Operative was told by a moving picture man of that city by the name of Zandre that there was plenty of intercourse to be had in the City of Rhinelander and that a fellow didn't have to hunt very hard to find it. He said "He at least never had any trouble in getting it when he wanted it." Operative asked him if he was a married man and was told he was but he said that did not make a difference as he had to be a good fellow with everybody in his line of business.

Lady operative went to the Alpine Hotel and told the clerk that she wanted to have her gentleman friends come to her room as she made her money by sporting. The clerk said that she could have anyone she wanted in her room. He told her that he would throw her trade as he had lots of men that come in and wanted girls. He told the operative she would have no trouble in getting a lot of trade as the fellows liked good looking girls. He asked the operative if she drank beer and when the operative said that she did he went downstairs and soon returned with a bottle of beer which he handed the operative and then went downstairs.

Downtown Rhinelander in the 1940s. Reardon's drugstore is still in business on the right.

Lady operative went to Reardon's Drug Store and asked Mr. Reardon where the Model Restaurant was. He told her and after she bought a ten cent bottle of perfume he asked her what she was doing in Rhinelander and she told him that she was traveling. Operative opened her purse and put the perfume in and Reardon saw a key in the purse. He said "Gee, I see you have a key, but I have a better key than that." Operative said nothing to this. Just then a Policeman came down the street and operative remarked to Reardon that that was the first Policeman she had seen in Rhinelander. Reardon told operative to go out and make a date with the Policeman as he was a good fellow and a sport. Operative asked if the Policeman was married and was told he was but that did not make any difference as the married men are the best.

Eau Claire - January 19, 1914

Operatives visited Fourniers Dance Hall on Friday and Saturday nights of last week and report that the dancing is outrageous. The dancers dance the Tango and the Hesitation Waltz in as extreme manner as possible. This dance, when danced extremely, is enough to arouse the passions of anybody. It consists of the dancers pulling each other right over the top of each other and they hold each other so tight that is an impossibility to dance this and not have ones passions aroused. People do not need to know each other in order to ask for a dance but the fellows go right up to a girl and ask her to dance whether they know her or not. Lady operative was asked by three different fellows to go outside with them. Man operative was asked by two girls where he roomed and when he told them yes they said they would come up and they would have a game of cards before he went away…

…There is a slot machine on the bar at Alphons Couture's Saloon located on Barstow Street. This is a chance machine as sometimes you win and sometimes you get nothing…

It is rumored that the sporting element from Chippewa Falls come down here to do their sporting but have been unable to locate things as of yet…

Lady operative visited Mrs. Stuart who runs what was formerly the Montreal House and was told she only had eight rooms and that for the present she would have to room with their daughter. She told an operative that a girl by the name of Katherine Stevens had been staying there and that she sported. She said she never did any work while she stayed at the Hotel but that she made enough money sporting… Operative said that this Mrs. Stuart is a very sporty looking individual and that her hotel is a dirty place and smells of onions and garlic. In the opinion of the operative this Mrs. Stuart is a sport. She asked the operative to have a glass of beer.

A young fellow by the name of Shorty Eddy who rooms at the Commercial Hotel has been in the habit of having girls come to his room. He has them register and get a room of their own and then when no one is looking they go to his. The proprietor of the hotel left the hotel on the evening of January 19 and left his son in charge of the place until he returned which would be a few hours. The son had complaints come into the office about this fellow Eddy having girls in his room and making so much noise. He went up to Eddy's room and rapped. Not receiving any answer he opened the door and was pitched on by young Eddy and received a black eye and a swelled nose. He said there were two girls in

Walter's Beer Wagon

Eddy's room. Those girls were working at either the Eau Claire or the Galloway hotels. Nothing was done until the next morning when the proprietor himself came back and hearing about the rumpus went up to Eddy's room and rousing Eddy from bed gave him five minutes to get out.

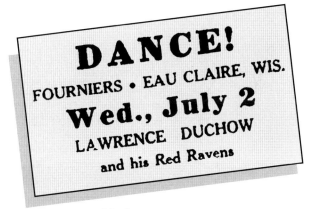

Ad for dance at Fourniers 40 years later

Janesville - May 15th, 1914

...I proceeded to secure some dinner and then boarded a car (with a girl the investigator had met by the hotel) for South Janesville, where I entered the Dew Drop Inn Roadhouse. There are gambling machines in this place, and there are signs posted to the effect that "No Gentlemen Are Allowed in the Wine room Without a Lady," and "Only One Gentleman with one Lady Permitted." From here I went across the street to another road-house. There were gambling machines in this place and young men dancing in the bar room. I could plainly see in here also that in order to get into the wine rooms one would have to be accompanied by a lady...

We went into a basement door, where there were four round tables, a carpet on the floor and a piano in the room. There were three other couples in the place besides ourselves, all of whom were drinking whiskey at their tables. A young girl and a young man were dancing the Tango, the girl raising her skirts far above her knees every time she would bend down. The man was holding her tight to his person while dancing and would love her up as they danced, at the same time talking to her about going to bed. This place has two signs, reading as follows; #1 - Some people come here to sit and think, while others come to buy a drink. #2 - No gentlemen allowed in here without a lady, and only one lady with a gentleman allowed. There is not very much light in this place, there being only two small lights, covered with red shades. Some heavy paper is pasted to the glass door leading to the wine room... All the girls in here appeared to be very "sporty," and one occupied her time flirting with me, and she appeared to have been drinking rather heavily. The conduct of all in here was really unbecoming for any lady or gentleman. The charges for drinks in this place are very high, for they charge 15¢ for either bottle beer or fancy drinks. Leaving this place we went to Smith's, across the street from the Dew Drop Inn, where there are two divisions of wine rooms, a partition between the two. These wine rooms are dark, more so than the Dew Drop Inn. There is an electric piano with an organ attachment here. There were two other couples on the other side of the partition. I walked through there with the intention of going to the bar room. I found all the doors closed, and these two couples were loving up, they being all bunched up. It was too dark however to see their faces. I could see the skirt of a woman over the man's lap. In order to remain there, I played the piano, but they would not dance, the fellows being too busy loving the girls. The girl I was with said she would not go upstairs in a place like this, as the place and the Dew Drop Inn were "too tough." In leaving the wine room we passed the Barroom on the outside of the building along the porch where we observed drunken men dancing within. They used bad language in such a loud tone of voice that it could plainly be heard on the outside. Leaving here, we drove back to Janesville, and I took the horse back to the livery barn, after which we went to McDonald's Lunchroom. While eating, the girl I was with said 'You should have taken a "gamer" girl than me to South Janesville and you could have had a better time." I asked, "Who is a "gamer" girl in town?" She mentioned the name of Vera Lentz, who is a bookkeeper at 319 West Milwaukee Street. Miss Wenger told me that this girl goes out with her "boss" and other men for a good time. I asked "Does she have intercourse with men for money?" and the girl answered "Yes, for money. She is a nice, stout girl, and her "boss" just gave her $200.00, with which to go to Chicago and buy new clothes. She goes out to South Janesville very often in a machine." Upon leaving McDonalds Restaurant, I took Miss Wenger home and then returned to the hotel where I discontinued for the day.

Janesville
May 16, 1914

On arising at 8:25 a.m. I had breakfast and then went to Joe E. Cockey's Saloon. He has about 12 pictures of nude women hanging about the bar. He has about one large-sized punch board, with about 40 holes in same, costing 10¢ per punch. There is also a gambling machine in there… I proceeded to the People's Drug Store, where I bought a cigar, while taking the clerk to one side, I asked him for a French Safe. He said "We do not carry them and have not for sometime." I said to him "I am all right, you are not taking any chances on me." The clerk said "You could have them if we had them in stock." I thanked him for this and then went to the Badger Drug Store. Here I purchased a cigar and asked the proprietor for a French Safe, designating a middle-sized one. He answered by saying "Nothing doing! We do not carry them, and in fact have never had them in stock. We do not carry anything that is not legitimate."…Without a doubt the city has greatly improved in a moral way and the only place that I can truthfully state where immorality is being practiced and which are hell-dives for fostering prostitution are the road-houses in South Janesville, such as Smith's and the Dew Drop Inn.

Stevens Point - June 9, 1914

"I visited several saloons, where I inquired where I might get a woman. I was referred by all to Polack Mary's place on Patch Street. Later on I visited this place and found she had two girls. They solicit their business in the bar room and take their trade upstairs. They charge $2.00 for a single service. From here I proceeded to Barney's Place, where I found "Red" tending bar. He was not very talkative, so I left here and met T.J. Cohn, the officer. I attempted to "rope" him, but without success. After leaving him, I proceeded to the Soo Hotel, where Ryan, the bartender, had two girls - one named Joe, who is 16 years of age and the other, named Mary, who is 17 years of age. There was quite a crowd around here. Ryan told me about taking them upstairs and about taking what they wanted. Scharer, the proprietor, also told me about two girls stopping there whom they had picked up at the Depot, and that everyone helped himself in regard to taking what they wanted from these girls. They finally put both of the girls to bed in an intoxicated condition. All the fellows also helped themselves in regard to a girl named Rosie, who formerly worked at the Railroad Hotel Lunchroom. A fellow named Kelly had a disease, which he gave to this Rose. Rose was here at the time, and Scharer was telling her that he did not know that Kelly had a disease. Leaving the Hotel, I visited the sporting houses and found at Cad's, the first house, five girls. They charge $2.00 for a single service and $1.00 for a round of drinks. The girls receive half the money they take in for intercourse, but not for selling beer. At Bell's the prices are the same. I later visited Barney's and met Bernel, the proprietor, who was intoxicated. He was giving away drinks, and later on Martin, with a crowd of about 12, started to fight. Accordingly, Bernel hired autos and hacks, and together went out to the sporting house. The fight was finished between Martin, Knopp and McDonald, who had his jaw cut open and some teeth knocked out. We went into Bell's place, and Bernel said that he still thought he could lick Martin, so we all went out again, and Martin beat up Knopp again."

June 11, 1914

On arising this morning I took up my duties by first paying a visit to the Saloon known as Barney's Place. I asked the bartender if he could get me some "chicken." He said "You bet, but not until it was dark." …Following this I went to the home of Stella Seips who is the mother of a three year old child (illegitimate). This young woman frankly admitted that anyone looks good to her who has the price and she was willing to meet me at anytime or any place. From 12 noon to 5 p.m. I visited 20 saloons but found nothing out of the ordinary. At 5:00 p.m. I met Josephine Gullen at the cemetery, she is about 16 years of age. Her cousin Lizzie Gullen was with her and is about 18 years of age. This young girl was with their cousin Josephine when I called on her the previous evening at which time I found three men in the house and all were drinking beer. At Josephine Gullen's I purchased a 25¢ can of beer. As soon as we got alone in the cemetery Josephine said she "got a piece of tail" from Fred Sanders last evening and Lizzie Gullen said she "prunced Harvey Wade." These girls proposed to elope with me to Milwaukee and start a sporting house. They wanted me to buy them each a suit of clothes and pay their way to Milwaukee, stating in return they would F--- me every night. Josephine Gullen admitted that the young man she had arrested did not try to rape her and that she squealed in order to get some money out of him. She said "If I wanted to be mean I could say you tried to rape me and make you pay me lots of money." I consider these two young girls to be dangerous characters for any community for they consider the method of blackmail a way of securing money.

Teasdale Exhibit - Unidentified wine room

New London - June 27th, 1914

Leaving Waupaca at 7 a.m. I arrived here at 9 a.m. and made my first call on Reverend Cochran who had previously been visited by Senator Teasdale. The Reverend gave me many leads which I proceeded to investigate and found some to be true. I found the conditions as follows: Mrs. Schroeder near the Fair Grounds with her daughter (supposed to have been married recently) are entertaining men and were arrested only about two or three months ago on this charge. Mrs. Klish, a married woman with a nice family, is always ready to meet men for immoral purposes. This woman lives just back of the Post Office. Young men visit Remmel's Saloon at the corner of Pearl and Spring Street. There is a small wine room at this place. There is a public gambling den at the Grand Hotel. Jack Hickey is operating a gambling den upstairs in the building next to the Grand Opera House. One man lost $500.00 and another $700.00 just a short time ago, at this place. Mr. Cochran operates a gambling hall over the John Harris Saloon. The roadhouse formerly operated by Mrs. Cass (now at Oshkosh) is closed. This was the only real open sporting house in the vicinity. All the others are what may be called private houses. I called on Mrs. Downer, Mrs.

New London High School (circa 1915)

White, Mrs. Butler, Mrs. Ponta and her daughters finding all the above to be lewd characters. Marie Ponta is but 16 years of age and yet she wanted me to take her to Milwaukee to make some easy money. Reverend Cochran of the Methodist Church told me that it was a conservative estimate to say that 9/10 of all the girls in New London are loose characters and he gave me the information that about half the High School graduates this year were diseased.

3 Members of the New London High School Class of 1914

Bernadine Yost
"Ca-Plunk, Ca-Plunk, Ca-Plunk, she's coming"
Student Senate
Thesis, Superior
Civilization of
Germany

Evva Jepson -
"Gypsy"
"I wish there were nine evenings a week, and a fellow for each"
Thesis, The
Convention system

Mabel Rohloff -
"Mae"
"Silent- but if aroused can be heard for miles"
German Club, Sr,
Thesis, High Prices

Oshkosh

I went to the South Side Park at 6:00 p.m., where it is the custom for a number of young girls to loiter until midnight. I devoted my time this evening between this park and the Electric Park up to 11:00 p.m. During this time I met eight girls who were willing to have intercourse for a stipulated sum. Many of the girls were from 12 to 17 years of age could be seen on the seats with men and boys, embracing and kissing each other. The young men speak of these parks as "Lovers' Paradise" and they are certainly on a level with their reputation. Young girls meet young men in the park and then walk outside of the parks where they linger on the grass for the evening.

At 11:30 p.m. I paid a visit to Menomonie Park which stretches along the lake and covers many acres of ground. Within this park is what is called a bathing beach, the boat landing, picnic grounds, etc. In the picnic grounds there are no lights and it is to these places where young men and girls retire. This part of the park is covered with heavy timber and here I found many couples at 2:00 a.m. I was informed by some of the park workers that it is nothing unusual to see young girls and young men leaving this resort at daybreak. The park commissioner is Ed Burkhart, who has police power, but seldom goes over the grounds to ascertain just how things are going. There should be special policeman for this park by all means. I retired for the night shortly after 2:00 a.m.

Very truly yours,
G.E.

Girl in a park wastebasket, circa 1914
(not a Teasdale exhibit)

At 2:00 p.m. I visited William Pueppke's Saloon, which is a meeting place for boys and girls. This is a real H---hole. A very tough class frequents this place. There are no rooms to be let here.

At 3:00 p.m. I went to Feinreich & Stoppers Saloon, #31 Main Street. Two young girls were recently arrested in this place. There are no rooms here, but it is a noted meeting place.

At 4:00 p.m. I visited Simpson & Koeplitz's Place, #71 Main Street, which is frequented by young girls.

At 5:00 p.m. I paid a visit to the Ozark Flats which are located at 20 Light Street. Pearl Johnson, the former manager of these famous flats, has vacated the place, and the madam formerly in charge is out of town.

At 1:00 (sic) p.m. I called at the Commercial Hotel and met Mrs. Fellows, who is cook at this place. She is a free drinker and is willing to go out any evening for $1.00, but will have nothing to do with a man in the daytime.

Phoenix House in Oshkosh, circa 1890. The name of the woman in the upstairs window, or what her occupation was, is unknown.

Oshkosh's South Park circa 1914

"Dirty Auto Livery, 124 North 3rd Street carries sports to the road houses and to other parts of the country. The drivers will call per phone all the prostitutes you choose in order to make up a party for a trip. The drivers know all the sporting women and the prostitutes know all the drivers. All of the big auto services have the same reputation."

Courtesy of Oshkosh Public Museum
Janis Bar on Main Street

Oshkosh area saloon, circa 1914

There is also a road house out 2-1/2 miles on the Lake Shore Drive, Jess Gokey, Proprietor. He has no inmates but the couples come out there for the afternoon and evening for a good time. Investigator treated a party of three-two whiskeys and a glass of beer. Investigator also took beer to be sure it was beer, paid 35¢ for same.

Hotel Roadhouse resort about 1-3/4 miles from town, on the Lake Shore Drive, E. Black, Proprietor. On the first floor is a neat bar room, at the side of which there is a large wine room. In the wine room there is an electric slot piano and a nickel in the slot gambling device. Upstairs are furnished rooms let to couples for assignation purposes, price $1 to $1.50. They have no license, but found them drinking whiskey and what appeared to be brandy. A young woman was tending bar. Bought a bottle of beer, which investigator paid 25¢. Said they had to ask that because of the risk they took in selling it to accommodate their friends.

Emma Graves at 332 8th Street, a regular parlor sporting house with 3 inmates and a hustling housekeeper, price $2.00.

Ella Stewart at 427 7th Street, a parlor sporting house, price $2.00. Has 7 inmates, sells beer at 50¢ a bottle, also sells whiskey.

Ozark Flats, six inmates, Landlady says she usually has between 14 and 16 girls.

Mrs. Nelly Merry at 360 Division Street, usually known as Calamity Jane, lets her rooms out for this purpose, says "she has a good trade for which she is well known."

Saloon at 31 Main Street, has 13 booths formed by seats, and has tables at which girls and women prostitutes gather. On the day the investigator was there 16 guests were there at the same time; six girls without male escorts were at the tables and were seen there to pick up men and go off with them.

Wants A Vice Inquiry

Jacob Paul was here from Farmers Valley, Monroe County, Monday morning looking for Senator Teasdale, head of the Vice Commission, who recently stirred La Crosse with his Vice Commission. Paul said someone up the valley saw a brakeman on a passing Northwestern train throw a kiss at a Hickory Hill School Marm and they want an investigation.

1914 PRICES

Small mansion in best section of La Crosse	$15,000.00
6 room, up-to-date house in Hudson with a barn	$2,100.00
6 Cylinder, 48 HP, Mitchell 6 Automobile (new)	$1,750.00
Small House with 2 lots, Hudson	$500.00
A "date" with the Widow Liddlefeld	$5.00
A weeks wages for a Girl to do housework	$4.00
Pair of ladies White Canvas Pumps	$3.00 & $2.50
A "back scuttling" in Milwaukee	$2.00
A "date" "On the peg" style in Milwaukee Dive	50¢
Ladies Summer Drawers, tight waist with loose knees and lace	19¢

Southeastern Wisconsin newspaper, 1914

Another Ashland Girl...

"This girl appears to have had a good upbringing, and from what she told me I think that she wanted to have good clothes and (illegible) looking for a good time. She went out automobile riding and had drinks with a man, he got her intoxicated and refused to take her back to the city unless she gave in, which she did as the man said he would take care of her. Her parents found out that she was running around and her father raised so much hell that she left home."

October 8, 1913

Dear Sir:

In reply will have been out of the area for sometime which leaves my correspondence somewhat behind.

As to vice and immorality, it is everywhere. The Catholic is catered to by the Politicians and no doubt you know what Priest and confessional means. And our girls are not <u>staying home with Ma.</u> But working in factories, shops, stores for <u>more</u> money and less virginity.

George A. Baker
New London, Wisconsin

Not only not staying home with "Ma," but out smoking stogies, drinking beer, and cross-dressing from the look of this contemporary photo. Besides being a writer of nearly incoherent letters, Mr. Baker was an agent for "Hupmobiles" and presumably in complete agreement with the Reverend Cochran.

A Helpful Letter From a Concerned Citizen...

Dear Sir:

  As you are the Chairman of the Vice Investigating Committee I just wish to write you a few lines.

  Although vice or sexual intercourse is wrong when it is for money there are three causes for the same and they must be removed before vice will ever cease.

  Now do not think that this letter is from a fool or some crank because what I have learned has come, under my personal observation.

  When the Red Light district was flourishing in Milwaukee I visited the houses and after visiting them I come to the conclusion that 3 nuisances must be removed before the vice problem will be solved. Those three evils are the Saloons the Dance Halls and to keep ignorant foreigners from coming to the country.

  Now these three evils must be nation-wide and not state wide.

  Now listen to me through. When I visited Milwaukee I asked these girls why they were in there and 9 out of every 10 said they did it to hide their shame which was caused by getting in the family way. And there some of them said also that they were ill-treated by drunken husbands and what was still worse these undesirable foreigners would get some girls and marry them or go through the ceremony and then put these girls in the houses of ill-fame and live off their earnings. I know this to be so.

  And there all saloon keepers will cater to white slavery. In regards to those girls who were in these houses to hide their shame I asked them if they danced before they came in to these house and they said "yes." Now I have had acquaintances of mine tell me that when they were dancing with girls that they always got a hard-on and had a desire for sexual intercourse with that girl and could always be satisfied. Now that is what the dance hall and the dancers will do.

  Now the only solution of the vice evil is to drive the three nuisances I mentioned out of the country. If you are going to have the saloons and dance halls and allow the greasy foreigners to come to these shores for God sake have the whore houses too.

  The way I should do if you are going to let the saloon run is to put the whore houses on a license and have a law passed allowing a whore house to every 1,000 population and make the license fee the same as a saloon.

  Now I am not signing no name to this because I do not want any one to know where it come from. But believe me this comes from one who has personally investigated this evil.

A less helpful letter from another citizen...

Say you Dirty Dog Running around the Country getting your name in it. If ever I get a chance at you I (illegible) put a bullet into you and the rest

–Citizen Correspondence to
The Teasdale Committee

37

GIRL ENDS HER LIFE BY TAKING POISON

Miss Luella Gamble, 24, known also by other names, committed suicide by taking poison early Tuesday morning at a roadhouse on Highway 13, south of the city. Authorities questioned Miss Beulah Spillman, companion of Miss Gamble, both of whom were inmates of the house, and learned that the latter had threatened on several occasions to end her life. On Monday night two Marshfield men drove out to the roadhouse and there was considerable drinking. Miss Gamble went to her room declaring that she meant to take her life but the other three paid little attention to her, until she came out screaming that she had taken poison. Death occurred before a physician could arrive there...

–*Marshfield News Herald, December 1, 1932*

Dear Sir:

I just happened to read of the evidence given by the police about whether the keepers of resorts were protected or not. Now I have a brother who is working for the city and he would be hounded out of his job if he went and told what he knows, without being called on, so I won't give my name. He did not see this but was told by the man who is the night Watchman at the City Hall. He is now an elevator operator and his name is John Oldenburg. He said one very cold night there was a young girl who was in a room of the Arlington Hotel. She was naked on the bed, with two men rubbing her to bring her to life. And another girl was in the room crying. It could all be seen from City Hall. The one man went away with an automobile and got a doctor, they worked from about 11:00 until 2:00 in the morning. The watchman called Policemen and they all watched it and when the watchman told them to go over, they said they didn't want to burn their noses. That looks like the place was protected. The girl was even carried naked to the window 3 or 4 times. If John Oldenberger is called before the politicians get at him he can tell all…

The above letter describing a long forgotten episode is typical of the anecdotal evidence that was the reason the committee was formed and the report issued. The Senator and his Committee were as appealing and fun filled as a 12 pack of O'Douls, yet just as well meaning. In all likelihood this investigative work was not undertaken due to needless blue nosing, or prurient interest on the part of Senator Teasdale and his fellow legislators. More reasonably, it was their concern for the welfare and safety of young women and morals of the society in general. The amount of vice the committee discovered was less than was predicted, and they uncovered no incidents of actual White Slavery. Some who were in poverty made a choice not to live what they thought would be the tedious life as a shop girl or factory worker and took what seemed to be the easier route to material rewards. Most were compelled by the circumstances in their lives to trade one undesirable existence for another when they left violent and drunken husbands, trading injuries for disease, or those unhappy with one turned to meaninglessness with many. Whatever the reasons, they made their beds and laid in them. And laid in them. And laid in them. The following pages show that prostitution continued long after the report was forgotten. But it is the exception, rather than the rule, that makes the newspaper. Local papers occasionally reported a raid or incident at some tavern or roadhouse, but excluding Hurley and Superior, taverns in Wisconsin were more Prosit Institutions than places for prostitution.

Hurley Taverns Raided Again

Hurley was raided again last Sunday night when 21 investigators for the state Beverage Tax Division simultaneously swooped down on seven Hurley taverns and one in Mercer... The agents leveled charges against 10 persons for gambling law violations, two with operating houses of ill fame, and two with soliciting for the purposes of prostitution. The agents hit Hurley and Mercer about the same time, 10:30 in the evening. Details of the raid follow:

Down Beat Tavern: Licensee, Joseph Moselle, charged with operating a house of ill fame. Jewel Johnson, about 35, charged with solicitation...

TryAngle Tavern: Licensee, James Shields, charged with operating a house of ill fame... Joy Wood, about 24, charged with solicitation...

Club Fiesta Tavern: Licensee, Eugene DeCarlo, pleaded guilty of operating a gambling house, fined $300 and costs, Mary Kaye, bing table operator, fined $50 and costs, Len Mallick, crap table operator, fined $75 and costs; bing, crap and blackjack table and all equipment and $23 cash confiscated...

Billy's Bar, Mercer: Bing table operated by Rose Hunter confiscated. She was fined $50 and costs and Walter Mazerka, Licensee was fined $100 and costs...

The Club Fiesta and Showboat Taverns had the distinction of being knocked off for the ninth time in seven and three years, respectively. Two months ago, after their eighth conviction, the Division forced Fred Fontecchio, Jr. of the Fiesta and Richard Matrella of the Showboat to surrender their licenses as tavern operators.

–*Iron County News, July 15, 1949*

The authorities might have been tipped off to illicit gambling at Billy's by the illegal slot machines shown in their advertising photos

A glimpse of stocking wasn't too shocking at the Downbeat Tavern.

39

Museum Bar

"During the daytime the streets of Hurley are more or less deserted, a few cars parked along the curb, the taverns empty except for a few stray locals, who stand at a bar sipping slowly the amber mixture or sit in the back room, head in hand. The Museum Bar attracts attention. Inside the place presented the neatest appearance of any establishment in town. Behind the bar presided a silver-haired man, tall and friendly, with the looks of a state senator. His great pride was a fabulous collection of wood carvings made by a local Norwegian. Under a glass cabinet which extends from floor to high ceiling and thirty feet from end to end are basswood carvings portraying individuals and groups in action - skiers,

the village blacksmith at his anvil, dancers, wildlife, hunters, archers, and scores of other pieces. Someone had remarked that the proprietor was the most gentlemanly saloon keeper in town. Yet, two weeks later the newspapers reported that he had been heavily fined for selling intoxicating liquors to minors... Night life in Hurley begins at ten o' clock. As the parked cars disappear from the streets of Ironwood, Bessemer and Wakefield, Michigan, and from Mercer, Wisconsin, the streets of Hurley begin to fill up. Few old-time cars are in evidence at night. Cadillacs, Buicks, Chryslers and Pontiacs are in the majority. There is a game carried on by the local citizens to count the licenses of

Michigan cars along the street. There are ten Michigan cars to one bearing a Wisconsin plate. "If the Hurley Taverns depended upon the patronage of Hurley people," remarked a local citizen, "the tavern operators would starve to death." The neon lights are ablaze, flashing their inside attractions to the gullible and the thirsty as well as those who seek slum conditions. The bars are filled and raucous canned music making a bedlam. In the few taverns which serve food the tables are filled by men and women, the high-pitched shrieks of the latter pierce above the hubub. Club Rondevoo's aluminum front, in cheap imitation of the night clubs of the big cities, is outwardly the most attractive on Silver Street. Inside the building is a bar on one side and on the other are tables jammed with patrons sipping their cocktails and beer, waiting for the leg show which will soon begin on a crude stage. As the evening advances the crowd becomes maudlin, demanding a show. The proprietor knows that as soon as the stage show begins there will be less drinking, so he delays as long as possible. Soon a few half-dressed women appear on the boards to shake and sing in hoarse tones amid the shouts and hand reaching on the part of the men patrons."

–by Lewis C Reimann
Hurley - Still No Angel, 1954

BABY FACE NELSON NEAR EAGLE RIVER?

Sheriff John Farmen, Sheriff Del McGregor of Vilas County and two carloads of Department of Justice operators and deputies from Oneida and Vilas counties, raided a resort 45 miles Northwest of Eagle River late Sunday afternoon looking for George "Baby Face" Nelson, a Dillinger gangster who was thought to be in hiding at the resort.

According to Sheriff Farmen it was reported that the gangster was masquerading as a woman.

–Rhinelander New North
Sept. 13, 1933

Burlesque dancers from a carnival or nightclub, somewhere in Wisconsin, sometime in the 1940s

OFFICERS SEEK GIRL FOR NUDE DANCING HERE

Miss Lona Drake, Chicago, was being sought today on a charge that she danced nude at the Garden Lunch Roadhouse on highway 12 and 18. Miss Drake was named in a warrant sworn to by E.D. Ballard, musician, who told officers he resigned a position at the Garden Lunch because of Miss Drake's dances. The warrant charged that Miss Drake "did unlawfully and publicly expose herself in an obscene and indecent manner by being completely nude in the presence of the complainant and several other persons on July 12 and 13." The warrant was sworn to Saturday afternoon, but when sheriff's deputies visited the roadhouse Saturday night they were informed Miss Drake, a professional entertainer, had left. The proprietor denied that the girl danced nude, claiming that she did not dance, but sang songs at the road house and was fully clothed. Ballard told officers Miss Drake was scantily clad when she danced on the night of July 12 and on the night of the 13th, Ballard said the doors were locked and she danced in the nude.

–Wisconsin State Journal, July 16, 1934

"I lived only 3 blocks from the Terrace Night Club, I seen it go up and down. I also worked there six years. One night (about 1933 or 1934) there was a big poker party - all the business men and big wheels were invited. They had naked dancers. Two ladies from town decided to go sneak a peek through the bay windows, overlooking the Apple River. There was barrels to hold rain water in case there was a fire. They put one barrel over the other to see what was going on. They seen the naked girls, so the next morning they called the Catholic Priest and did they (the business men) get hell. I met Al Capone and Baby Face Nelson, Big Mary, their mistress from Chicago. That night I told my husband 'Let's get the hell out of here.'"

–Anna Belisle, Somerset

Eight Men In & Out

Frank "Seagan" Lange, (the tall fellow next to his wife in this circa 1940 picture), was with the Chicago White Sox and compiled a fairly respectable record through 3 seasons from 1910 to 1913. He was teammates with several of the soon to be infamous Chicago "Blacksox," the team that threw the 1919 World Series. Although Fred was off the team before that scandal developed, he might have picked up a few bad habits from his crooked teammates. He was released by the White Sox midway into the 1913 season and journeyed northward to Columbus where he purchased the Fountain Saloon. During Prohibition, Frank operated the downstairs as a speakeasy and the upstairs was a "house of ill-fame" for the "sporting crowd." The place stayed in business until Prohibition ended in 1933 and reopened as legitimate saloon.

Courtesy of the Hard Head's Bar

Courtesy of the Art Helm Family

Around 1946, Olga's Beer Rats are beered up and ready for a game. At this point though, it was too late for a road trip to Frank Lange's Saloon, upstairs or down. Frank died in 1945 and passed the business on to his widow. She later sold or gave it to the round faced fellow on the left in the picture at the top of the page. The new owner, a life-long bachelor, did not restart the upstairs business.

It is not shown, but a missing scene to this late teens advertisement might have been where the Old Style Grenadier got tossed out of the upstairs of Frank Lange's Saloon for dressing like a sissy. After the humiliating incident, the jaunty fellow wiped off his silk pantaloons and ruffled blouse and then attempted to restore his manliness. In this illustration he has headed over to the local diamond and is tossing a high hard one past the bottle-wielding slugger while grasping a foaming mug of Old Style.

Window Tappers

My father got most of his beer for his Blue Moon Tavern from the Northern Brewery. He could not read or write English, just Slavic. One time during the Depression or right after, things were slow and the brewery said he could come down to the brewery and work the debt off. We made brandy in the basement and one day my Dad went and got a bottle, gave it to me and told me to take it to the foreman and give it to him and work for him that day. So I operated a bottle washer. I stood on two beer crates and put 4 bottles at a time into the big wash tub. At morning break the foreman got everyone and we went to the tap room. He said we could have a bottle of beer from the cooler or a glass from the tap. Same thing at noon and afternoon break and after work. I was only 15 at the time. It was good beer. The next day my Dad told me to go back again, I ended up working there all summer. At the Blue Moon we also made wine and brandy in the basement. All of us kids would wash our feet and help stomp on the grapes. The first wine was excellent, it was like champagne and we kept that for family and friends. Then Dad took the pulp and added water and sugar and made a new batch. It was OK too. We sold that over the bar and at the back door of the tavern to the winos. He also made a plum brandy called Slivovitz. This is how he managed to make a living and raise 9 kids, from just the bar. It was difficult back then.

I tended bar at the Blue Moon when I was 18. You should have been 21, but the law at the time said it was OK for family members. Some of the girls from the bordellos down the street were customers. I got to know them all and be friends with them. At the time there was seven large bordellos in Superior, this was between 3rd and 5th late in the 1930s. I knew most of the owners. They would stop in and show their appreciation if we referred any business to them. Sometimes in the morning they would be doing their socializing, they didn't want to drive drunk and they wanted me to chauffeur them around to the taverns. Sam Coker, operator of the St. Paul Rooms, and his wife were out for two days with me. He came in days later and threw a $100 bill on the bar for me. Those guys had money. One time I looked in his dresser drawer and it was full of wads of cash. Tens and twenties in bundles, could have been $50,000. At any one time there would be four or five ore boats at the docks, and in addition to the sailors there was lumberjacks and even miners from the range. There was 314 John, the upstairs of Tony's was called Rosie's, The St. Paul Rooms. Then off the downtown from Ogden to Grand there were little cottages for the "window tappers." You'd walk down the street, and in these little brown cottages there would be ladies in the windows tapping on the window and motioning you in. Next door to the Tip Top was Herman's Pool Hall, it was run by a guy named Dave. In the back room was gambling. In the afternoons some guys would play pinochle and cribbage, but at night it was three tables of high stakes poker. There was a gambling house across the street from the Ritz. In the basement of the Ritz were the only slots in Superior.

–Alex O'Kash

"Silver Boots" Mona was a well known figure in the nightlife of the tavern-filled area near Third Street and John, Superior.

Mona, Lady of the New Years Evening. At the Tip Top, December 31, 1959.

Hard working Mona, ready for the seamen of the Twin Ports.

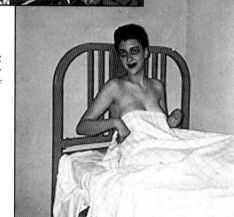

Down To The Cabaret

Courtesy of Angie Bronson

"We brewed in the basement during Prohibition, the police knew about it but no one was ever thrown in jail. We had a small brewing set-up in the basement-bottles only. I would fill up the baby buggy with beer and everything else. My grandma would be sitting in a chair, and you know how they would wear those big dresses. She'd sit in one spot with bottles under her dress on the floor, ready to sell. Of course federal agents would come around once in awhile. They would come into Tony's, we had a partition made there, by the door there, and if we knew who it was we would let 'em in. There was a counter there, cigars for sale and snuff. My dad used to go for a ride every night to see if the federal agent was at his home or if his garage door was open. If the door was open we knew he was out and that we would have to be more careful. After a while we moved the beer making upstairs. And then we made wine. Two bottles of beer for a quarter and you got a bottle of wine for free. That was the gimmick and everybody liked it. We always had a pretty nice dance floor. We had a wonderful band. "The Biggest Little Band," three brothers and a cousin. This was before 1948 when Frankie Cox started in as the

house band. My dad heard them at the Log Cabin by Chippewa Falls and hired them to come up here to play. They were so fabulous we just couldn't believe we got 'em. Saxophone, piano, drums, and bass, and they would all sing. The girls used to come in alone and never worried about a thing. And another thing, I was one of the instigators to let women sit at the bar, they could at Tony's. This was not allowed in those days. If a man came in and talked to a woman at the bar, you could get arrested for that. When the beer came back my dad was the first one to go and get a keg of beer. The first beer we served after Prohibition must have been Peoples. We were across from 1608 Third, a House of Ill Repute and Indian Sadie's. She was a colored woman, blind too, prostitution house.

I used to have girl friends come over and we would watch to see who was going in there. Club Superior was the biggest club, live music seven nights a week. The Ritz was a big club too, at Third and John Ave., and they were open almost all night. There was the International Club run by the Vucovich's, the Blue Moon was down the street and was run by the O'Kash's. Herman's Pool Hall was around the corner, the Savoy next door."

–Angie Bronson, owner of Tony's Cabaret in Superior

Courtesy of Angie Bronson

Tony at the bar

SHERIFF RAIDS BLAZING STUMP

Sheriff Gerhard B. Jensen and deputies raided the Clover Inn, more commonly known as the Blazing Stump, in the town of Harrison Tuesday night and arrested six girl inmates of the place and two men patrons. The girls pleaded guilty on a morals charge before Justice Franklin J. Schmieder at Chilton Wednesday morning and were fined $100 and costs and ordered out of the county. The men patrons were fined $15 and costs for frequenting a disorderly house by Justice of the Peace Oscar Schaubs early Wednesday morning. Including costs of girls paid a total of $693 while the men paid $32.95 each or a total of $65.90. The Clover Inn was at one time a tavern but its license was revoked by the Town of Harrison last summer.

–Chilton Times Journal, March 16, 1939

RAID TAVERN SOUTH OF CITY

A raid on the Green Roof Tavern, just south of the city on Highway 22, resulted in the arrest of two women inmates Monday night. Charged with being members of a disorderly house, they were freed on $300 bail. They gave their names as Bernice Donnelly, 26, Milwaukee, and Betty Carson, 25, Marinette. The license for the tavern is issued to Mrs. Vivian Roberts. District Attorney James Larson said that undercover agents have been working in Shawano County for sometime, checking up on taverns. The Green Roof was one of seven taverns raided last fall when a large number of defendants were brought before a night session here.

–Shawano County Journal, June 3, 1940

Trixie's Private Funeral

Long before Ma Bailey's in Woodruff existed, the most famous whorehouse in the Northwoods was Trixie's, in Minocqua. Trixie's was on the west side of the present Highway 51... This tale is told by aged Minocqua resident, Al Ray: "Trixie was marvelous, or at least my father said she was. My Dad went there frequently. Trixie's was a class place, and well run. It's not the gents of the community that wanted the place to die, but their wives. When Trixie died, the do-gooders and the holy rollers of the community barred Trixie from being buried in the so-called "Christian" cemetery. This marvelous woman had given so much of herself to the community, and in the end she wasn't allowed to get down in the dirt with the girls, so to speak. My dad took Trixie's body in his boat on Lake Minocqua and found her a permanent burial place. That place is just east of Jossart Island. He never told anyone on what part of the island he buried her as she was placed in the grave with all her diamonds and jewels-which were considerable.

–Gangster Holidays

45

MURDERS & MAYHEM

ROOSEVELT'S FRIEND ARRESTED FOR DRUNK

John Garrity, the "Rough Rider Orator," who claims to be a personal friend of Col. Theodore Roosevelt in whose famous regiment he says he served during the Spanish-American War, was arraigned in the municipal court this morning charged with drunkenness. Garrity was even more eloquent than usual this morning. After a voluble plea in which he told the story of his life and imparted much information, valuable and otherwise, on subjects too numerous to mention, he asked that he be freed. "I've been in Superior twenty-four hours this time. Give me fifteen minutes, Judge, and I'll be out of the city and on my way to the Frisco fair." Judge Parker was so moved by Garrity's eloquence that he suspended sentence. "Let me go, too, Judge," suggested John Wyman, an Indian from the Cloquet reservation who was up on the same charge. "No, that speech isn't good enough to get you out," responded his honor, giving Wyman his choice between a $5 fine or a ten day term at the workhouse.

*–Superior Evening Telegram
March 5, 1914*

Drunken Sailor Removes His Shirt And Dives Through Saloon Window

While crazed with drink, an unknown sailor this morning pulled off his shoes and threw them through the windows of the saloon of Anton Kruprenski, 425 Tower Avenue, after which he tore the shirt from his back and dived headfirst into the splintered window pane. The man's head was badly bruised and his arms were torn to shreds by the glass. Detective William Mead and Patrolman Zimmerman, who were nearby hurried to the scene and called the patrol, in which the man was rushed to headquarters, where City Physicians C. M. Gould and D. R. Searles took him in charge. Several arteries and veins in the man's arms were cut and he lost fully a quart of blood before the bleeding was stopped by the surgeons. The floor of the room in which the man was treated was covered with blood and the place had every appearance of a slaughter house. Excepting for the weakening effect of the loss of blood the man is none the worse for the affair. He is being held pending his recovery for the effects of his injuries. According to the saloonman, the sailor had been in the place and became ugly, threatening to "clean out" the place. He was put out and immediately commenced wrecking the glass front of the thirst emporium.

–Superior Evening Telegram, May 8, 1913

PUTS HAND THROUGH GLASS BARROOM DOOR

"Texas" Owens, recently returned to this city from Racine, where he has been working for some time, "butted into" the limelight Saturday night about 10 o'clock when he shoved his hand through the glass front of the storm door of the Branigan Hotel barroom, severely injuring his hand and arm and shattering the glass. He bled so freely that he became frightened and hurried to the Beloit Hospital whither the police traced him by the drops of blood on the pavement. At the hospital the deep cuts were dressed, Owens nearly fainting from pain and loss of blood. Several stitches were taken. He is said to have been drunk at the time and it is supposed that it was some vagary that caused him to smash the glass.

–Beloit Daily News, December 23, 1907

Young Girl Soaked With Gore When Porter Hits Boy Patron With Beer Bottle ————————•

Saturday night in the wine rooms in the rear of Duval's Saloon at 1104 Tower Avenue a prominent Superior young man was hit over the head with a beer bottle by a Greek porter employed at the place and known as "Johnny" or "Tony" Palush. A doctor had to take several stitches in the wound and says it's a wonder the boy's skull wasn't fractured. For a quarter of an hour the place was in an uproar that would rival the best efforts of any "Bucket-of-Blood" booze joint in the country. Companions of the injured man threw beer bottles and glasses at the Greek, who fled in terror to the back room and took refuge behind the bar. Efforts of the proprietor, "Bill" Duval, and his bartender, Earl Childs, to pacify the warring elements were fruitless and the porter would probably have been the victim of considerable harm but for the fact that he armed himself with a huge butcher knife and dared his enemies to come on and get "carved." The trouble started when the porter was delivering beer to a wine-room party which included at least two men who may have been of age but didn't look it and two young girls who certainly were not 21 years old. The beer was not being served to the liking of one of the boys and and when the porter objected to the criticism of the service one of the young men "took a slap at the Ginny," to quote a description used by a spectator. The porter defended himself with a beer bottle used for a weapon. With one husky swing he split open the scalp of the boy who had struck him. The lad went down in a heap with blood spurting all over the room. The dress of the young girl sitting at the table with him was saturated with blood. The companion of the injured lad started after the Greek to get revenge but the latter fled, pursued by what bottles and glasses remained. The boys followed the fleeing porter to the bar and would have continued the fight but for the butcher knife. Order was finally restored, the injured boy being taken to a doctor, the girls sent to another room and the porter spirited out of the place before threats of "raising a gang to get him" could materialize. No arrests were made as a result of this riot and there is no record of the battle at police headquarters. The Duval place has been open every Sunday for months, apparently being so confident of its protection that it did not even follow the example of a number of other saloons and close up for a couple of Sundays during the recent activities of the "crusaders." The patrons were watched a little closer, that's all, and anybody who "looked right" could get in. Yesterday nobody was barred. It snowed a little in the forenoon and there was a beaten path to the back door of the saloon five minutes after the snow ceased…

–Superior Evening Telegram, February 16, 1914

No Arrests Follow Gory Stabbing Affray Which Results In One Death, Police Get Assailants Name And Description From Lips Of Dying Man

On Friday night, February 13, Matt Eskolie, a Finnish laborer, was stabbed in a brawl on North Third Street, between Tower and Banks Avenue, on the north side of the street. According to half a dozen men who were questioned by a Telegram reporter concerning the affair the assailant was one Herman Maki, who has the reputation of being a "bad man," having been mixed up in at least one cutting scrape prior to that of last Friday. Eskolie's injuries became so painful that he went to the Soumalainen Saloon, 1807 North Third Street, where he was taken in and given a bed upstairs. On Saturday a doctor was summoned. It was at once apparent to the doctor that Eskolie was in a very serious condition. Blood poison had set in. Sunday morning Eskolie was removed from the room over the saloon to St. Mary's Hospital. His condition became steadily worse. The blood poison advanced to that stage that the amputation of the injured leg was the only chance to save his life. But as the operation was about to commence it was found that he was already dying. He was consequently taken back to his bed where he died at 8:50 o'clock on Wednesday night, February 18…

–Superior Evening Telegram, February 20, 1914

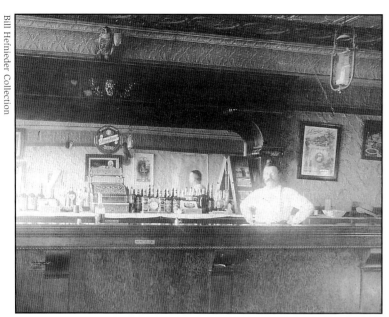

New Richmond Area Tavern (circa 1906)

Street Brawl at New Richmond ────────●

Old Feud Culminates in a Row in Which Two Are Hurt Seriously

A feud that has been existing for a long time between members of the Emberson and Christianson families, farmers residing near Deer Park, some miles from here, culminated in a five handed riot in this city last night.

The fracas started in a North Side saloon, and it was fought out in the early evening on the principal business street. Beer bottles, boots, and fists were the weapons used, and they were used promiscuously without referee or timekeeper or any sort of interference until the belligerents all appeared to have had enough. As a consequence Gilbert and Oliver Emberson are laid up for repairs, and Chris and Tom Christianson, brothers, and Christopherson, a cousin, are held awaiting the outcome of Gilbert Emberson's injuries.

Emberson was horribly cut up by beer bottles about the face and head, then he was kicked and beaten beyond recognition. Some of his forty stitches were taken in his wounds by Dr. F. S. Wade. His brother Oliver was also quite badly beaten up, but he has only a few stitches to his credit.

−Hudson Star Observer, April 17, 1906

ASSAULT AND BATTERY

A scrap with beer bottles between some young men on the north side Saturday night resulted in badly bruised heads for Gilbert and Oliver Emerson; 30 days in jail for Christopher Ellison, and a fine of $10 each and court costs for Christ Christianson and Torvial Christianson. Officers Lynch and Brickley quelled the disturbance, and the trial was before Judge Hough.

−New Richmond News, April 20, 1906

3401-B

Couture's Saloon in New Richmond, in calmer times about 30 years after the big brawl

Somerset Cat Fight

Jack Boss (left)

"Next door to Henry's house was a large building. When I was real young it was a tavern. I believe it belonged to Art Morrissete. Art and his wife and family lived above the tavern. At the time I guess Somerset was the capitol of moonshiners. Many moonshine stills throughout the area. Usually every Sunday and Monday mornings after the weekend drinking, some of us kids would get up early and walk around the town in all the alleys, etc. to look for empty moonshine bottles to sell back to the taverns for a nickel. I suppose they would just fill them up and sell them again. One time Willard and I saw Art leave the tavern and walk back by Uncle Delors warehouse and reach under the building and take out a bottle of whiskey and took a drink, then put it back. Willard and I would go and take the bottle and empty it and then go sell the empty bottle. We did this three or four times then I guess he hid the bottle in another place. Don't know why he wouldn't take a drink in his own tavern.

"In those days everyone had to prove how tough they were and Archie's was the site for many fist fights that we observed when we were kids. We'd watch through the large front windows and when we noticed two fellows arguing the word got around in a hurry and all the kids in town soon had their noses up against the windows and sure enough when they started fighting. It seemed like the whole tavern erupted in a bunch of fights. I believe Jack Boss was about the toughest fighter there ever was around Somerset. Archie's could hold his own with most. Bill Beseau, I believe was the strongest of any except for perhaps Jack Boss, but he lacked skill.

"One day Jack Boss came into town. Don't know where the fight started but I know it ended up in Henry's Barber Shop. I saw five guys grabbing onto Jack and he would just smack one and then the other and either knock them off or knock them out. Henry was not a fighter but he tried to stop them from wrecking his barber shop. Jack hit Henry and knocked him cold.

"I will tell you about one of the most famous fist fights that ever took place in Somerset. Believe it or not, it was between two women, and I missed it. Willard and I were up river fishing for northerns. When we walked into town there was a very large crowd gathered by the fancy restaurant in Dr. Phaneuf's building. It seemed as though everyone was hollering and shouting. After a lot of questions, etc., this is how it was explained to me. Mary Lou, who was a dancer at the Terrace Night Club, did not get along with one of the other dancers. In fact, they were bitter enemies. This other dancer knew a professional woman fighter, and she hired her to beat up Mary Lou. One day around noon this dancer and her fighter came to Somerset to beat up Mary Lou. It happens that Dave and Mary Lou were out of town but that they would be back later in the afternoon and they always ate supper at this restaurant. Practically everyone in town had heard about the big fight that was to take place. It seemed like even the country people had heard about it and came in to witness the fight. One of the boys heard about it and came home and told my mother about it. She thought it was just terrible. She kept calling the eating place to see if Dave was there or Mary Lou. Finally Dave and Mary Lou drove into town from St. Paul in Dave's big car. They later told me they wondered why there were so many people in town and they were all telling Mary Lou and Dave "hello" as they were walking into the restaurant. They sat at the table for a few minutes and someone called and asked for Mary Lou. She went up and answered the phone and came back to the table and sat down. Dave asked her what was the matter because she looked so pale and frightened. She told Dave that Mrs. Shay was on the phone and told her that a professional fighter was in town to beat her up. They got up and started to leave and a cup came flying through the air and just missed Mary Lou's head. I guess they made it outside and this is where the other lady caught up to her and they began fighting. Some of the men later said that they would have hated to get into a fist fight with either one of them. I guess it was the surprise of her life. It is claimed that Mary Lou gave more than she received. After a lot of fist fighting and hair pulling, etc., a deputy sheriff for the town of Somerset stopped the fight.

"Through the years Mary Lou and Dave would hire practically all of us kids that asked them for a job. Donald worked there and I worked there. I believe Elaine worked there. I often wondered why they were so good to our family as jobs were very scarce during that period. My mother then told me one night a group of women were playing cards and when Mary Lou met my mother for the first time she thanked mom for that call. She said that of the friends she thought she had in Somerset, who were all aware of what was about to take place, a woman who she did not know at all was the one who warned her."

–Marvon Shay of Somerset

One Of Three Shots Found Its Mark

Tuesday evening about seven o'clock, John Nelson, a farmer residing in the town of Hughes, was brought into town suffering from a gun shot wound in his right arm. He was shot by George Hughes, the bartender at the Half-Way House, a saloon located on the Iron River-Barnes Road, about 6:30 in the evening. Nelson is in an Ashland hospital and may lose his arm, while his assailant is in the Bayfield County Jail, awaiting trial in Circuit Court upon the charge of assault with a dangerous weapon with intent to murder. Nelson, who is of small stature and sixty or more years of age, was in Iron River on Tuesday, and, as is his habit, got drunk. In the afternoon he and three companions hired an auto from a local garage to take them out to the Half-Way House. There the party and some other men, drank and made merry. The Half-Way House was, we are informed, sold about a week ago to a Superior saloon man named Hogan, who sent down a man to run the place. The latter's name is George Hughes. Hughes was on the job Tuesday, and there was also a woman there, whose identity has not been clearly established. Hughes has stated that she is his wife; she has made other statements that would lead to other conclusions. Be that as it may, she was in and out of the ballroom frequently during the course of the afternoon, mingling with the men and partaking of drinks at the bar.

Iron River circa 1918

Nelson paid attentions to this woman that aroused the ire of the bartender, who "called Nelson down," according to the stories of witnesses. Hughes came from behind the bar, caught Nelson by the arm, and shoved him toward the wall but in the general direction of the door leading to the highway, remarking at the same time: "You dirty ------, go through the door now!" Hughes' anger apparently increased and as he stepped behind the bar he kept talking to Nelson, who made no reply or offer of resistance. Finally Hughes turned around, extracting a pistol and fired three shots at Nelson in quick succession. At the time Nelson was standing in the open doorway, steadying himself by leaning against the door casing. One of the three shots found its mark, striking Nelson in the arm several inches above the elbow and passing downward and backward, coming out at the elbow. Soon after the shooting, Hughes hired Everett Moreland to take him to Gordon with an auto, and he there secured another car to take him to Superior. He was arrested there the next morning in a rooming house and brought down last night by Under-sheriff Long. When arraigned in Municipal Court he had nothing to say other than that he desired to waive extradition.

–Iron River Pioneer, June 20, 1918

Chief Dies From Injuries Suffered In Fall ─────────────────●

Mel Bloomer, proprietor of the tavern in front of which Police Chief Antone J. Steffes was found unconscious about 1:30 o'clock Easter Sunday morning, availed himself of his constitutional rights and refused to testify Wednesday afternoon at the inquest into the circumstances in which Chief Steffes suffered the fracture at the back of his skull which resulted in his death. Mel's wife, Mrs. Julia Bloomer, did, however, submit to nearly an hour of the most minute questioning by Walter J. Clark, a special assistant to the special prosecutor… In her testimony, Mrs. Bloomer said that Mr. Steffes had come by the tavern a few minutes after 1:00 a.m. Sunday while she and her husband were discussing whether to go up town for a lunch. She said she saw Mr. Steffes strike Mel with a blackjack and then stumble backwards about three yards and fall on his back. Questioned as to whether Mel or she had hit or shoved Mr. Steffes, Mrs, Bloomer declared positively that neither of them had hit or shoved him. She said that Mr. Steffes had not said a word to either Mel or herself. She said that she went to Mr. Steffes when she saw him fall, that she heard him moan, that she went to the tavern and fetched some brandy for him and that Mel carried him into the living quarters on the east side of the tavern and laid him on a davenport. Questioned as to whether she thought Mr. Steffes was seriously hurt in the fall, Mrs. Bloomer said that she did not think he was badly hurt. In response to questioning, Mrs. Bloomer said she was aware that Mr. Steffes had cautioned her husband about the 1 o'clock closing hour several times. She estimated that this had happened "about a dozen times" to her knowledge "in two and a half years." …Dr. Minahan, the first witness called at the inquest, testified that he was called to the tavern about 1:30 a.m. and that when he got there he found Mr. Steffes lying on the davenport in the tavern living quarters unconscious from a brain concussion and a skull fracture. He immediately called an ambulance, he said, and had Mr. Steffes removed to St. Agnes Hospital, Fond du Lac, where he died without regaining consciousness at 3:50 a.m… The autopsy report described the skull fracture at the back of Mr. Steffes' head and discoloration from an injury on the left cheek. There was no finding of any chest injury. Herman Rau, who has been operating a tavern since April 1 a few doors from the Bloomer Tavern, told of meeting Mr. Steffes outside of his tavern and of talking to him. This was about 10 minutes after 1:00, Mr. Rau said. He had closed his tavern and was about to leave for home, Mr. Rau said, and he asked Mr. Steffes if he wanted to ride up town in the Rau car… Steffes replied that he had his own car down near the depot. In the course of their talk, Mr. Rau said, Chief Steffes had commented on having had some trouble with Mel Bloomer, about closing on time… Adolf Kulick, a sign painter who was staying at the Bill McGrath tavern said he…was sitting in the McGrath tavern when he heard loud talking outside. He identified that voice as that of Mel Bloomer, but was unable to understand what was said. He looked out, he said, and saw the form of a man lying in the street in front of the Bloomer tavern. Later he went out to look around and the body was gone. Asked why he was not more curious about what happened, he said he thought it was an intoxicated person.

–Chilton Times-Journal, April 9, 1942

FRIGHTFUL ACCIDENT

Oman is the man who stabbed a fellow quarry man at Fairwater last fall during a drunken brawl in Hilderbrand's saloon. Judge Gilson, of Fond du Lac, has released upon his own recognizance, Michael Oman, who has been held since last September on a charge of assault with intent to kill. The case is a peculiar one. Oman, who is a Finlander, cannot be tried for the reason that he does not speak English and that no one can be found who can converse with him in his own language. During the months he has been in jail he has learned to say "tobacco" and "matches."

–Green Lake County Democrat, January 10, 1884

Speaking of frightful accidents…

Yeggs Abduct Two Women, Rob Tavern ————————————————●

Efforts are underway to apprehend three men who abducted two local women Saturday night, stole the car they were driving and later that evening held up Nellie's Tavern at the Bass Lake Crossroads, where they lined up some thirty patrons in the place and robbed them of their cash and jewelry. The women, Mrs. C. J. Reiter and her daughter Julie, were taken six miles out in the country, gagged, and tied up with tape and picture wire and abandoned at the pea viner on County Trunk N. After this was completed, the men drove away in the car, apparently taking the same route through the "badlands." The yeggs then drove to Burkhardt where they purchased five gallons of gasoline from Mrs. Glen Batten, who became suspicious and jotted down their license. After getting the gas the men drove directly to Nellie's Tavern at the Bass Lake Crossroads. Mrs. Mahler, the proprietor, stated "one of the men came in and drank about three glasses of beer. Then the other two came in, drew their guns and ordered all of us to stick up our hands. I started to run upstairs but one of the men, who I recognized as Jack Solis, grabbed a hold of my arm and pulled me back down the steps. After searching and robbing everyone in the place and looting the cash register, one of the men took several bottles of Irish whiskey and several cartons of cigarettes. Before they left they jerked the telephone from the wall, shot up the tires of two or three cars parked outside, and took the ignition keys from several more."

–Hudson Star Observer, Sept. 22, 1933

PULLS "TEMPORARY" HOLDUP OF TAVERN

A friendly bandit made what you could call a "temporary" hold-up of a tavern here Monday night. The man, unmasked, walked into E.A. Brievogel's tavern near the west city limits just before closing. Brievogel was alone. Brandishing, Brievogel told officers, what he thought was a .32 caliber revolver, the man asked for money. "I only want to borrow it for a few months," Brievogel quoted the man as saying, "I'll pay you back in a couple months." Brievogel said the man took about $250 from the cash register and his wallet then tied him loosely in a restroom and drove off. Brievogel freed himself and called authorities.

–Wisconsin Rapids Daily Journal, December 30, 1952

Would-Be Tavern Bandit Roughed Up, Yells 'Uncle'

The guy had in mind a quiet, little tavern holdup but it was like falling into a cement mixer. Carrying his artillery and wearing a mask, he walked into Frank Schneeberger's tavern early Friday and announced the purpose of his visit. Then the fun started.

A backhand wallop from Louis Zimmerman, 38, a patron, sent him reeling. A cuff on the wrist sent his gun flying. A beer bottle launched by Cecil Sorenson, 31, dropped him to the floor. Punches from both assailants kept him there. When the police came, the would be bandit pleaded "take me out of here quick before they kill me." The officers accommodated him. First to the hospital for repairs, then to the police headquarters minus four teeth. The prisoner identified himself as John Tomlinson, 28, Ashland, who completed a five year term for burglary and car theft at Waupun State Prison 17 days ago. He was charged with assault and intent to rob while armed.

–Superior Evening News, August 1949

Man is Shot to Death ●

Frank Liddlefeld, a bartender in the Stacey Saloon, was killed Monday night by Peter Culbis, who fired two shots at him, they taking effect in Liddlefeld's body. Liddlefeld died just as medical aid reached him. It is reported that Culbis entered the Stacey Saloon Monday evening and played a game of dice in which he was beaten and refused to pay. Some words followed and Culbis left, to return later with a gun which he shot at the bartender twice. It is stated by the police that last fall Liddlefeld was tending bar at the Soo House and had some falling out with this man Culbis who vowed to get even. Culbis was then sentenced to 15 days in jail. The murdered man was about 36 years of age and leaves a wife and two children. He was at one time a fireman on the north side. His remains were taken to New London where they were interred Wednesday. Peter Culbis was arraigned Tuesday morning in municipal court and admitted to the shooting but was not able to understand the court fully. The hearing was continued until Wednesday and again to Thursday morning. Thursday morning Judge Walker held the preliminary hearing in the courthouse... Dr. H. J. Westgate testified being called to Stacey's Saloon Monday night finding Liddlefeld dying and he testified that Liddlefeld died immediately after. He said he found but one wound which he believed was caused by a bullet but blood was flowing from the man's mouth. He could not find a wound there or in any other part of the body. The bullet had severed a large artery and Liddlefeld had bled to death. Guy Daly testified that he had worked in a lumber camp with Culbis and came to Rhinelander with him. He said that he was going to shoot someone with whom he had a quarrel in the Soo House... Frank Wilson, a bartender in Stacey's, told of Culbis quarreling in the saloon over a game of dice but was not present at the shooting.

–Rhinelander News
March 14, 1913

VET GOES BERSERK IN OCONTO

An evening of drinking and shooting which tallied three holdups landed Ben Trepanier of Oconto in jail where he is awaiting deposition of his case... Trepanier started the evening about 4:15 when he entered Alice's Bar on Pecor Street and after a short conversation with Mrs. Lancaster, the proprietress, he brandished a gun at her and told her it was a holdup. He ordered her from behind the bar, and after scooping about $30.00 from the till, he struck Paul Larmay on the head with the gun, and fired several shots at random before leaving. Mrs. Lancaster went to her 2nd floor apartment and notified the authorities. In the meantime, Trepanier had gone to Chubby's Bar, having driven there in his 1930 Pontiac. Here he repeated the performance, getting about $14.00 from the till after ordering the proprietor, Herman Debbins, away and firing four shots, one barely missing a customer. By this time Officer Henry Toole was on his trail, and was told that he might be going to the Log Chateau operated by Mr. and Mrs. Ernest Pecor. This was a good hunch as by this time, Trepanier had the owners, six adults and two children lined up against the wall. Toole was ordered to do likewise, but, keeping up a steady stream of talk, the officer managed to get his gun after a final blast. He had taken about $28.00 at the Chateau. According to his story, Trepanier does not recall what happened between the time that he took the gun from the home of James Blucher, an Oconto fireman, and the entrance of Officer Toole at the Chateau.

–Oconto Falls Herald
January 18, 1951

1,000 Rounds For The House, Please

Hundreds of federal agents and posse men swarmed through a huge wilderness area today searching for John Dillinger and a half dozen associates after three desperate battles in which two men were killed and four others wounded, one critically. Three girl companions of the gangsters were captured and held incommunicado.

The battles, which raged through the dark forest of this resort country, followed 48 hours in which Dillinger and his henchmen had held Emil Wanatka, proprietor of Little Bohemia Lodge, captive in the resort with his wife, his 8-year-old son, and two employees. More than 50 federal agents and local officers engaged in the three battles, in which the gangsters answered assaults with flaming machine guns, and the attackers literally blasted doors and windows out of two resorts with buckshot and rifle fire... Capture of Dillinger and all of his companions probably was prevented only by the unfortunate exit from the Little Bohemia Resort, at the very moment that 17 federal agents prepared to enter, of three youthful conservation corps workers. Despite shouted orders to halt, the three entered a motor car and started away. Someone among the ambushed federal men opened fire with a machine gun, sweeping the car from front to rear. Eugene Boiseneau, 27, died at the wheel and the car careened into a tree. John Hoffman and John Morris were taken from the wreck, wounded and injured internally. "The radio was playing in the car," moaned Hoffman, "and then something hit me. I didn't think anything was wrong before that." Realizing their error, the agents hastily reformed their lines around the resort. It was learned later that Dillinger, John Hamilton, and another gangster had seized the opportunity to flee afoot during the excitement. Other members of the gang, warned, opened such fire that the attackers retreated... The night's fiasco came after a week of intensive detective work. The Department of Justice officials were believed to hit upon the Little Bohemia Lodge hideaway after questioning numerous persons close to the Dillinger gang. The building was known to be owned by Emil Wanatka, former Chicago night club owner and an intimate of Frankie Lake and other Chicago bootleggers...

–*The Wisconsin State Journal*
April 1934

GREETINGS FROM LITTLE BOHEMIA

Emil Wanatka

THE FAMOUS LITTLE BOHEMIA LODGE ~ MANITOWISH, WIS.

THE FAMOUS LITTLE BOHEMIA LODGE MANITOWISH, WIS.

Gimme A Bloody Mary, And Make It A Stiff One... —————————————•

A person who apparently killed and then carried away the body of a 55-year-old town of Pine Grove tavern keeper Wednesday afternoon is the object of a state wide search today. Sheriff Harold S. Thompson was called to Mary's Tavern on County Trunk D, five miles west of Highway 51, about 6 p.m. Wednesday after a neighbor had found the tavern empty and bloodstains leading from the bar room through the door to a spot where a car or truck had been parked. The victim, apparently, is Miss Mary Hogan, 55, who has operated the beer tavern for several years. She lived alone in a bedroom and kitchen behind the tavern. Seymor Lester, a neighbor, came to the tavern shortly after 5:15 p.m. to buy ice cream. He opened the door, saw blood on the floor and notified Vilas O. Waterman, the town of Pine Grove chairman. Waterman came to the tavern and then notified the sheriff.

Searching the tavern, authorities found a .22 caliber cartridge case of the type used in automatic pistols. Two one dollar bills and a roll of nickels were found on the floor. A cash box behind the bar and a cigar box used to keep money had been rifled. Neighbors believed Miss Hogan kept a considerable sum at the tavern, but Sheriff Thompson said he had no idea the amount that is missing. A coffee cup was upright in the center of spilled coffee at a table in the bar room, and the chair next to the coffee cup had been tipped over. A book was on the table. A few spots of blood were on the floor near the chair and a trail of blood, through which a body had been dragged, led from a spot four or five feet from the table to the door, then across the snow to a point where a car or truck had been parked.

–Wisconsin Rapids Tribune, December 1954

Shoot The Bartender —————————————————————•

Less than 24 hours after his capture, George DeMo, 31-year-old ex-convict who has served time at both Wisconsin and Minnesota prisons, was sentenced to life imprisonment by Judge A. Walter Dahl in Superior Court on a charge of first degree murder. "I'm sorry it had to happen," was DeMo's only comment when asked by Judge Dahl whether he had anything to say before sentence was passed and he pleaded guilty. DeMo will be transferred to the state penitentiary at Waupun as soon as the arrangements can be made. DeMo had been brought before Municipal Judge Claude F. Cooper for arraignment shortly before noon, and was bound over immediately to Superior Court, and appeared before Judge Dahl at 12:30 p.m. DeMo, 31, was charged with first-degree murder Thursday by District Attorney Andy Borg in a fast-moving sequel to the brutal slaying of Hite H. Snow, 33, the wounding of Mrs. Catherine Frederick, and the looting of the "Hite and Kay" tavern at the junction of Highway 13 and Highways 2 and 53. The crimes occurred early Wednesday afternoon, and DeMo was captured two hours later by Superior and Duluth police as he attempted to escape to Duluth in a taxicab. The cab was stopped in a roadblock set up at the Interstate Bridge... An ironical touch to the murder of Hite Snow was provided by an "electric eye" game at the Hite and Kay tavern. The game is one in which the player uses a rifle with an electric beam and fires at a tiny figure which walks back and forth in a glass cage when the patron inserts a nickel. The sign on the game, designed to lure players, is this: "Shoot the Bartender." Snow's body lay in the tiny washroom a scant 10 feet from the game...

–Superior Evening Telegram, January 8, 1948

"He told me he got up about 5:30 in the morning and that he had a bottle of whiskey under the porch. He was staying out at Billings Park at 2003 Wisconsin Avenue... After he drank this whiskey he then went back to bed. He then got up and did a little more drinking about 9:30 a.m. and then went to downtown Superior. He went to to a tavern at 7th and Tower known as Billard's Tavern where he had a few more drinks and then made a call to the Asylum at Parkland. He wanted to contact John Walz, the Superintendent at Parkland, for a job. After making this call he decided to go out to Parkland. I might also tell the court that he also informed me that the day before he had purchased a .32 revolver at Gordon's, a second hand store in Duluth and also purchased six shells at Marcus Loan in Superior. So at the time he was to go out to Parkland he had in his possession the gun and the shells. He got on a bus and went out to the East End where he stopped at another tavern where he had a couple more drinks. He then boarded another bus and went out to Itasca where he had a couple more drinks. He then walked out to a tavern that was formerly know as McCafferty's now being operated by Mr. Hite Snow and a Mrs. Frederick. When he arrived in this tavern there were two to three gentlemen in there and Mr. Snow and Mrs. Frederick. He hung around the tavern and had a couple bottles of beer..."

–Portion of DeMo trial transcript

Cadaver's Tavern

A full-scale investigation is being conducted by local and state authorities here today into the brutal slaying of an elderly town of Grand Rapids woman. The body of Miss Clara Bates, 76, was found about 6 o'clock Monday night in the living quarters attached to Cad's Tavern, a beer tavern she operated seven miles east of Wisconsin Rapids on the Portage County line… Time of her death has not yet been established, although it is believed to have occurred sometime after 11 p.m. Sunday when she closed the tavern, authorities said… Authorities have as of yet advanced no motive for the murder. A robbery motive has been ruled out, however, since the tavern till had apparently not been touched and jewelry on the victim had not been removed. The body was discovered by Edward Kanieski, 620 11th Street South, and Alvin Phipps, Rt. 1, who lives about a quarter mile north of the tavern, at about 6 p.m. Monday. Kanieski told authorities that he had been driving with his wife and child on County Trunk U, which runs past the Tavern, and decided to stop in for a beer. He found the tavern door locked, he said, and walked around to the rear of the building, where he heard noises inside that sounded "like a woman or child weeping." Puzzled by the sounds, Kanieski said, he returned to his car and drove to Phipp's home. They went back to the tavern, entered the house by way of the open rear door and found the victim's body in a bedroom. They immediately called the sheriff's office on the house telephone, Kanieski said.

–Wisconsin Rapids Tribune, July 1, 1952

It is not known how much time George DeMo, who so quickly received justice, spent at Waupun State Prison. His prison records could not be recovered. But hopefully he spent a long time locked away in that dismal location and far from the gaiety of Waupun's Greystone Tavern.

Kanieski, the fellow who found Clara Bate's body at her tavern, was later charged and convicted of the murder. During the trial, the defendant stated that Cad's Tavern was a "sporting house" and that the back living quarters were occasionally used by visiting prostitutes and their johns. Could the "Cad," briefly referred to in the Stevens Point section of the Teasdale Report many years earlier, be the same person? Probably so, she would have been in the same profession, her tavern was only about 20 miles or so from Stevens Point and she would have been about 30 at the time of the Teasdale Report. Kanieski spent about 20 years in prison, but was then freed on appeals, despite what would seem to have been an overwhelming amount of circumstantial evidence. The mystery of the missing Mary Hogan was finally resolved 2 years later in a horrific manner. A County Sheriff found her remains on the farm of the notorious Ed Gein who lived a few miles from the tavern. She is thought to have been his first victim. Alfred Hitchcock's 1960 movie, "Psycho," was the film version of the novel "Psycho" written by Robert Bloch of Weyauwega. The

novel was inspired by the crimes committed by Gein. Whether the murder at Cad's Tavern, which occurred a couple years before and 50 or so miles from Weyauwega, was the source of the "Bates" family name in the novel is not known. If so, the forgotten and childless Cad Bates might have at least passed on her name, not with a normal line of progeny, but forever linked, at least in a tiny slice of cinematic history, with the warped and deranged character of Norman Bates.

CONGENIAL EVENINGS

Pleasant Times...

Many of the preceding pages recall incidents of prostitution, acts of lawbreaking, and violent events. As we have offered earlier, these episodes made the local papers, or were recalled by old timers, due to the fact they were exceptions. Sing-a-longs to "Who Stole the Kieshka?" were the closest brushes to criminality that most taverns ever encountered. As Ma Gordon might have sung, "There's a dark and a troubled side of life, but there is a bright and sunny side, too. Though you meet with darkness and strife, the sunny side you also may view." There were 100 Buttsy and Evies, Ervin Ressies and Ma Gordons for every George Hughes. The main attraction of the tavern through the years has been the gemütlichkeit, the camaraderie. As it was at Oscar's Tavern it was the same 10,000 times over: "A pleasant way to spend a congenial evening." The following pages are happy slices of Wisconsin tavern life to refresh that point, and leave the cheerlessness and troubles of the previous pages behind.

Courtesy of Doug Dahl

"Here's To You" in Hammond about 1940

THE CITY TAVERN

The City Tavern, managed by Leo Hickey, has recently been redecorated and remodeled. A new backbar and other improvements have transformed the tavern into an inviting place where thirsty patrons may enjoy their favorite beverages amid delightful surroundings. Hickey is noted for his ability to remember faces and names. Many a stranger, visiting the tavern after an absence of several years, has been pleased and amazed when Leo has greeted him by name. The tavern is popular among both local residents and tourists.

The Tomahawk Leader, 1930s

Who can say what can cause a new love to bloom: a casual look, a little glance, a well turned phrase, or maybe the accelerant of Cupid's arrows could be the arrival of your favorite beer on tap! This Ready Teddy, with a gleam in his eye that could lead from beer to paternity, and his nicely coiffured lass blinked on and off all night long, being part of a Peerless light-up advertising sign.

Speaking of Walter's Beer Garden...

For many years this piece of property, situated on the North Side on Forest Street, has been well and popularly known to the people of Eau Claire, and has held its place as one of the most attractive pleasure spots in the community. It was here that the people gathered to forget their troubles in the afternoon or for an evening concert by some local band. A dance pavilion at one time was filled to capacity by the young people, while on Sunday the entire family gathered there.

–Eau Claire Leader, 1911

Oscar's Tavern at Wauzeka, owned and operated by Oscar Bieloh for 37 years, is the spot in Wauzeka to spend a pleasant, congenial afternoon or evening. Here you may purchase beer on tap or in bottles, mixed drinks, soft drinks, cigars, cigarettes, candy, gum or shoot a game of snooker or pool. You will find congenial company and a courteous host on the person of Mr. Bieloh, who has had a lengthy musical career, and was with the Ringling Brothers Circus for many years. You will also find the services of an experienced bartender at the 30 foot bar, one who knows how to mix your drinks as you wish and as you order them. Seventy-five patrons can be accommodated at one time. Ladies are invited. Atmosphere and conduct of this tavern are all that could be desired.

–Crawford County Press, Prairie du Chien, July 8, 1937

As they lingered over their lager, do you suppose this couple realized what an ephemeral pleasure they were partaking in? These folks are enjoying a couple bottles of "Highlander Beer" from the short lived Highland Brewery, open from 1933 to 1942.

At The Rustic on Highway 61

Phyllis

and her
Incomparable
Melodic Organ Rhythm

Currently appearing

HALFWAY HOUSE
GORDON, WI

Management: Central Booking Office .. 203

1960's

At the Halfway House, Phyllis allowed all to enjoy the incomparable rhythm of her organ.

ENTIRELY AIR
CONDITIONED
Phone 3366

WONDER BAR

Most Modern Bar In
Northern Wis.

Frank A. Handrick, Prop.

206 Washington St.
WAUSAU, WIS.

A national sensation in the 1950s and 1960s, Liberace was born in Milwaukee and was supposedly reared in Wausau, where he met his first love while playing a gig at the Wonder Bar in the 1940s.

When Your Spirit LAGS take a SWIG at SWAG'S

You could have a swig with "Swag" if your spirit lagged in Burlington.

61

Once A Mill, Local Tavern Started in 1907

The reconversion of a feed mill into a saloon forty-three years ago brought Denmark one of its most familiar business places. Chris Larsen sold the mill to Lawrence Hendricksen in June of 1907 for $1,000 and after several months of remodeling the tavern was opened for business. It has remained in the same hands and with the same furniture and fixtures since that time. John Jorgensen did the carpentry work. In the fall of 1907 Mr. Hendricksen and Miss Minnie Rasmussen were married. Mrs. Hendricksen has been operating the tavern since 1935 when her husband died. Hendricksen's brick fronted tavern is located in the heart of the village. With the exception of the remodeled front the Hendricksen's have preserved the quaint atmosphere of the "old style saloon." A few fixtures in the tavern, dusted with history, include a black poker table with built in shelves on each leg for bottles of beer and four matching wood arm chairs with rounded backs. The table and chairs have become somewhat of a relic and Mrs. Hendricksen explained that if she would ever sell out they would stay with her despite the many offers by her customers to buy them. Above the bar hangs a picture taken 40 years ago in the Kellner Milliner Shop, once in business across the street. The gents in the picture are all donning large flourishing hats popular in 1910. They are Lawrence Hendricksen, Frankie Hershman, Jake Strickel, John Jacobson, Frank Wanek, Henry and Frank Kellner, Willie Hansen, Henry Gelmer, and Jack

Hershman. The caption written on the picture reads, "Oh you kids." Flipping back the pages of history about 12 years, Mrs. Hendricksen told about the children that used to play football and pitch horse shoes on their lot on the side of the tavern, where the Denmark Cleaning Establishment is now located. She remarked that they would play whenever they had a chance then run in their tavern for a bottle of pop when they got tired or warm. Mrs. Hendricksen is very pleased with her business and intends to run the tavern for as long as possible. She is also proud of the village she lives in and the improvements that are constantly being made.

–The Dairyland Review
Denmark, Wisconsin
December 1954

Shaded in age only by the back bar at the Monarch bar is this old German card table with corner shelves to place your stein of beer. Customers here play skat, an old German game. From left are Jim Scholmeier, Laude Giverson, proprietor Carl Heitman and Allen Funke.

Courtesy of The Monarch Tavern

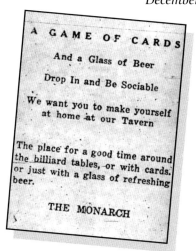

A GAME OF CARDS

And a Glass of Beer

Drop In and Be Sociable

We want you to make yourself at home at our Tavern

The place for a good time around the billiard tables, or with cards. or just with a glass of refreshing beer.

THE MONARCH

Customers in the 1950s were still accepting the invitation offered in the 1933 Buffalo County Republican to have a glass of beer and a game of cards at the Monarch bar in Fountain City.

Ed Chaney ●

Ed Chaney had been operating the tavern he built, and rebuilt, outside of Spooner on Little Spooner Lake for about 20 years when he married his wife Darlene. They then operated the business and raised a family over the next 30 years.

Ed's family moved to the area from Iowa in 1909. They built a log cabin and farmed on 180 acres just down the road. Ed was born in 1911. He liked to cook and wanted to open a restaurant, but the county clerk at the time said he should start out with a tavern. It was easier to get started and make some money to buy the restaurant equipment. A beer license was only $5 at the time so he did that. I don't know why he never did go through with the restaurant, I guess he did just fine with the beer and drinks. Ed sold a lot of Walter's and Schoens. We had an auction here a few years ago and sold a round Schoen's mirror. He always had hamburgers and polish sausages, but that was as far as cooking went. He built the building himself in 1944 with stone and logs and a wood roof. It burnt down once but he put it back up. The first couple years the place had a dirt floor. Sometimes on a Saturday night, they would have to wet the floor down because the dancers would raise too much dust. Ed had a Wurlitzer jukebox for the dancers, it was turned up as loud as it could go. He had to chain it to the wall, it would get to vibrating on the uneven floor and fall over. When he started out, there was an outdoor pump for water, and on the inside was a horse tank filled with ice for the beer, and boards over pop boxes to sit on. When I first visited the place he had a wood floor, but there were still outdoor bathrooms, that was in about 1966. In the 1950s he built a small motel on the shore of Little Spooner Lake, but that burned, too. Afterwards he built three cabins up near the bar. Ed always had a good business with lots of friends. There was some occasional trouble, sometimes some drunk would make a smart remark and Ed would put them in their place. He was big and strong, he could place one hand on the bar, vault

Ed Chaney outside of his Spooner area tavern about 1960

over it, and be right on top of things in a hurry. He knew how to box as well. His father taught him. His dad had been a sparring partner for Jack Johnson at the turn of the century. Yeah, he was in good shape. His last child was born when Ed was 71. He was still working the bar until he was 86. He passed away three years ago. He had a lot of stories. We wanted him to write a book of them, but he never did.

–Darlene Chaney

Hilma Willa

In 1937 my father John O'Brien and a friend decided there were not enough taverns in the area where we lived in St. Croix County, so they rented an old mill in the tiny village of Boardman and made it into a tavern. They called it the Monte Carlo and ran it for two years. It had a bar at one end, booths down the sides, and a few tables. The middle of the room was for dancing. We had living quarters at one end of the building. There was only a door between our area and the barroom. There was a kitchenette to one side where my mother made sandwiches, soup, stew and coffee. We weren't allowed in the bar except on Sunday mornings when we helped our mother wash the beer and shot glasses. I hated the smell of the stale beer. On Saturday nights my father would hire a piano player and a group of three or four tap dancers and singers who would put on floor shows. This really would pack the tavern. Since we kids were not allowed in the tavern, sometimes the performers would put on a mini-show for us kids in the kitchen. We thought that was grand. The area was mixed with French, Irish, and Germans—lots of good beer drinkers. The piano player was a chubby lady. She was out of New Richmond and her name was Hilma Willa. All you had to do was keep a full glass of beer on her piano and she'd play all night. She got louder and louder as the night went on. She wouldn't even get up to go to the outhouse. We didn't have bathrooms, just an outhouse out the

Monte Carlo, Boardman, 1940s

back door. She would play Schotizhes and old time waltzes and everyone would be dancing. Everyone had fun. Everyone was poor, but didn't know it. Mother finally got pretty burnt out on it, raising seven kids and all, and cooking and helping tend bar and we sold it and moved to the south part of the state.

–Lola Huber

Neither snow nor rain nor gloom of night nor lack of heat from a broken furnace stays these males from the swift completion of their rounds of Point (or Schoens or Rhinelander Shorties).

Buttsy & Evie's One Night in the Late Fifties

Buttsy & Evie

My dad sold moonshine back in Prohibition. When I got home from school, my mother and I would bottle it up by hand. They later had a store in Doering where they sold a little out of. When Prohibition was over, I remember my dad got a half barrel of beer tapped in a washtub filled with ice in the front room and sold beer right there.

…I wanted to work in the Leideger Brewery so I quit high school. My mother went to the owner of the brewery and said she had to get her kid back into school, she didn't want to see me drop out. So he told me if I didn't drop out, when I got out I could have a job there. So when I finished school he gave me a job as a shipping clerk. I dispatched trucks and I also went around in a brand new 1939 Pontiac to service the beer coolers in the taverns. The taverns didn't have much cooler space so we'd bring one in and the owners had to put in a quarter a day to make them run. So I went around and collected money from these coolers. My boss told me at every stop I should buy a round for all the boys. By the time I got back the sack was nearly empty. At every place they knew when I was coming and they'd be there for the free beer. Had that job for a couple

Buttsy & Evie, about 1955

years. When I was in the service I stopped in a bar in Tennessee and I ordered a beer and the bartender says the beer comes from Merrill, Wisconsin. He said it was the only beer he could get. Boy, did I feel good drinking Leideger in Tennessee.

We bought the place in 1947 after I got out of the service. I took it over from a guy named Gieshart. I changed the whole thing, smashed up the old bar and put in a new one. We sold lots of Rhinelander Beer and Marathon, too. I worked awhile as a distributor and hauled Rhinelander from Portage through Herb Schultz.

I had it about 25 years and always had good times, we never had any kind of trouble. We had music here, mostly country & western groups. When we had a group they would set up on the pool table. Sometimes I'd play Hawaiian music. I'd wear a grass hula skirt and play my Doodlesucker (a stringed instrument made out of a frying pan and broom handle). My dad invented it and we all had a good time with it. The bar opened at 8:00 in the morning. We had hamburgers, bratwursts and Bar-B-Ques. No television then and people would come out and have some fun. The best years were from 1955 to 1960. Things started to change after that.

I'd have something made up every Christmas to give away. One year I had some ashtrays made up. The ashtrays said on them, "Your Pleasure, Our Success." It must have been from the late 1940s. Awhile back a fellow came up to me and asked if I had any of them left. I said no and he gave me one. He said, "I don't have long to live, so I'll give you this one." Gee, a week later he was dead. I was at an auction a little bit ago and some other fellow said he had one of my key chains. He said I could have it because I didn't have one of those left either. That same day they took him to the hospital for a heart attack. I went to a bar after that and some guy there said he had some of my bar chips for me. I told him the story of the other guys and he said, "To hell with you," and put them back in his pocket.

–Buttsy Mosser, Merrill

65

The Gingerbread Barman

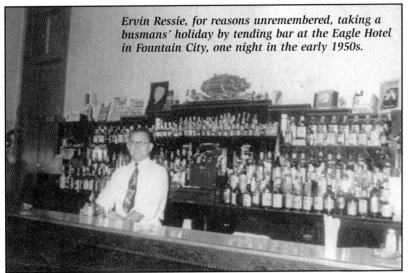

Ervin Ressie, for reasons unremembered, taking a busmans' holiday by tending bar at the Eagle Hotel in Fountain City, one night in the early 1950s.

Courtesy of Ervin Ressie family

Ervin Ressie operated the Gingerbread Tavern for almost 50 years, in a converted river boat just a little north of Fountain City.

My business came out of Winona. The Gingerbread actually started out as a boat! It came from the boat yard, it was a quarter boat. They used to use it for dredge work. Chopped the cabin right off the hull. Towed it down the highway. I was in there eighteen hours a day. I started in 1936 or so, for 47 years. I went to work at 5 o'clock in the morning and we would open at six-thirty in the morning. We usually did, too. Sometimes I stayed there until one or two in the morning! We didn't have no competition. Now there's six of 'em. The beer I sold the most of was Grain Belt. Shit, I paid more here than they did in Minneapolis for a case of Fountain City beer. They sold it out there for two-fifty a case and here I had to pay two-seventy-five. I sold Walter's and Miller's, too. Potosi was a good beer,

too! I drank beer when I was twelve years old over at the Bub's brewery in Winona. You know what's wrong with tavern owners today? They think they're big shots. They don't want to work. They want to sit on the wrong side of the bar. You can't do that. I never drank when I was behind the bar, never in all those years. When I first was in this business, if you came in and you were fourteen years old, I'd serve you a beer, but you'd better behave yourself. If you were lipping off that meant you didn't come in here no more. We didn't have no trouble. The state inspector came in and said 'How come in all the twenty or thirty years you've been in business you have never had a mark against you?' I said I treated 'em right when they came in and told them they better behave themselves. Some kids came in and they were buzzed up and I asked them if they were 18. They said, "sure." I said, "I'm sorry but you've got to be 21." I remember one time there was trouble. It was one Labor Day and the place was packed. It was four o'clock in the afternoon and it looked like midnight, a big storm coming. All of a sudden everyone left and I'm in there by myself. A car pulls up and in walks two guys, oh, were they drunk! "Give us a drink," one said. "No," I said, "I'm locking up." Smash! One threw a bottle at me. I hurled over that goll damn bar and I hit that son-of-a-bitch, and they ran outside and I give 'em another one and he fell over the railing. They got in their car and drove off real fast. Pretty soon the sheriff pulled up. I said, "What the hell do you want?" "I got a warrant for you 'cause you hit those guys, you attacked them." "Damn, there's two guys and only one of me and they threw a bottle at me." I went up to the judge and he said "You're nuts"... let me off. I always tell people what I'm thinking. You know what I said to my doctor when I saw him two weeks ago? He said, "You drink much beer?" And I said "Yeah... about fifteen bottles a day... and I spill a lot, too." I told that one girl to bend over and take your medicine, and she said, "What for, I'm not even sick?"

–Ervin Ressie

66

Courtesy of Ervin Ressie family

The Gingerbread Tavern, about 1962

At least in the early days, Ervin operated with some of the same serving rules that many country taverns used. The qualifications to buy beer were not a reaching a certain age, but a minimum height. If your nose could reach above the bar, you could get a beer.

Courtesy of Two Rivers Historical Society

This pair of Two Rivers young-uns, circa 1938, were on the wrong side of the state to patronize the Gingerbread Tavern.

Courtesy of The Art Helm Family

The era between World War II and television was prime time for taverns. A crowded jukebox Saturday night in Saukville. A jolly group crowded around the Rockola jukebox at Olga's Tavern.

There Once Was a Grocer named Ol' Sam Drucker... ——————●

The Spa in Hammond was quite a place, a little place but real good food. In Glenwood City they built a tavern that is still there, the Boondocks. Out of town on the north was a place a Belgian guy built and they called it the "Belgian Church," The Catholics would go to early Mass and then stop there and drink because he would open early there. Wilson was open but Glenwood City and Baldwin were closed on Sundays. Highway 12 was the main road from Chicago to St. Paul. Down in front of the Shady Rest there was a drunk that wandered out in the road and a semi-truck hit him so hard it left his shoes right in the road where he stood. That Shady Rest was quite the place. A lady named Esther ran it as a speakeasy and then a tavern. At the Shady Rest you could get a beer for a nickel, a hamburger for a dime and a piece of tail for a quarter. She later sold it and headed up to Trego to another place. Down the road from there, just after Prohibition, a guy named Shultz had a real nice place, a little tavern. In those days it was hard to get a hot shower being out in the country. Well he had hot showers there for a dime. You could work out in the field like the farmers did and then bring clean clothes and clean up out behind the bar. He also had German bands in from Menomonie for a big birthday party he would have for himself every year. Right in Wilson there was a bar there, it had outside biffies. I went there one time back in 1949 with my niece and her boyfriend. Well he was a

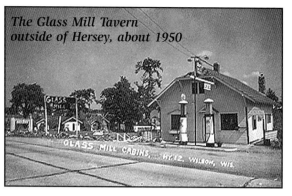

The Glass Mill Tavern outside of Hersey, about 1950

tall guy and he went out to use the biff and he reached up and caught a sparrow that was flying around. He kept it in his hand and brought it in and let it go and said, "Happy New Year" and it flew all around that goll darn bar all night. If a guy was drinking a lot and it was affecting his family, they would put his name on a list in the county bars and no one could serve him, so the drunks would just take off and drive to the next county and drink. I used to drink triple brandies, quit cold turkey 30 years ago. I drank a lot of booze but I never got on that list. I sure got on my wife's shit-list though...

–*Russ Thorsen, Glenwood City*

The Gray Goose

The Gray Goose was a fun place; they really had some good bands there: Whoopee John, Lawrence Welk, even Cab Calloway played there once. My sister and I would put up flyers on the telephone poles in Hammond and get in the dance free. It was for a long time just a dance hall. They didn't sell liquor. If people at the dance wanted a drink or a beer they would go across the street to the two taverns there. But toward the end there they put a bar in the Gray Goose but it kind of spoiled things. It seemed people would just stand around the bar and drink instead of dance. We used to go to Roberts, too. There was a rickety old dance hall there. It's gone now but they would have the Old Time Music there. If you wanted big band or swing or the modern music we would go to Hersey. The White Owl was a fun place, too. We had a friend who met a soldier there while he was on leave. They danced all that night and a couple of nights after, too, then he had to ship out. They wrote each other and then one day she took the train east and they got married. The day they got married was the first time they had seen each other in the daylight.

–*Adrienne Bruckner*

I remember the night the Gray Goose fell in. It was on a Wednesday night in 1962, January. George Zastro owned it and he hired a bunch of guys to shovel off the roof but they never showed. I helped sweep the floor that night and hauled in a bunch of beer with Agnes. At 8:00 they were to have a bunch of square dancers in there. At about 10 to 7 that thing fell down. I walked out of there about 6:30, went across the street to the other tavern and got my $2 and then walked home. When I got in the house we heard a loud cracking and banging and Arnold looked out the window and said "the Gray Goose is gone" We went up there and saw nobody was inside, but an hour later it would have been full of square dancers. – *Jim Keuhl*

**HARD TIME
DANCE
GRAY GOOSE
PAVILION**
HERSEY
Saturday, June 21st.
Music By
Elmer (Lars) Larson
and the Northern Knights
Coming Saturday, June 28
"SPIKE" HASKELL

Beer 'n' Bullheads

"Uh, bartender, howzabout a plate of Bullheads, some slaw, and a glass of Fox Lake, please. Oh, and yeah, how fresh are those Bullheads?" Add a bratwurst and you have "Surf & Turf" Wisconsin style. Badger barhoppers probably suffered as much from clogged arteries as they did from cirrhosis of the liver. The taverns of the Dairy State were on the whole, hospitable, homey and happy, but not healthful.

"THE WORLD'S LARGEST TAVERN OWNER"
The Host with the Most…
No Brag, Just Fat

What qualities does a good bartender need to have? Well, one is to be someone you can chew the fat with while you have a beer or a cocktail. Ed Bauer of Campbellsport could not be licked in that category.

Annual COON DINNER
AT
SIMON'S LOG CABIN
Jct. Hwys. 12, 18, and 51
Wednesday & Thursday — Dec. 8th & 9th
Served Family Style $1.50
also serving
HICKORY SMOKED PIT BAR-B-CUE RIBS
STEAKS, CHICKEN, SEA FOODS
RESERVATIONS for parties of four or more persons for Coon
Dinner taken any time during December.
CALL - CH 4-9741

Harry Fosch's Tavern (in Sauk City) once a year, at least, had a 'Coon Fest,' and it was absolutely delicious. When I asked him how he did it, he told me he roasted it, and then basted it with 7-Up and covered it. Boy was it good!

—Marion Korfmacher

Don't Miss the
Fried Turtle Feed
SATURDAY, JANUARY 27
AT
Bode's Tavern
SERVING STARTS AT 5:00 P.M.
On Hwy. 133 between Cassville - Potosi

Nejedlo's Tavern
COOPERSTOWN   HAROLD & MILDRED
BUTTER CRISP FISH
Served Every Friday Night
DAILY LUNCHEON—Tender Steak Sandwich, Home Made Chili
Vennerhke, Fresh Jumbo Shrimp.

PLAY CARDS
FOR CHICKENS
SUNDAY AFTERNOON
At
BUNGALOW TAVERN

Don't Miss the
Fried Turtle Feed
SATURDAY, JANUARY 27
AT
Bode's Tavern
SERVING STARTS AT 5:00 P.M.
On Hwy. 133 between Cassville - Potosi

Charley's of Medford… Home to Bar-B-Ques and probably Medford Lager

Chicken Chop Suey 25¢
For Your Dinner
TONIGHT
Serving Starts at 6 P.M.
At The
Rosebud Tavern
on the Sun Prairie Road
Music by the Rosebud Trio
and Smiling Jobo
Jack Kramer   B. 4892

Your Friday Night Treat
TURTLE PLATE LUNCH
Includes Mashed Potatoes,
Cole Slaw, Rolls
KEULER'S TAVERN
Hwy. 55 — Stockbridge
Phone 60 for Reservation

MANTHEY'S
Little Rib Tavern
Frog Legs Plate Lunch
AFTERNOON and EVENINGS
25¢ plate
FREE FISH FRY
EVERY FRIDAY

WHEN IN NEW RICHMOND—STOP AT
JACK'S PLACE—Jack Goodwin, Prop.
BEER
On draught and in bottles
Try One of Our Famous Dutch Lunches

Beer and a "Dutch Lunch" at noon, a "Dutch Oven" for the Mrs. that evening.

70

Happy Meal '41

Paul's Tavern of Spooner had everything you could want in a bar. Cigars, whiskey on and off sale, a local beer or two on tap, a peanut machine and dance music provided by an orchestra! Look closely and the photo reveals another, somewhat peculiar attraction, a little structure called the "Hamburger Hut."

Saturday, June 21, 1941
Dad & I went in and had a whiskey...
Burger, fried onions, pickle, fries, and a shot of Ancient Age...
Happy Meal circa '41

PAUL'S TAVERN
Dine and Dance — Orchestra Music
Spooner, Wisconsin

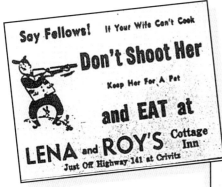

Presumably, one of the benefits of Peerless was there was no need for the traditional "Morning After Wisconsin Breakfast" (3 aspirins and a glass of Pabst).

The First Martini in Prescott

In the town of Prescott, William "Stingee" and Rose Stark bought a tavern from the Park Brewery in 1915 for $1,500. They owned and operated the tavern until 1945. In 1978 Rose gave an interview about the bar.

"When we bought the building it was about half the size it is now. The basement door on Orange Street was at the end of the building. When we had the tavern at first it was not common for women to come in. We had 5 and 10 cent beer; whiskey was 10 cents a shot. We treated customers to fried liver and onions, or pretzels that we bought by the barrel. Every so often my brothers, Fred and Albert "Carp" Schmidt, brought in some fish. I'd cut the fish into small pieces, fry them up, and put them out for customers.

"I remember the first martini mixed in the tavern. Most of the local people drank beer or a shot. But not too long after we bought the place, a university professor who was spending his summer on Lake Street came in and asked for a martini. Mr. Stark had never mixed one so the fellow gave him directions. It was probably the first martini mixed in Prescott."

—Rose Stark & Rick Foley, Prescott Area Historical Society

71

A newspaper can be read to review the latest local and national news, gain some perspective on politics, analyze stock prices or check out sports scores. The good folks at Medford Brewing thought it an activity that went well with beer drinking. In Chilton, during the summer of 1941, it could have been a blueprint for a paycheck-blowing weekend toot. They're all fun: dinner, dancing, or beer parties. "Choose One, Two or More." Can you pick beer parties twice? God Bless Wisconsin. The center ad, which reminded the area wives to keep a few cool ones on hand for hubby, concluded with a wink and the oddly suggestive line, "We Deliver As You Desire." These drivers, delivering to neglected wives of semiconscious, beer sotted husbands, might have had the best gig since the Teasdale Dicks of 1915.

"In those days the beer trucks would deliver to homes cases or pony kegs, or, if they were having a big party, the full size kegs. The driver would tap it for them and get it ready for the party."

–Nellie Bird

Ich Bin Ein Spoonerer

JFK's Irish campaign team sure knew where to hold a speech in a small Wisconsin town. Stopping in the midst of the October 1959 Wisconsin primary to do some street corner politicking, they chose the right end of the block in Spooner. This was outside of the Buckhorn and across the street from the Coral and Kurth's. Let's hope the future president is trying to make a political point with his hand gesturing, or better yet ordering a round of Walter's for the crowd, but not trying the old "pull my finger" joke on the open mouthed fellow in the front row. The brief article in the local paper did not report that after the speechmaking the senator headed straight into the Buckhorn where local Ed Ackley bought him a cold one.

Courtesy of The Buckhorn Tavern

SEN. KENNEDY GETS CORDIAL RECEPTION HERE

Senator John F. Kennedy received a warm welcome in Spooner Friday as he stopped in the city on his strenuous campaign tour leading up to the Wisconsin primary on April 5. Seeking the Democratic nomination for president, Senator Kennedy said he was impressed with Wisconsin's great vacationland, and placed the improvement of the farmers' station as vital to the economy of the state and nation.

Kennedy climbed on the hood of his car to give his short address, then answered questions from the crowd.

–Spooner Advocate, March 18, 1960

Courtesy of the Hartford Historical Society

We don't know if JFK tried the same tactic in Hartford, but he could have tried to win a few converts by doing so in what was the tap room of the Republican Hotel.

A wooden plaque on the Buckhorn's men's room door commemorates a visit the future president made after quaffing his beer. It could just as well have read:

"Kennedy's Johnson was here, but it wasn't Lyndon."

74

Dirty Taverns

Some Taverns Dirty, Says State Official

A story of unwashed glasses, dirt an inch thick and "indescribable" filth in many Wisconsin taverns was relayed to the senate state and local government committee yesterday.

Clyde S. Tutton, head of the beverage tax division, told the story in backing a bill to give his agency power to make taverns clean up their premises. At present, Tutton said, the state is powerless on checking sanitation of 10,000 out of Wisconsin's 14,000 taverns. The other 4,000 are inspected by the Board of Health because they also serve food. Many of the unchecked taverns are dirty, Tutton said. Some of the filth, he added, was so bad it could not be described at a public committee hearing. He quoted reports from beverage tax agents which told of several taverns throughout the state that washed glasses only in the morning and merely rinsed them with cold water the rest of the day. Another tavern used water from a contaminated well for glass rinsing and cleaning. In a rural Waukesha tavern, he said, rinsing tanks were "rotted, dirty and leaking." In a Chippewa tavern agents found beer tapped from a keg only three feet from a toilet. Dirty bars, floors, and washrooms were found in a number of other taverns. The filth is particularly bad in small towns and rural areas which have no sanitary regulations, Tutton said. Beverage tax agents have received no cooperation from small town local officials, who say that sanitation is "none of their affair."

–Ashland Daily Press, March 14, 1945

"One Man's Vice is Another's Virtue"

Among other traits, Germans are known for their admiration of neatness and cleanliness. Playing to that sentiment, John Baechler proudly advertised to his mostly German fellow Fountain-Citians, that "every glass was freshly rinsed." This would not have been acceptable for the overly fussy Clyde Tutton, who probably spread out lace doilies on the barstools he sat upon to make his persnickety inspections. More to his liking would have been the Wonder Bar of Rhinelander.

STOP AT
FOUNTAIN HOTEL
For Beer to Suit the most fastidious tastes.
Every glass rinsed in fresh running water.
JOHN BAECHLER, Prop.

Buffalo County Republican, 1933

The Wonder Bar - Air Conditioned

The Wonder Bar located at 230 South Pelham in Rhinelander, phone 512-W, not only designates the place but also signifies the entire atmosphere of the interior, majestic service, courtesy, and quality of the drinks served to you. Here one may drop in any time, especially on a hot sultry day and have his or her favorite cool and refreshing drink. Possibly you would like a sip of burgundy, a mint julep, a cocktail, a glass of fine wine, or maybe a cold glass or bottle of beer; whatever it is you can get it here. Amid the pleasant surroundings you are served your favorite drink. Everything is spotlessly clean and sanitary. Every glass is washed and polished until it shines. Such an institution as this one adds to the reputation of the community of being alive and wide awake. It brings favorable comment, not only from the locals, but from the traveling public as well and assists in making this a better place to live. People from every walk of life have found this the ideal spot to complete the pleasures of the day, and in the review of this community, due mention should not be omitted to the leading position occupied by the Wonder Bar in the social life of the community.

–Advertisement, Three Lakes News, June 1933

MUSIC & MERRIMENT

Wisconsin State Historical Society

Bessie Gordon, August 1941,
in her Schofield tavern

The Round Mound of Sound ———●

A small wooden structure in the center of Wisconsin might well have been the best example of all that was ever right and good with Wisconsin Tavernania. In what was then a rural area of Schofield sat a tiny tavern that was kept filled with song and good times courtesy of owner Bessie Gordon. From the early 1930s to some 40 years afterwards, she raised a large family and cared for a disabled husband on the proceeds of the tavern, as well as raising a few crops and serving as the county clerk. At Ma Gordon's, the distinctive focus of fun was a reed organ that was tucked under the bar. From there, the five foot tall, 300 pound Ma let loose her rich voice to entertain local farmers and townsfolk. She sang standards, folk songs and weepy old-timey ballads. More than one time an Aunt Flo pulled her Uncle Joe off a barstool by his bib overall straps to dance a schottische or a polka. The bantam barroom was as packed with fun and merriment as a Christmas stocking. Evidently that reputation went considerably beyond the borders of Marathon County. It was a long way from the little wooden beer hut in a rural area, not really far removed from frontier life, to the ivory towers of the University of Wisconsin. In the early 1940s a folksong collecting professor of music by the name of Helene Stratman-Thomas stopped into Ma's swing shack. The patron's befuddlement at her hyphenated surname perhaps equaled the professor's shock at the abbreviated wine list. Going past the initial Green Acres-like cultural discord, if the good professor had any smarts that went beyond vibratos,

continued... **77**

Photographs courtesy of the Gordon Family

staccatos, glissandos, and castratos, the tape recorder-toting egghead would have knocked back a couple of Schoens' Old Lagers, wolfed down some pretzels, and settled into her recording sessions. Maybe the combination of Ma's cheerful hootenanny and the effects of the local brew, led the scholarly barhopper to the conclusion that in not every instance does a 5 x 5 x 5 cubic polyhedron equal a square, especially when the object in question was the rocking and rollicking Ma Gordon.

The Country Club

As the great American philosopher Bo Diddley once sang "You Can't Judge a Book By Looking at the Cover." The La Crosse Area Country Club on the outside appeared to be a bit of a plain Jane, but inside you'd find an elegant backbar fully stocked with liquor, adorned by some paintings or artistic advertisements, and best of all, a wind up Victrola on the bar. The stylishly dressed proprietress stood at the ready to pour a shot or spin a platter in the pre-jukebox era.

Courtesy of U.W.- La Crosse, Murphy Library

Courtesy of U.W.- La Crosse, Murphy Library

Mood Swings

A splendid Wurlitzer 24 reigned over the floor of the Blue Heron Tavern in the Hayward area sometime during 1950s. The selections are out of view, but due to the musical richness of the era, one would be hard pressed to press wrongly on a typical jukebox that would be filled with 78s or 45s of Frankie Yankovick, Larry Lee Phillipson, Raylene and the Dairylanders, or the Six Fat Dutchmen. Those discs were among many that would start taps flowing and feet tapping. Whether providing music for dancing, boozy sing-a-longs, or just playing cheerful background sounds, a well stocked jukebox was the leading source of merriment for a tavern. Of course, where there is alcohol there are mood swings. Countless times a lonely sad sack would lead off coin fired concerts with records containing the braggadocio of Buddy Holly's "That'll Be the Day," and beers and tears later would be pumping in more nickels and dimes to hear Jim Reeves sing the forlorn "He'll Have to Go" eight or nine times in a row.

Wisconsin State Historical Society

79

67TH YUBA TWO-DAY DANCE MARCH 8-9

The 67th annual Masopust old-time two-day dance will be held at the Yuba opera house on Monday and Tuesday evenings, March 8th and 9th. Sponsors of the dances, which have become famous through many years of tradition, are now making all preparations to insure that this two-day dance will be one of the best in history. A different orchestra will provide music each night. The first night will feature a mask dance with many prizes to be offered. The prizes are: best representative couple, first prize $5.00, second prize $2.75, third prize $2.00, fourth prize $1.50, fifth prize $1.25; to couple coming the longest distance $1.25; seventh prize, to the oldest couple masked, $1.25; eighth prize to best clown $1.00. The judging of prizes will be decided by three persons picked by floor managers. Dancing will begin at 8:30 sharp. The grand parade will be held at 11:00... For sixty-seven consecutive years the two-day dance has attracted dancers from a wide area throughout this portion of the state. It is a tradition which has become interwoven with the history of Yuba. For the past many years the dances have been sponsored by Robert Novy, who this year again will be the genial host.

–Hillsboro Sentry-Enterprise, February 25, 1943

A tavern was the community center for dancing. The special amenities which led out the round of pleasure in that day, which made existence harmonious and agreeable, were feasts and dances. For those pleasures some were willing to endure real hardships, for they often rode miles in wagons drawn by oxen to join in the excitement of the evening. The dance was the quintessence of social events. Old people were rare in those days; all were fair, none were fat, and few were over forty.

Welcome was a word large with meaning when invitations were extended for an old time dancing party or other social affair in the tavern days. People liked people then as now and accepted and extended invitations for various social pleasures. The shams of modern society had no place; hypocrisy and selfishness were seldom present in these rustic entertainments, often the whole family would go to the ball, the children stowed away in bedrooms or below.

–Stage Coach and Tavern Tales of the Northwest, 1930
(from Harry Elworth Coles first draft, not used in book as published)

Yuba's Celebration

Martin Rott, Jr. and wife Tena recall the flavor for the earliest celebrations:

"At first I remember we had it in a tavern. We sat in one corner and played; the bar was in the other corner. As they danced, the women came within a few inches of the bar, but they never drank there - just the men in those days," Martin said. Dances began about 8 p.m. and lasted till 3 or 4 a.m. "Sometimes if everyone was feeling good even a little later." For years they played the entire dance both nights. He couldn't remember those long nights, but his wife, Tena, laughed and reminded him that the band members all came over to the hotel for oyster soup about midnight. She worked there then and remembered them well. They married soon after in 1907... Kate Marshall recalled the celebration as well, and how it took its toll on everyone: "Well, for one thing... they had their Masopust. That means, they tell me, in Bohemian, "Season Without Meat." And they celebrated that, before the Season of Lent. Usually it started on Monday. They'd have a two day dance, Monday night and Tuesday night. But they told me, some of them, that it was about a week long. They would dress up. And they'd play from sundown to sunup. They played clear around the clock almost. I mean, all night. Then in the daytime they'd take their bobsleds, load 'em up, some of them with musical instruments, and they'd go out and serenade the farmers out in the country. The farmers, in turn, would give them grain or something they could take back and trade or sell and get money to pay for any expenses. Yes, they had their Bohemian music...umpa umpa music they used to call it. There was some of those old fellows in the band, and they told me that playing from sundown to sunup and all of that, that their teeth, by the time that season was over, would be so loose they could just wiggle them."

–Yuba: A History of a Wisconsin Czech Community
by Phillip C. Braithwaite, 1998

My Dad Was A Moonshiner

My dad was a moonshiner. We started out in town at 213 John [Superior], he bought a big house down there. In the late 20s we moved out to the country, out by Pattison Park... Dad had at least 25 men working for him, it was a big operation. The whole house reeked of mash. He had a big still out in the woods and the mash upstairs in the house and dozens of five gallon Red Wing jugs sitting around there waiting to be filled. He had holes in the floor of the garage with cement tops, caverns under there for hiding booze. We had a lot of business from West Duluth. He made the best! We had money and dresses of black beads. He had maybe a hundred thousand dollars in 1931. Do you know how much money that was in those days? I was maybe five or six years old when one day a bunch of cars pulled up and these guys went upstairs with axes and chopped the whole thing up, they didn't care, they could do what they wanted, they were the Feds. There was a big trial, it was front page news. Al Otto, that was my dad, ended up in Leavenworth, Kansas. When he got out of prison he started up again, only on a smaller scale. He was arrested again and sent to a jail in Two Harbors for six months. It was real tough. It was a real hard time. My mother turned into an alcoholic. My sister and I

Glen and Nita Hope loafing circa '53

Courtesy of Nita Hope

thought she was going to get better but she would beg us to go down and get her another bottle. My dad did what he liked, he fought and lived to be 93. We had some good times and some bad times, too. My uncle made moonshine, too. One time somebody stole from him. It was winter, but he tracked 'em down all the way down Highway A to Amnicon Lake. He knocked on the door and had a confrontation, the guy shot and killed him right there! Eli Savitch shot him, got off on self defense. When I was a teenager I worked at Tony's Cabaret, must have been around World War II. I shouldn't have even been working there. I was a teenager and a cocktail waitress. They had music, of course, Frankie Cox was just starting there. My sister was working there, too. She met her husband there, he was home from the service. The Main,

continued...

Jonnny's, Club Superior - there was a lot to do on Third Street. We used to go to the Pickwick in Superior and "the Gitch" too, a supper club and dancing out in Billing Park. There was quite a gang of us. All good friends and good dancers, too. There was no TV. You had to go out and make your own fun. I got drunk on wine one night and crawled under our car; all that was sticking out was my feet. When they came out they were all plastered, too. It's a good thing they saw me; we had a good time!

Glen and I bought Neumann's summer cabin in the fall of '49. We sold a cow to make the down payment on the mortgage. We were both 21 at the time. We called it the Loafer's Lodge. At that time we could sell beer to 18 year olds. We put in a bar and four booths with the help of our neighbor Tony Kowlowik, who also helped us build a small house close to the tavern. Friday and Saturday nights were always busy; folks came from all over Superior, Duluth and the county. We had a shuffleboard and a nickelodeon and punch boards, too. The place was small but many couples found room to

Down the road from the Loafer's Lodge at Pattison Park

dance. We had a keg night two times a month; everyone who walked in the door paid a buck and they could drink from the keg all night long and eat free peanuts, too. Many times the hardwood dance floor was covered with a layer of beer foam. There was at least one fight a night, usually over a gal, everyone would go outside and watch. Glenn was very strong and could usually get things under control. We sold fishing and hunting licenses and had a biggest-buck pot, often gave away $100 to the largest buck by weight. At one o'clock we had to have plenty of beer in the cooler because we sold six-packs hand over fist when the bar closed. We purchased plenty of beer from the Northern Brewing Company, sold an awful lot of it, especially their Bock Beer. I'd ask 'em and get all the trays I wanted. We sold Blatz and Miller Beer, but mostly Northern. We had a nice Coke machine, too, it cooled with ice, an old one even back then. We had all sorts of advertising on the walls, clocks signs and trays. I guess that stuff is collectible today. Once in awhile we had live music —the Red Caps from Duluth. They were a country band. It was packed with 18 year olds. We had somebody at the door to check IDs. We couldn't let 15 year olds in. They played for about a year but it got to be too much trouble. There were cars parked all the way up and down Highway B. The sheriff would be tagging them and there were an awful lot of fights outside. Some who were doing the fighting are real well known now. One being a judge now and some lawyers, too. One of the guys took me for a ride on his motorcycle to the Oakland Town Hall —never again, hangin' on for dear life. It was terrible. That one is a banker now. The truck drivers that delivered beer would meet and play Schmeer all afternoon. One afternoon the Miller driver had too much to drink and he rolled his truck on Follics Curve. He lost his job but the neighbors had a good time. Anybody who came along would load their car with cases of beer. In no time the place was cleaned up. We sold the place to "3 Shot Annie" in '54 and then bought the Happy Hour.

–Nita Hope

I Got So Lonesome It's Funny I'm Alive ———————————●

I put the record out about '61 or '62, that's right. The picture on the record was a mural they had at the photography studio. I went in the studio over in Sauk Center at Cuca. He was in a hurry that day and I wasn't happy with the record. That guitar wore out. Wherever I would go, they would call up the tavern and book me. Word of mouth. A couple came over to Monroe to pick me up; they insisted I come out to Jersey. That was a long way to go. Lefty Frizzell played out there and so did Carl Smith around the time I did. I'll tell you I was shakin' in my knees that night. A six piece band comes walking off the stage and I'm up there all alone. A big crowd, there was a big crowd. They made me feel good. Then I stayed out there. I went out there for a hundred bucks in 1960 for the fun of it. I pissed off a lot of musicians, too, when I was out there. "You ain't gonna be cuttin' prices," they said. They were probably getting fifty or sixty a night and, well, I could cut prices 'cause I was one man. I practically got beat up. The mob was in control of the clubs out there, too. I just wish somebody would have copied me. No one copied me! I heard so many guys say when I was playing "Well, I'll show that Boyd off. They never did. I think what killed 'em was that snare drum; that fooled 'em. That was tricky. Bass drum, the foot, no problem. I made a gizmo that attached to my knee that would hit the snare drum. Why couldn't anyone copy me I don't know. There was a guy from over in Jefferson. I tried to help him, but he couldn't get that rhythm. I said you got to get that rhythm, sing or something. He died a few years ago, nice fellow. There was a one man band from Dodgeville who played the bass drum only. I played lead on the guitar, too, and the mouth organ. It was hard work standing in one spot, but I didn't mind it. After a while it was just like shifting a car. I started playing the mouth organ when I was five or six and it took me about twenty-five years to get that thing together. See how I really started out was playing with my neighbor who was an accordion player. He was very young and very good. We started out playing in the night clubs. First thing you know they found out his age and he was

out. I already played the mouth organ and I thought that would take care of the accordion. I played nothin' but country songs. Played at a drive-in over by Madison before the movies would start; it was the Badger Big Sky Drive In. Played all over down through La Crosse, Bear Valley, Monroe, Dodgeville, New Glarus, Ridgeway, Mt Vernon, all down through there. Mostly taverns, but hospitals and wedding dances, too. I did have a good rhythm and made it easy for them to dance. Five piece one man band! A guy named Lawrence, he has a tavern up in Spooner now, owned the Junction House in Monroe in 1960.

Yeah, I was down there most every Saturday night. Oh, did we pack 'em in. We played till one and the other places closed at twelve. Ridgeway and Dane, they were two wild places where they had a time. They weren't mean, just having a good time, they were all hammered. Having a few beers and dancing. Yeah, everyone was happy! I had a lot of beers but it never bothered me a bit. I worked it right off. I would get twenty-five bucks for a party and bands would get ten, but then a lot of times I would get fifty or sixty. Sometimes I would play all night long. They were primed and would say 'Come on over to the house.' We would go all night long. They'd pass the hat and keep you there until ten in the morning or until I played the next place! Some weekends I'd play for days at a time. For many years I played every night, except for Monday night. Sunday morning was hard on me. I'd play Friday night, and Saturday night, and then I'd play Wednesday and Thursday, Sunday morning, Sunday night again. Then try to keep up with your farm work or other work. It's funny I'm alive. Everybody's buying you booze, shots and all. I never smoked except being in all those smoky places. I did stop smoking when I was twenty-one, though. The only thing I couldn't take was on the road. I traveled out to New York and Georgia, all the way up to Maine. I didn't like it up there, I'll tell you that. When I went to New York, I got so lonesome! I didn't want to leave my family and go out playing. I guess that's what saved me.

–Boyd Skuldt, Mt. Horeb

83

Highway 35 Revisited

Nobody had ever seen that before?! If any of those artsy-fartsy folkies would have ventured out of their coffee houses, beatnik pads, and art parties near the University of Minnesota and into the Badger State they could have caught Boyd Skuldt doing all of that and more. Interestingly, there is a one in a million chance Dylan himself could have done so. In the late 1950s, the then teenaged Bob Zimmerman spent a couple weeks of several summers at Camp Hertzl, near Webster. At the time, on Highway 35, was a roadhouse named the Log Gables, which featured live music and was just down the road a piece from the camp. It was just the type of establishment that would have been a natural for Boyd. Could a youthful Dylan, after grown bored and restless sitting around the campfire roasting marshmallows and singing "Hava Nagihlia," been attracted by the sounds of far off music, set his boot heels a-wandering down the highway on a summer night to see Boyd? Peering in the window he could have seen a bar full of juiced-up Badger Barhoppers, drinking and dancing to the jumping one-man accompaniment of Boyd. One would think that Bob would've sopped up the unique sounds like a bar rag does a spilt beer. Maybe at that point the young Dylan at last figured out what Elvis had in mind when he said, "Let's get real, real gone now." Did it happen? Doubtful, about as much chance as Gene Vincent being a session man for the six Fat Dutchmen. Just the same, it will never be known. The answer to that question was blown in the wind down Highway 35 a long time ago.

Boyd Skuldt, with harmonica, after 10 + years on the road, circa 1960.

Bob Dylan, no harmonica & three years away from his first record.

1959 Hibbing High School Yearbook, The Hematite

A fellow student who knew Dylan during his year after Hibbing High School at the University of Minnesota and before his move to New York City.

"For awhile, people mostly went to parties to hear Dylan play. Later, nobody wanted to give a party because Dylan would come and play. Then he became the first guy to put the guitar and harmonica together, with the frame holder around his neck. Nobody had ever seen this before. As far as I know, he was the first white performer to combine Sonny Terry harmonica with the Woody Guthrie guitar."

–No Direction Home

Briggsville

"This place has been a tavern or inn since the 1850s. It is along the shore of the oldest manmade lake in Wisconsin. In the 1940s a gentleman named Otto Byer purchased it. The photo shows a very rustic looking place. There were wagon wheels in the bar and the walls were decorated with all sorts of Indian artifacts: bead work, moccasins, and things like that. But in actuality he turned the place into something quite elegant. He was a concert pianist from Chicago and brought a grand piano up here. He would play the piano for the guests, mostly rich people from the Chicago area. They also had a game farm here and raised pheasants and other fowl and served them to the people on some very fancy gold-trimmed china. Quite the place! He owned it until about 1954. In the end he developed arthritis in his hands and while he couldn't play any more piano, he could pick up a cocktail glass and he started drinking very heavy. Sadly, he crashed his car into a tree and was killed. We bought the place from his widow who also passed away shortly after that. I don't know what became of the piano, and most of the Indian artifacts ended up with the Wisconsin Historical Society.

–Susan Hilliard

While traveling in Wisconsin, America's Dairyland, and the Nation's all year Playground, on city highway 41 and through the north limits of Fond du Lac, be sure to stop at THE BEER HUT for a brief rest and a fine lunch. You will find that Wisconsin Hospitality and our Services are unequalled.

Keg-Liga

The great Hank Williams had a hit record in the early 1950s with "Kaw-Liga" which told the musical story of two cigar store Indians. Kaw-Liga's lack of ambulatory ability left him in a permanent state of unrequited love for a lovely wooden princess. Hank made at least one concert trip, in 1948, to Wisconsin during his too brief career. Could that road trip have been the source of the record? The scenario is even less likely (if that is possible) than the convoluted conjecturing offered on the previous page. But suppose his journey took Hank and his band past "Tibbies" of Indian Ford and the "Beer Hut" of Fond du Lac. The fried chicken featured at Tibbie's would have been irresistible for a car load of hungry hillbillies. The beer would have been as equally tantalizing to Hank. After a meal, and several bottles of Old Style, Hank could have stumbled out of the place, tipped his Stenson goodbye to the wooden Grenadier, lit up a Camel and flopped in the back of his waiting Cadillac. The Grenadier was the last thing on his mind as he drifted into a lengthy booze-snooze. Several hours later could have landed the band on Highway 41 outside of Fond du Lac and the "Beer Hut." The Miller Girl perched on the giant beer keg would have been as overpowering a lure as her counterpart to the south. With that vision presented to him, Hank would have then had the catalyst for a song: Two characters sharing similarities in proportion, composition, and vocation, unable to establish a romance due to the fact they were made out of wood. One of the two was located at Indian Ford. All that was left was for Hank's alcohol-fueled imagination to put the pair together, at least musically, add a few chords, and make a role change to characters more readily identifiable to record buyers outside of Wisconsin.

The Night The Greyhound Died ———————●

January of 1959 had been colder than usual through Wisconsin and the Upper Midwest. One of the few things to interrupt the bleakness was the fact that a traveling rock and roll show, called the Winter Dance Party, featuring Buddy Holly, Dion and the Belmonts, Richie Valens, and the Big Bopper, was touring Minnesota, Wisconsin and Iowa. Rock and roll was only about 4 or 5 years old at the time, and there was a real excitement among midwest teenagers that these big stars would be in their little corners of the country.

The concert in Duluth was about the midpoint of the tour chronologically and the northern most point geographically. The daytime high that January 31 was only -1. That evening the outlying regions would see -35, extreme even for northern Wisconsin. However, those frigid temperatures were not enough to deter hundreds of teenage fans from Duluth, the Iron Range, and northwestern Wisconsin from filling the Duluth National Guard Armory. The concert lasted a couple hours and for the time being the performers did not have to worry about the bitter cold or the long bus trip ahead. By all accounts it was a great evening for everyone. Afterwards they packed up their instruments and boarded an outdated bus with substantially inadequate heaters and a failing mechanical system.

Courtesy of Shawn Nagy

Buddy at the Armory that evening.

BUS WITH ORCHESTRA GETS STALLED

Bob Ekert and some other Mercer drivers were called out real early Sunday morning to rescue members of an orchestra, whose chartered bus became stalled on Highway 51 near Pine Lake. The ten members had played Saturday evening at Duluth and were on there way to Green Bay to keep an engagement for Sunday evening. The men were lightly dressed and suffered from extreme cold of 35 below zero that morning with no heat in the bus while they waited for someone to come along. Four cars went to take the men and their musical instruments to Hurley. Some had to be taken to a doctor to be treated for frost bitten feet and fingers and severe chilling.

–Iron County Miner, February 6, 1959

The bus left the Armory and headed down Superior Street which took them through the deserted downtown area and to the Duluth-Superior Toll Bridge. This bridge crossed from Duluth to Connor's Point in Superior. There are not many businesses or buildings remaining that they would have seen through the frosted windows of the bus. The art-deco styled Mom's Cafe still stands near where the base of the Interstate Bridge was, but it has been idle for many years. The Old Town Tavern, farther away from the bridge is another survivor, but for the most part the original streets were rerouted or eliminated to allow for exit ramps and access roads to the High Bridge, which opened in 1960.

Within minutes they left the glow of the street lights and bright neon of the city and headed out on Highway 2. From that point the only illumination was the stars, a quarter moon, an occasional farm house porch light, and the headlights of the bus which brightened the frozen highway and crystal ice pellets that were whisked along by a brittle northwest wind which sent them swirling over the concrete highway and the crusted snow on the dormant fields. One would think any conversations on the bus would had given way to a quietness as the band members hunkered down to what they thought would be an uneventful seven hour ride to Green Bay. As the bus traveled on down the highway and through the small towns and villages of Poplar, Blueberry, Maple, Brule and Iron River it became apparent that the heating system could not keep up with the severe cold. More significantly, the mechanical problems which had been a persistent headache from the start of the tour were aggravated by the extreme weather. About three hours after they began their journey, the old bus completely failed, rolling to a dead stop in the -35 Wisconsin night, about ten miles outside of Hurley, the little town with the big reputation. They successfully flagged down a passing car which got word into town for a wrecker. Now most accounts say that a tow truck and several passenger cars arrived and hauled the broken bus and the frozen musicians the rest of the way into town. Arriving there, some members of the bands found hotel rooms and others whiled away the wee hours at an all night cafe named the Club Carnival on Hurley's infamous Silver Street. But at least one longtime Hurley area resident says that, at the time, not only was the Club Carnival a cafe, but also had strip shows going every night. The wee hours might been the whee hours for the boys. According to this witness, once entering the club, the Crickets and the rest of their entourage parked themselves front row center. A perfect perch for the Big Bopper to view some chantilly lace and less. Anyway it would have been a major rave up for Buddy especially, if this story is true. After hours in the absolutely quiet chilling stillness of the Wisconsin countryside, it must have been an enchanted, transitory moment when the fog and ice melted away from his coke bottle bottom glasses to reveal a lively tavern, hot and steamy, noisy, smoke filled and neon lit. One of the many sights to appear might have momentarily taken his breath away. At the time, the dancing girls on stage in Hurley were not wayward farmers' daughters, but out of state Puerto Rican gals!

Courtesy of Shawn Nagy

Lithe young dancers, of the same ethnicity as his pregnant wife, Maria, who was back in New York City, awaiting Buddy's return. Buddy in surprised wonder had to think, if not outright exclaim, "Well, all right and oh, boy!"

On hearing the story, you hope it is true. Buddy would have only one more full night on earth, within 48 hours he was shaking hands and saying "How do you do" with Hank Williams and Johnny Ace, and it is nice to think that some of that precious time was spent viewing Latin lovelies and maybe drinking a bottle or two of Breunig's, Northern or Royal 58. Maybe he had a delicious pasty to munch on that evening.* Any chance that the tale is true? The facts are probably irrecoverable whether Richie pumped nickels in the jukebox to play "La Bomba" or "Donna," or how much the Bopper blew on overpriced drinks for the dancers.

Although there are bits of circumstantial evidence for and against the story, no one will ever really know for certain how and where that evening was spent. It is best to leave it at just that: Buddy enjoying the visions of sexy señoritas, Richie in a jukebox induced reverie, and the Bopper laying a dollar on the runway and saying, "You know what I like."

* That is P-A-S-T-Y, which is a type of meat pie, filled with potatoes and pieces of meat, enclosed in a crust. They are sold all around the Hurley area as well as the Iron Range in Minnesota. P-A-S-T-I-E-S, are, of course, the adornments worn by strippers. Although, with enough Royal 58s in him, anything could have been possible.

The Hoople House

"Oh, that Hoople House was a fun place. The owner, Ed I think his name was, had a big handlebar mustache like those fellows in barbershop quartets. On nights when it was real busy and everyone was having quite a time, he'd ring this bell he had behind the bar and lead everyone in singing a few of those old saloon songs."

–A longtime Marshfield resident recalling the musical Hoople House in the 1950s

The perfect potion for song at the Hoople House, their private label beer, brewed by the Berlin Brewing Company.

Wisconsin had at least two Hoople Houses. And if you can believe matchbook covers (as the authors do), the West Allis version was a cheerful establishment in its own right.

Short & Stout Wave Broadcasting

Music was, and is, as essential as bottle openers or tap knobs to a successful tavern. The source of most music being either a jukebox or a live musical group. However, the busy downtown taverns of Two Rivers had something unique going for them. Rose "Ginger" Gordon, was the so-called "Automatic Hostess" of the town. Although the details are sketchy, it seems in the late 1940s she operated some kind of broadcast system, probably via shortwave radio coupled with telephones or intercoms, that was linked to the taverns. To add to the oddity, the music to all those bright and lively spots emanated from the basement of a local funeral parlor. During the weekly Saturday night platter party, patrons would call in from various locations with dedications to other barhoppers. Her breezy patter between the platters must have been enough of a hoot for the patrons to allow the bar owners to forgo what would have been a tidy sum of coinage that would otherwise have gone into their jukeboxes.

The Lovely Beaver Damsel ————————•

I may be sad, I may be blue, But I'd be a fool if I'd cry over you,
You played a trick, surely was slick, So listen what I say to you.
It's better to be single, Than to take one that someone else had,
It's better to be free, 'Cause her past would mean nothing, you see.
She may be an angel to your face, But think of the bygones, Oh, what a disgrace;
It's better to be single than to take one someone else had.
You may be sad, I may be blue,
When you think of how you tore my heart in two,
You took a dare, Girlie, beware,
he maybe sang these same words to you.
It's better to be single, than to take one that someone else had.

A boar, if things do not go successfully during his first attempt at intimate relations, will sometimes give up and reject the opposite sex forever. Thankfully, um, very thankfully, this trait rarely shows itself in humankind. "Birds do it, Bees do it, even sophisticated Fleas do it," went the jazz age song. One jazz age musician who didn't do it was Otto "Windy" Jacobs of Beaver Dam. He was possibly the most talented barkeeper in Wisconsin. Known to all as "Windy," he was skilled with as many as a dozen musical instruments. He was a virtuoso at music, but not at the ways of romance. At some point in the 1920s his story goes, he had become infatuated with a well-to-do young girl in town. Unremembered are the specifics of that pairing. Were they engaged, did they share occasional dances, or was it a case of unrequited love for Windy? Was it similar in nature to Mr. Bernstein's story in Citizen Kane? When the character wistfully told of a girl in a white dress on a ferry boat, whom he'd merely glanced at many years previous, yet carried the memory of her throughout his life. Whatever was the relationship of Windy and his lovely Beaver Damsel, it ended when she was courted and wed by another. With sorrow, Windy became a reverse Jay Gatsby and retreated to his working class tavern where he served beers, shots and pined for his Daisy Buchanan. When Windy was 36, after about a decade of brooding, he wrote and recorded the curiously ambiguous ballad, "It's Better to be Single (Than to Take One Someone Else Had)."

He lived his life in accordance with the record, and remained a bachelor. Windy tended his combination bar and sheet music store from the early 1930s to sometime in the 1960s. All the while his true love, lost but not forgotten, happily lived her life on the other side of town with her husband, who was a prosperous Chevy dealer, and their children. This circumstance did not keep him holed up on lonely street though. With a heart that was broken but big, he was often out and about, performing his music at parades, the local calliope, and with his band at dances. He was also always at the ready with loans or gifts for those acquaintances down on their luck. While free spending with others, he spent little on himself. He owned a house in town and rather than live in it, he rented the house and resided in a garage near his tavern. A constant saver, Windy one day walked into a local car dealership and paid in coins for a new vehicle. The Dodge dealer though, not his one time rival's Chevrolet outlet.

PROHIBITION
1919 - 1933

Knapp

The Knapp House was owned by a fellow named Ben Harling, that used to be a place we'd stop when my father was with us. He could go there and have a little something, some "juice." Down the road was Teagarten, there was a little town there. Now, that was a place to party, there was a home there during Prohibition where homebrew and moonshine was always served. At the barn dances some guy would always show up with a trunkful of bottles and be parked out in the dark at the edge of the field. My dad would go to Somerset and buy the moonshine and come back down and sell it. He had a 1930 Plymouth and the back would open and it would hold five jugs of booze and then he put more in the back seat. It was all white moonshine. My mother would burn some sugar and put it in the bottle to make it brown. They would hide the bottles all over the farm, bury it out in the fields. I remember us kids would look out the window sometimes late at night and see flashlights moving around out there. Some guys would be snooping around out there trying to find our Dad's hidden bottles.

–Fred Colburn, Wilson

Courtesy of Hartford Historical Society

On a sunny afternoon, or maybe morning, workers stop to sample the product of the Schultz Brewery in Hartford. They were all out of jobs when Prohibition came a few years later.

DRAGGED BY THE CRANK FOR TWO MILES...

To find a body of a dead man hanging on the crank of your car must be startling, to say the least. Elmer Mountain and Marshall Farr, both of the Town of Salem, drove down through Dodge Coulee Sunday at about 7:30 p.m. Their car hit something—the boys didn't know what, but feared it might have been a man lying in the road. They drove on. At the Halverson Gas Station on Rush River, they stopped to fill up. Stepping ahead of the car to crank up, they found the body of Edward Gibbs, a man of 60 who lived with his brother in a cabin on the river. The crank handle had pierced Gibb's body so that it hung there for about two miles. The body was cold, and Gibbs had evidently been dead when his body was hit and the car rounded one of the many bends in the road. It was found that Gibbs had been drinking earlier in the evening. At the side of the road near where the car picked up his body, blood was found, and it is believed he fell and hurt himself there. Dist. Atty. T. A. Waller and the coroner were called, but found no reason to doubt the boys' story, and the relatives of the dead man asked that no inquest be held. "Booze did it."

–The Osceola Sun, 1930

Bottle Of Beer Is 31 Years Old ⎯⎯⎯⎯⎯•

Hello Chris and your sixteen year old bottle of beer! We see by the public prints that Chris H. Roepeker claims ownership of a bottle of beer brewed sixteen years ago. We will take off our hat to Chris for having a bottle of real beer in his possession that long without pulling the cork. We will admit that the "old sparring partner" was a hard ticket to beat while running for office, but when it comes to real beer, he's just an infant. We suggest that Chris make a special trip to the New North office, bring along his glasses and cast his optics on a souvenir bottle of real beer brewed by the old Rhinelander Brewing Company thirty-one years ago. This was given to Oliver S. Rogers, 716 Wabash Street, by George Hilgerman, manager of the brewery. Oliver Rogers and Chris Roepeker each possess a bottle of old beer but, going into the stronger beverages, we know a certain man about town who has a bottle of genuine champagne twenty years old. We would mention this man's name except for two reasons-fear of being robbed of his valuable possession and fear of being raided by the "feds." His willpower, however, must be tremendous as Schnozzle Durante would say.

–Rhinelander New North
March 30, 1933

BEER PENCIL BRINGS BACK MEMORIES

Memories of the "Good Old Days" in Hudson were brought back this week to the old-timers here when Martin Michaelson, a former resident who has been visiting here for the past six months, displayed among his friends an advertising pencil distributed 40 years ago by the Artesian Brewery of Hudson. The pencil advertised the fine qualities of Hochstein's Pure Artesian Beer. Mr. Michealson, who plans to return to his home in Seattle in a few days, said he found the pencil while rummaging about the house.

–Hudson Star Observer, March 3, 1930

Find Bottle Of Old Beer ⎯⎯⎯⎯⎯•

Under direction of Emil Birchler, Milwaukee architect, reconstruction on the Hillsboro brewery is being done at a rapid pace… Workmen at the brewery Friday found an old bottle of oldtime Hillsboro beer, made here about 15 years ago. Although the bottle was opened Friday, even as late as Monday afternoon quite a head of beer was to be seen on the beer. Incidentally the beer was so old that it tasted flat and was not suitable as a beverage. The half emptied bottle with the original label may be seen in the window of the Sentry-Enterprise building.

–Hillsboro Sentry-Enterprise
July 13, 1933

Wildcat Breweries Continue To Operate

It will be interesting pastime for the local public to estimate, although exact data cannot be gathered on the subject, how much equipment used in Ozaukee County's wildcat breweries and alcohol stills will be left idle with the repeal of the Eighteenth Amendment. Rumor in the county has it that a number of wildcat breweries will continue in operation and that the product will be sold on the same basis as any other brewery. The owners will, of course, have to comply with the same legal requirements by which large brewery operators abide. An attempt was made by the Herald to ascertain, roughly, the number of wildcat breweries and alcohol stills in Ozaukee County. Inquiries were made at all official departments of the city, county and towns but without fair success. Some estimated, since estimates were all that could be gained, that there were fifteen wildcat breweries in operation toward the close of Prohibition. There were considerably more than that when Prohibition was at its height. The number of alcohol stills in Ozaukee County has always been comparatively few, according to the views gained. It was estimated that there were about five or six in "good dry days" and only two or three toward the last.

–The Port Washington Herald, March 29, 1933

Booze Toter Ends Journey in Limbo

A.W. Kent of La Crosse (at least that's the name he gave the police) came to town Wednesday loaded down with two cumbersome grips. He decided they would be safer in the custody of the little parcel checking receptacle down at the depot than open to prying eyes. But alas, that contrivance was never intended to be a party to evasions of the dry laws. One of the precious grips was stored comfortably away, but the other was too large for the door, and so Mr. Kent checked it with the agent. As the baggage smasher set it away in one corner of the room, a suspicious gurgling sound was emitted from the interior. It reminded one very much of the gluk, gluk, sometimes heard when a well filled jug or bottle is emptied. The city police somehow got wind of the affair and an investigation revealed some eight or nine gallons of alcohol in the two packages. A John Doe warrant was sworn out before Court Commissioner Winchester and the officers settled down to wait for the return of Mr. Kent. He came in the station shortly before midnight, slapped down his check and called for his grip. The obliging agent referred him to Marshall Stowe and Constable Schelden, who stood at his side, and he spent the rest of the night as a guest of the city. His hearing was held yesterday afternoon, but a disposition of his case had not been reached at the time of closing our forms.

Reedsburg Times, December 29, 1922

While waiting for an order of steak in a Kenosha restaurant, John Kuzins, 35, fell dead. Friends, who were there with him, carried him out believing he had fainted. An investigation by the coroner revealed the fact the man had been drinking heavily of moonshine and that death had been caused by heart failure.

–Reedsburg Times, November 17, 1922

Oliver

I remember the Blind Pigs. In fact there was one just around the corner from this house even. I was just a kid at the time. We could go into their living room and there was the slot machines. That was the only way people could survive. Seven's tavern opened up in Oliver in 1932. There was plenty of bootlegging before that, though. Seems like there was one everywhere there was a creek to cool the coils. Of course I knew where the stills were because you can't keep anything from a kid. We were always exploring the woods and all over. People had to live; they had to survive. There was a couple local constables and they'd be cooking moonshine, too! The taverns are all gone now. The Carriage House, the 105, the DeLuxe, the Palace Bar, there was also the Pal-A-Mar, the Red Top and the Garden Tavern, which was probably one of the oldest taverns besides Casey's Cave, but that one goes way back. Then there was the Brown Derby. There sure was a lot of drinking here. Sunday used to be the big day in Oliver. Superior and Duluth used to shut down so we got folks coming out here. Northern Beer was a big seller. It was a good beer, so was Fitger's. There were some people that passed through the village that most locals never even knew stopped by. Al Capone used to stop by one of the taverns regularly. I know this for a fact. Those guys would spend some time in St. Paul, they'd make a circle tour. They would come up Highway 61 and on their way back to Hayward they'd stop by the village of Oliver.

Casey's Cave in Oliver, 1912, seven years before Prohibition

Courtesy of Oliver Town Hall

I don't know if they had any connections here. They'd stop by and have some fun and drink. They kept it low key, this was not known by many locals though. They'd pull up in those great big fancy cars, big Packards. Nobody around here had ever seen a car like that before. People on the police force looked the other way. They didn't see them things; they were out of their league. They certainly weren't going to give them a hard time. When they passed through they left a lot of money. Waitresses and bartenders were happy...

–John Turk of Oliver

SAUKVILLE "COP" IS NABBED BY AGENTS

Constable Lawrence Feltes of the village of Saukville found himself sitting in a "hot spot" Friday afternoon when he was nabbed by federal Prohibition officers. The officers, led by Arthur E. Hamilton, deputy dry chief, were raiding a still on a farm near Fredonia when the Saukville constable entered. Feltes was promptly taken into tow by the officers, suspected of being connected with the operation of the still. The constable explained that he was the village constable and he was "looking for a man." Having given his alibi, Feltes was questioned by the dry agents who wanted to know why he was looking for a man on an out of the way farm like this and what the man looked like. The agents kept the constable in custody for 5 hours and questioned him thoroughly before they were willing to let him go...

–The Port Washington Herald, April 26, 1933

Eau Claire

My parents were what you'd call "bootleggers." They ran a speakeasy. They must of started that in the late 1920s... I was just a little tyke so they must have started in the business about then... I guess every city, hamlet, town or whatever had that kind of set-up, a speakeasy of some type... there were several of them in Eau Claire as I recall... My parents, as I remember, said that they moved 10 times in 11 years or 11 times in 10 years to keep one step ahead of the federal men... the local law enforcement tended to overlook selling liquor and beer because they enjoyed partaking in those kinds of things themselves... so it was the federal men who came to town that you didn't know who were unbeknown to anyone... that was the problem... As I understand it there was strong beer available... I remember as a little guy going toward Bloomer to a place that is still there... I think it's called the Gateway Inn right now... It's on the corner, I believe it is on Highway 40... It seems to me that the man who ran it was Hans Steffens. He had beer in kegs. I remember going up there with my dad

Bill Hefnieder Collection

and getting kegs of beer out of the basement of the place and putting them in the trunk and bringing it back to Eau Claire. So apparently strong beer was available. Near beer or non-alcoholic beer was available because it wasn't an alcoholic beverage, but people would spike it. In other words they would put a shot of this clear alcohol in it and make it strong beer... but, getting back to buying that beer up there. It was called Taylor's Corners. Apparently that beer was coming out of Chicago. It might have been something to do with the Al Capone Gang that was down here distributing that beer in this part of the country... There was a Gordon Gullickson that as I remember was considered a bootlegger. He had a rooming house up on the North Side. It would have been about a block west of North Barstow and Wisconsin Street called the Gordon House... At that time Gordon was the supplier of alcohol... in later years he was in a car dealership and still had that hotel up there... probably some kind of house of prostitution, that I don't know... but I'm guessing it

was because it was a rooming house and they had a bar in there... I'd go in there with my dad and he'd pick up stuff... Apparently he was in Eau Claire buying alcohol... One place, the Log Cabin, that I can remember, which was out off State Street on Grover Road... The place was built in the 20's. It was actually brand new when my folks went in there and ran it as a speakeasy. It was a regular nightclub. They had a five piece band on weekends, and I guess some nights of the week. Of course, growing up and living in the same building with a speakeasy that had a five piece band playing on you almost would have to plug your ears not to hear it, I'd go to sleep at night and hear that music all night long. Jazz, sweet music, the big band sounds that were popular. I guess swing music, dance music. People danced, of course. There was no closing hours, you could stay all night if you wanted. Sometimes they stayed open until 6 in the morning as long as people were drinking. They served meals, too, mostly chicken and spaghetti and beer... there were a lot of slot machines there... A fellow by the name of Stew Dorsey in Eau Claire had many slot machines around on a shared basis... They had nickel, dime and twenty-five cent slot machines in there... You could dine, you could dance, you could gamble the slot machines... It was all illegal then, except the restaurant part of it... the thing about a place like that was you couldn't get in unless you knew somebody... The proprietor obviously couldn't just let a stranger in the door. He'd hear a knock on the door, look and they'd open up a little slot on the door to look outside and see who was there... The place was always locked... There was a woman in town that used to come out there, a single girl. She used to pick up with traveling salesmen and take them out there. One time she picked up a federal man, so my dad, because he knew her, let her in with him. He observed what was going on, then left and came back later and arrested him. He brought back a whole bunch of feds. I can remember them because I was standing out by the back door and these guys were walking in and picking up slot machines and carrying them out. My dad was standing in the front room by the bar with his hands up and

continued... **95**

they were frisking him… He got arrested, of course. He had to go to federal court up in Superior. They went easy on him. He did serve six months in the Chippewa County jail for being a bootlegger but he was a trustee, so he could come and go. I suppose some of the law enforcement people frequented his place and knew him quite well… My parents were in that business all their lives, from bootlegging until the repeal in '33… Then they continued on in restaurants and bars… They had a place on the Chippewa Highway after repeal. They used to have free fish fries on Friday night to get people in…

I remember they had nickel beer, at that time tap beer. People would come late after a night out carousing. Two couples would come in and maybe the two guys would order nickel beer, and they would order four fishes. We'd say what do you girls want and they'd say, "We don't want anything, we just want fish."… My dad died in 1959 and my mother continued to run the business which then was Bud's Bar and Grill downtown, on South Barstow next to the Hollywood Theater…

–*William Culbert of Eau Claire*

Osceola Had A Brewery

Did you know, that at one time, Osceola had a brewery? It did, a brewery that turned out a very potable beer, and furthermore, the building in which the establishment was housed is still standing, in a good state of repair, and the caves used for beer storage, carved out of solid sandstone, are just as they were when last used for the purpose for which they were excavated.

The Osceola Brewery was started by the late Veit Geiger about 1867. Mr. Geiger had been a brewmaster in Germany and when he came to this country first settled on a farm in the town of Farmington, near where A. C. Nagler now lives. After a few years he decided Osceola would be a good place for a brewery and moved in town and started a business. He chose as the site for the new enterprise the spot where the Jos. Geiger residence stands, feeling that location was ideal, what with an abundance of water from the large spring and the possibilities for extending caves back into the cliff.

The first beer was made in a frame building, but before much time had elapsed, he began construction of the present building and the structure was built to endure. The face of the building is of stone quarried nearby and in the building proper was housed the simple machinery used in the brewing industry in those days. Practically everything was done by hand, the only power machinery being a malt mill which was operated by horsepower.

Mr. Geiger was ingenious, however, and had many labor-saving devices which greatly facilitated his work. He piped water from the spring to the brewery, and had a system of pipes and hoses to convey the liquid from one part of the brewery to another. The brew kettle was placed atop a large furnace and the liquid was drawn off by gravity.

The earth and stone excavated from the caves was used to fill in the lot facing the street. A sub-cellar was excavated beneath the main caves and used to store lager beer.

The local brewery was a quite sizable industry for its day but along about 1878 Mr. Geiger tired of the hard work of operating a small brewery such as his, closed down and went into the saloon business and later entered the mercantile business here in Osceola.

The writer had the privilege of going through the old brewery building and caves Saturday, with Joseph Geiger, son of the late Veit Geiger, as guide. One must marvel at the courage and faith in the future of this frontier community that the builder showed in erecting such a substantial structure in Osceola's infancy. By the way, the caves maintain a temperature of about 50 degrees even during weather such as we are having now, and one of the caves is being used at the present time for the purpose for which it was intended- Lenno Stelling, distributor for the Blatz Brewing Company, has keg beer stored there.

Mr. Geiger, while acting as guide to the writer pointed out the sites of other former Osceola industries, the flour mill near the cascade; there was a furniture factory on the north bank of the creek, off the east side of the road, operated in the seventies by a man named Whittier; Mel Nason had a blacksmith shop on the opposite bank of the creek and a principal part of his work was shoeing oxen used in the woods and for hauling on roads.

Osceola had a glorious past, and I hope a still more glorious future.

–*Osceola Sun, September 21, 1933*

The Plant of The Oshkosh Brewing Company is a model of cleanliness, most modernly equipped.
Our constant aim is to produce a healthful beer of finest quality from the best ingredients obtainable–
CHIEF OSHKOSH BEER – B'Gosh, It's Good!
Call for it by name. You are invited to visit our plant.

–A postcard courtesy of Chief Oshkosh Brewery (1894-1971)

HAPPY NEW BEER
April 14, 1933

Beer is Here

In the special statewide election of April 1933, over 600,000 of 750,000 voters cast ballots in favor of repeal. The results were closely aligned by nationality. In a look at the results in St. Croix County, Glenwood City, with a large population of Norwegians, narrowly voted in favor of keeping Prohibition in force. Many in the heavily French town of Somerset made money bootlegging: the Frogs voted by 204 to 19 to do away with "the Great Experiment." The Irish in Erin Prairie bested that proportion with a vote of 156 to 13, a 12 to 1 ratio. Within weeks, taverns began popping up faster than dandelions in spring, with everything from out of business banks, riverboats, mills and other available buildings being converted into taverns. Within a few years there were over 14,000 taverns in the state.

Stir Created By Return of Beer

The return of legalized beer to Chippewa Falls created some little stir as trucks bearing cases and kegs began arriving in the city shortly after 7 o'clock this morning. However, some of those who had ordered the 3.2 beer for sale had not anticipated the demand when they gave their initial order and as a result, their supply had run out before 11 o'clock. Further shipments were expected later in the day.

The first beer to reach here came from La Crosse, but as the day wore on, shipments began arriving from other points, including Milwaukee and Chicago. One dealer, who had orders for a large number cases, was not open when the truck bearing his shipment arrived in town, so the driver continued merrily on his way. However, he was expected to return sometime this afternoon.

As the trucks were unloading their cargoes at several downtown places, curious crowds gathered to watch the process, for it is thirteen years since the old-time beer wagons last made their deliveries in the city.

Opinions on the 3.2 beverage differed among those who were in time to sample the first arrivals, but a majority declared the bottle beer to be delicious. The draft beer, however, did not appear to suit the taste of some of those who had enjoyed the bottle exhibits. The difficulty, according to those who claim to know their beverages, is that the new beer is not as strong as has been some of the home brew, spiked beer and wort beer which has been sold in this vicinity for sometime.

Pint bottles were sold this morning for 15 cents each over the bar, while the draft beer was bringing 10 cents a glass, but the "collars" were reported to be of the high variety by some who had tried it. Perhaps it was this fact which made the bottle beer more popular than the draft...

The impression seemed to be prevalent today that the return of beer would have a tendency to do away with the beer parlor and beer flat and beer cottages of which there are probably several hundred in Chippewa County...

–Chippewa Falls Herald
April 7, 1933

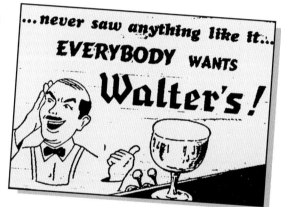

Beer Did Not Cause Much Local Hilarity

The coming of legal beer has not to date been the cause of any great amount of hilarity. The popular 3.2 beverage is being dispensed at a number of local places, there being no local regulation to date. Local authorities are waiting to see what the state measure will be like before they pass local regulatory measures. Beer is being sold at varying prices, five cents for a "snit," up to 15 cents for a bottle. Men who relished the beverage in the "good old days" before Prohibition are almost unanimous in their opinion that the present beverage is equal to any made in that period.

–Osceola Sun, April 13, 1933

Dance Well Attended; Fine Orderly Crowd

The Easter Monday Dance, sponsored by Henry G. Mallin Post, American Legion, was attended by a large crowd, the Legion Post clearing a nice sum of money. Excellent music was furnished by the Arnie Kuss Orchestra. By the way, the crowd that attended this dance, the first since the legalization of beer, was the soberest and most orderly the writer has seen in years.

–Osceola Sun, April 20, 1933

The first truckload of beer to arrive in Hudson was brought by the Casanova Beverage Company from St. Paul and reached the toll bridge at 12:30 a.m. A group of the more thirsty boys met the truck and negotiated the first legal sale of beer in the city. By Thursday no cases of intoxication have been reported as the results of the new brew. In fact, Hudson Police Officers report that the usual drunks and tipsters were not in evidence here last Saturday evening and it has been many months since the downtown streets were as quiet and orderly after 11:00 as they were last Saturday. "The boys drank their New Beer and went home sober." One observer stated, "If they stick to the New Brew and leave the 'Spikes' alone, we will have little trouble."

*–Hudson Star Observer,
April 13, 1933*

BEER ON SALE IN SEVERAL PLACES IN CITY NOW

The 3.2 percent beer made its debut here last Friday morning, April 7, and is being dispensed to the public in several places... Naturally the places open for beer sales last Friday enjoyed quite a rushing business that day and over the weekend, but to date have been conducted in an orderly manner, and little or no boisterousness can be attributed to the sale of beer locally. The reception of beer throughout the state and in other parts of the country seemed to be a cordial one, and breweries are being taxed to the limit to supply the demand for the beverage.

–The Spooner Advocate, April 13, 1933

Watch Parties Get Real Stuff

As news of the preparations to speed truckloads of beer to Hudson early Friday morning spread about town, local beer lovers planned to organize "Watch Parties" to formally greet the first load as it pulls into the city. Those who are in the know say the new beer will be "real stuff" and "just as good, if not better than the famous pre-prohibition brews."

–Hudson Star Observer, April 6, 1933

New Brew Not Hard To Take

Well real beer is here! Rhinelander citizens who have indulged in the new brew are delighted. It contains just the proper amount of alcohol to be palatable. One old Rhinelander soak who drank two or three cases, more or less, on the first day declared it to be stimulating but lacking in authority. During the last thirteen years this man has consumed enough high powered liquid dynamite to float the U. S. Navy, so it can be readily seen that it takes something more than a mild 3.2 percent beverage to satisfy his craving. Most of the beer sold here last Friday was brought in on trucks direct from the breweries. Friday afternoon a small shipment of beer came in by express and since then shipments to the local agencies have been in carload lots. Beers now on the market here are: Pabst, Blatz, Hamms, Kingsbury, Schlitz, Heileman, Old Time Lager, and several other leading brands are expected within a few days. Beer is retailing to consumers at $2.50 to $2.75 per case plus a one dollar bottle charge, which is refunded on return of the empties. In practically all the taverns the price is ten cents for a fair sized glass. To promote sales it is said some of the taverns will set up free lunches. The people appreciate having real beer back and it is believed that from now on there will be less demand for illegal liquor. From an industrial standpoint beer should be a step toward restoring prosperity.

–Rhinelander New North
April 13, 1933

ONLY ONE DRUNK PICKED UP BUT HE IMBIBED IN MORE THAN 3.2 BEER

The return of beer to the city brought little more than routine business to police here. Only one drunk was picked up Friday night and police are of the opinion that he had imbibed in something that contained more than 3.2 alcohol by volume. The only other untoward episode that might be blamed to the newly legal beverage was a family quarrel, the cause of which might be laid to anything, including beer, police said. No cases of reckless or drunken driving were reported to the police, and only one minor accident occurred, that on Farwell St. Friday afternoon.

–Chippewa Newspaper, April 10, 1933

Start Work On Rice Lake Brew

Work will begin Monday on the new brewery at the former plant of New Idea Potato Machinery Company, north of Rice Lake on Highway 53. Two carloads of equipment arrived here this week for remodeling the present structure to three stories and a large bottling plant is to be erected north of the present building. The plant will represent an investment of about $150,000, according to the owner, John Breunig.

–Radtke's Weekly
Shell Lake, November 29, 1933

Brewery Here Scene of Rush for Beverage ━━━━━●

Stevens Point was a gay old town last night and early this morning celebrating an event that occurs but once in a lifetime - the return of beer. Much of the glamour of the old days was missing but all the good fellowship was there. Beer flowed freely.

There was much conversation, the chief topic of which was a comparison of the newly legalized beer with the "wild cat" brew which has been sold to the public during the past 13 or more years… Several hundred people visited the bottling plant at the brewery, watching filled bottles pile up on movable racks. For some the temptation was too great. "There are racks filled with bottles of beer and a bottle or two won't be missed," visitors mused. And they'd pick a bottle off the rack and slink through the door to bury the warm beverage in the snow for awhile before consuming it. The bottling was started well before midnight, but except for a few cases, none of the bottled beer was sold until later in the morning. A labeling machine arrived on the late train last night and was set up and placed in operation at 3 o'clock this morning. The few who went away with bottled before 3 o'clock pasted labels on by hand, customer and seller sharing the work alike. Ten minutes before twelve men who had come to the brewery for keg beer had their trucks and cars in line, engines running on many of them, rarin' to go. When the whistle was blown at midnight signaling the return of beer there was a grand rush at the keg-loading platform for the first keg. To Anton Pejon of Custer went the first two "quarters" of beer. Next in line was Frank Sikorski, operator of the Congress, who got two "halves" and third in line was an agent of Jack and Mike O'Keefe,

operators of a tavern at First and Main streets. "I sent my man to the brewery at 7 o'clock," Mr. Sikorski said, "but the fellow from Custer was there ahead of us." No bottled beer was sent out until about 12:45, when Hiram Hansen conceived the idea of pasting labels on bottles by hand. He said, "I'll paste on my own labels if you'll just let me have a couple cases of beer." He walked out with the first two cases… After the first rush at the brewery the crowd started to thin out and many of the people visited taverns on the south side and up town. The Empire, the Dewey and the Congress bustled with activity. A keg was tapped at the Congress at about 12:11, believed to be the first tapped in Stevens Point after it became legal, and Walter Murat, district attorney, had the distinction of being the first to sample the beer. Pete Prais was the first to "rush the can" and Ed Zinda was the first to "rush the jug." The first half barrel of beer at the Congress was empty just 60 minutes after it was tapped.

–Stevens Point Daily Journal, April 7, 1933

Stevens Point saloon, before Prohibition

Hillsboro Beer Greets Market October 15th ——●

The first truckload of Hillsboro beer since Prohibition went into effect over a score of years ago, will leave the local brewery by the 15th of October, E. A. Aman, plant supervisor, announced Sunday. The local branch of the Hutter Brewing Company had demonstrated much speed in being able to produce sufficiently aged beer at this early date. A beautiful cream colored structure with appropriate green trimmings now looms up in place of the devastated ugly ruins which were apparent to every Hillsboro visitor early this summer. Every Hillsboroite now has reason to proudly point out "The Home of Hillsboro Pale Beer" to out-of-town guests… A trip through the brewery with Joseph Vogel, brewmaster, proved very interesting and enlightening to your reporter. The brewing operation begins at the mash tubs where the mash is manufactured. From there it goes to the kettle where hops are added. Then the batch is pumped over a cooler whence it is repumped into beer cellars. It requires eight hours to prepare and cook a batch of beer, Mr. Vogel stated. The brewmaster then offered us a dipper of sparkling Hillsboro beer which we graciously accepted. Although the brew was only four days old and we were compelled to partake in a cooling cellar with the temperature hovering around freezing, we are ready to vouch for the quality of the beer when properly aged…

–Hillsboro Sentry-Enterprise, September 14, 1933

Throngs Enjoy "Brewery Day" ——————————————————●

Throngs of people promenaded the streets of Hillsboro last Saturday afternoon and evening, participating in the big "Brewery Day" celebration, held under the auspices of the Hutter Brewing Company and the Hillsboro Commercial Association. The crowd started to arrive shortly before noon and by the time the free beer and free lunch was ready, a crowd of people stood in a solid mass, reaching from the Stanley garage to Wolf's store. Both the beer and lunch were served in the garage which had been converted into a temporary large-sized tavern, with the rafters appropriately decorated with branches of trees. Some idea of the size of the crowd may be gained from the fact that about 8,000 sandwiches were served, and more than 37 half barrels of the new Hillsboro Pale Beer. From noon until two-thirty the crowd milled through the garage, each to receive his portion of the beer and lunch. Four bands, including the Wonewoc, Trippville-Fox Ridge, Bezucha Brothers and Hillsboro German band, provided spirited music throughout the day. After two o'clock the crowd began to break up into smaller units, some going to the Hutter Brewery to learn how Hillsboro's latest product is made while others drove to the fairgrounds to witness the ball game between Trippville-Hills Prairie and Meadow Valley.

–Hillsboro Sentry-Enterprise, October 19, 1933

Charles "Heinie" Heinrich owner of the Hutter Brewing Company

Old Country Lager Now on Tap ━━━━━●

Jung's "Old Country Lager," the beer brewed by the Wm. G. Jung Products Co., is now on tap and according to tavern owners is in great demand. After being fully aged this beer was placed in the market, the first being tapped in the tavern of the Globe Hotel last Saturday where Charles Weingartner was honored as the first taster of the brew, and he pronounced it perfect. Orders for "Old Country Lager" have been coming in since the legalization of beer and the company anticipates a continuation of the demand. To take care of the big volume of business, a new bottling house forty feet wide and sixty feet long is under construction. It is being built of concrete blocks directly south of the main brewing plant. If you haven't tried "Old Country Lager," do so now. We know you'll like it.

–Random Lake Times, June 1, 1933

Pabst Says 3.2 Beer Is Best ━━━━━●

The first few days of beer consumption have provided an impressive demonstration of the fact that beer is a temperance beverage, and should quiet the misgiving of even the most skeptical, in the view of Fred Pabst, Vice-President of the Premier-Pabst Corporation.

"The fact that people have not had real beer for several years led to its being drunk in a volume greatly in excess of normal," Mr. Pabst said, "but in spite of this there was no intoxication."

A laboratory test, no matter on how mammoth a scale it might have been conducted, couldn't have demonstrated as convincingly as the events of the last four days, Mr. Pabst declared, that beer is a temperance beverage and not a liquor. The brewers have taken this position and there contentions are more than vindicated.

Asked if he would like to increase the alcoholic content of the beer to give that customer a little stronger "kick" from drinking it Mr. Pabst said:

"Decidedly not. Our beer, except for a few special brands, was never more than 3.2 or 3.3 per cent alcohol, and I am convinced that this light beer makes the most potable beverage. We would not avail ourselves of the privilege but would stick to the 3.2 beer. That is where we are putting our tests, about 3.16."

–Milwaukee Sentinel, 1933

MEDIC DECLARES BEER EXTRA SAFE

Now it all comes out-you can't get drunk on 3.2 percent brew.

You would drown before you could drink enough of the new legalized brew to become intoxicated. And those who have contended that the new beer was nice tasting, but without a wallop, can now back up their arguments with the scientific observations of Dr. H. A. Heise, of Uniontown, Pa., a speaker at a Milwaukee club meeting recently. Furthermore, the good doctor declared, the average person cannot tell when he is drunk. Experimenting for years with drinkers, in cooperation with the police department of that city, the doctor asserts a man may be adjudged intoxicated on the street, although not having a drink in years.

–Rhinelander New North
June 13, 1933

Imported Hops In Old Port Lager

Imported Bavarian hops! There's something about the smell of them that convinces you beer couldn't be anything but par excellent if made with them. Such are the hops used to manufacture Old Port Lager today, the beer that now as well as before Prohibition made Port Washington famous. It is a pleasure for Braumeister Scholl, like it is for any chef, to see use of the best ingredients in his mash. The pleasure is also shared with the public. This public, to judge from orders piled up in the office and compliments received, is not only Port Washington and Ozaukee County but the entire state and nation. Orders are coming in every day that cannot be filled. There is a limit to the amount that can be properly aged in the local plant so that is all that will be brewed. Braumeister Scholl and Herb Labahn, owner, will not sacrifice quantity for quality. A convincing illustration of this is the recent postponement of marketing bottle beer made in the local brewery. The bottle goods were scheduled to be put on sale a week ago but in the opinion of Mr. Labahn and Braumeister Scholl it will be held over until Saturday, July 29, to age it properly... an age that has not yet been attained by any of the amber fluid brewed since the return of beer. Visitors at the brewery are treated to a mug or two of beer in a novel manner, employing an automatic bar that has been in service more than a quarter of a century. A moon-shaped slug is inserted in the automatic bar, a handle is turned to allow a quantity of beer to flow from the kegging room into a glass container, and then with a pull of the faucet you get two brimming full copper steins of cold, foamy, Old Port Lager. It's only an old dark stained sort of cabinet but it's a wonderful fixture in the plant. Or, might it be the beer that is wonderful.

–The Port Washington Herald
July 19, 1933

Terry Post Collection

Down the road was their competition at Weber Brewing Co. of Grafton.

Medford Brewery Makes Its First Sales In The County Wednesday

Yesterday, October 30, saw the first sales of Medford Beer being made, according to Frank Mohr, brewmaster at the Medford Brewery. This was slightly in advance of the date set during the latter part of August when brewing activities started. The date set for sales at the time was Nov. 1.

The area that will be worked first will be Taylor County, Mohr stated Tuesday. Later, the brewery will expand its sales to nearby counties. Tuesday night and Wednesday the brewery was bottling the beer preparatory to loading and selling. The beer was put in barrels Tuesday.

Three new trucks have been purchased for delivery purposes. One of these is a pick-up and the other two are regular size. Each carries the name of the brewery and the word "purity" in the upper left hand corner. In the other corner is a picture of a grain shock done in golden and green color. The word Medford appears in large white letters on a red background above the words "lager beer." The artwork was done by Walter Kuse of Medford. As the brewery progresses and moves towards full capacity, the list of employees will be increased. There are about six employees, including Mohr as brewmaster, Frank Kraut and Norbert H. Laabs as truck drivers, Wm. F. Hoppe, bookkeeper, Emeron Meister, cellar man and Jacob Knippel, fireman and engineer… Capacity of the plant when running full, is between 20,000 and 25,000 barrels a year.

–The Taylor County Star, October 31, 1940

The
Beer
That Is
Preferred for Finer Flavor

MEDFORD LAGER BEER

Will Be On Sale At
ALL LEADING TAVERNS
on and after
Wednesday, Oct. 30th

THANKS A LOT

"Man, That's Beer That Is Beer!"

We want to express our keen appreciation to the people of Medford and other parts of Taylor County for the fine reception given our product—"MEDFORD LAGER BEER."

We have tried to the utmost of our ability to give you a beer worthy of your patronage, and the hearty response we have received leads us to believe our efforts have met with great success.

We want to assure you that we shall continue to brew this same high class beverage at all times. There never will be a "let-down" on the quality of our beer.

Ask for Medford Beer, "Preferred for Finer Flavor."

MEDFORD BREWERY

If you are going to "borrow" names or slogans from your statewide competitors it would seem to make the most sense to "Go for the Gusto" and lift something worthwhile, as it looks like the Casanova Brewing Company did with their version of "High Life." By 1906 the "High Life" from Milwaukee was being nationally advertised. The good folks at Medford instead opted to share the remarkably simplistic "Beer that is Beer," from Walter's of Eau Claire.

The Finest Beer

That ever was brewed in Hudson; the

"High Life Brew,"

Good for men, Better for women, Extra Fine for Sweet-Hearts

Order by Phone No. 160

Casanova Brg. Co,

Hudson   Wis.

Ray Small Has A "Little Willy"

A winter beer party with some of the boys around the Plum City area.

It was in 1933 that the first little bar was built with the help of a neighbor, Carl Steffenhagen. Upon completion, with the rapid growth of business, and in the same year, it was decided to build so there would be "room for the stove." The new addition, to the north of the original bar, included several booths, to accommodate the public when stopping for a bite to eat. This became a popular spot for barbecues when returning home from dances being held at the Plautz Pavilion. As time passed, this little bar became the perfect place for neighborhood parties, anniversaries, and various celebrations. The post-Prohibition days were filled with memories in and around Schuster's Tavern.

An interesting family of German descent, the Plautzs, most of them bachelors, would get together on Sunday evening at Julius Plautz's Garage. They had a standing order of an eighth barrel of beer at Schuster's that they wanted warmed when picked up, so each Sunday, Ervin Schuster would roll a keg over by the stove. One could write a book of the stories that were told while sitting around the keg. Goldie recalls one springtime there were bad "sink-holes" in the hollow by Steffenhagen's on County Trunk F which the Plautz boys would not attempt to cross; consequently Goldie would put the keg in her car and meet the boys on the other side of the hollow as she always managed to make it through. One snow-stormy day, four neighborhood fellows, namely: Oscar Landrath, Ray Gramzow, Ray Small, and Herman Dillinger also planned on picking up a keg of beer; but the roads were drifted shut, so the guys walked and picked up their beer. According to Goldie, "they rolled the keg down the hill to the east and started carrying it up the next, but by the time they reached Ed Sabatake's farm, they gave up on the idea and sat down and drank it on the spot." On another occasion, these fellows decided they'd like some beer, but all were broke. By pooling their change, they came up with 35 cents, the cost of a "Little Willy" and made their purchase, and shared it all alike.

–Berlin's Memories Book

Bar Closes But Memories Remain

During the Depression, it was a haven for a famished man to get a piece of bread and a beer to wash it down. During election time it was a political forum for Portage County candidates to show their wares and woo voters. During spring planting it was a general store to buy feed, fuel and hardware. During deer season it was a stomping ground for hunters to register deer and relate tales of their escapades. Now, after nearly 43 years of meeting nearly any need, Tony's Bar is closed, to reopen again under new owners. The wood building with a brick front was "only a skeleton of a tavern" when Tony and Regina Bembenek left North Star to become its new owners in June 1939. They stocked the bar, and built shelves and a meat counter for housewares and food. That was when whiskey was 10 cents a shot, beer 5 cents a mug, gas 20 cents a gallon and a semi-truck load of food cost $68. Starting a business during the Depression was not easy, Mrs. Bembenek recalls. While she taught in rural schools for $65 a month, Tony opened the bar and store at 8:00 a.m. "If we made $3 a day (at the bar) it was good business." She said during that time men would walk down the road and stop in, starving for a piece of bread. She would make them a sandwich and her husband would draw a beer, even though the men could not pay for it. If a neighbor was short of money and needed something badly, the Bembenek's would sell as much as 100 pounds of flour on credit. Back then people could be trusted, Mrs. Bembenek said. "If you were busy in the store and someone came for $5 of gas you could trust them to put in only $5. Now they'd turn it back and put in $5 more," she said. Mrs. Bembenek said she has seen many changes over the years. "There were still those who went on two-three day benders. Tony would drive them home in their car and I'd follow in our car to pick him up... but most would

come in only when they needed something." The men would have a beer while the women bought groceries and then they would leave. And drinks were never mixed. Liquor was served straight unless an older person asked for it mixed with hot water to warm him up in the winter, she said. Bembenek's fresh cold cuts were popular also. Myron Orlikowski, Ellis, said her sausage "tasted better from her than the big stores in town," and people from Stevens Point often came to buy the cold cuts. They came from farther away than Stevens Point, too. Tourists from Illinois and Southern Wisconsin would refuel at Bembenek's en route to and from cottages up north. Mrs. Bembenek said the bar would always fill up at 11 p.m. Friday and 4 p.m. Sunday.

–Regina Bembenek, Stevens Point Journal

Gordon

In the Gordon area, this is what I recall hearing of and what I remember as it happened... Joseph Terry and Pete Nelson were the two oldest saloon keepers I remember hearing of around World War I. Joseph Terry got tremors real bad and had to be hospitalized. After quite sometime, his son, who was in active duty, was released to come home and take a job he did not like. Many Indians were around at the time, and they could be quarrelsome and unruly. A half-breed, Al Thayer, who was a very quiet, soft-spoken person would be around, especially on Saturday nights and helped the young man to keep things under control... Ernest Wilkinson then took over. This was at a time Gordon was still selling liquor but Superior was not. The Soo Line Railroad put on two extra coaches on Saturday night to accommodate those coming from Superior to buy liquor at Gordon and would return on the next train with their booze. The man who hauled liquor from the depot to the saloon also had a job hauling empty cases away. He was building a new home at the time, so he used the liquor cases which he took apart to sheet up his house. So you can imagine how much liquor was consumed. The hauling was all done by team at this time, no trucks around... Danbury was also dry so Saturday

Courtesy of Ron Finsted

Above, the arrival and probable consumption of Leinenkugel's Bock, brings joy to the Buckhorn Tavern about 1958.
Left, an interior shot of the same vintage.

Courtesy of Ron Finsted

continued...

109

nights many from there headed to Gordon. They could always find their way to Gordon but I well remember they had a time finding their way home. At that time my dad and the neighbors were away working so two women were left with families and these men would go up and down the road cursing, yelling, singing, trying to find their way home. A scary time for these women… one man's daughter was a teacher and then getting paid would give her dad the check and list of groceries needed. He would go to Pete Nelson's Saloon and spend the check and then go to Joe Terry's and borrow money to buy groceries but never thought of paying him back. Ed Thiede took over and ran the Saloon then until Prohibition came into effect. He was arrested for selling moonshine. Sent to Green Bay for five months, ending his career. Carrine Fisher then took over and ran the place for several years until she bought land along the St. Croix River … A man I never knew bought the Old Bar as it was later known. He had a grand opening, ran out of beer and went to Solon Springs to get more, hit a bump on the way back, car flipped over and he was killed… Palmer Finstad from

Drummond area rented space in the old store building and ran a tavern there until Harry Cosgrove bought the building and forced him out. He built a quick building across the street and on the other side, called the Buckhorn Tavern. He ran this place for many years, raising a family of eight… Walter Pooler had a bar near the Town Hall. I remember well when a neighbor came into the bar to cash a check and Mr. Pooler told him he'd cash the check but to go buy groceries and take them to his wife and family. They were destitute. After, Mr. Pooler walked over to the stove, opened the door, and threw the check in. When Mrs. Pooler died, he took to drinking heavily so he had to give the bar up… There was a bar run by, I believe, Art Taylor. It was on Main Street and had a big glass front and going by there at noon you could always see the Soo Line Depot agent laying asleep on the pool table… Years ago you saw many drunkards, today not too many. I remember years ago when I first came to Gordon (around 1919). If a woman was seen coming from a tavern you did not walk on the same side of the street as her. You quickly crossed to the other side.

–Jenny Terry of Gordon

110

The Silver Rail, Solon Springs

Galesville

The military's worst nightmare nearly erupted in June of 1945 when Staff Sgt. Jim Cram finally returned home to Galesville on a six day pass from a military hospital in Chicago. During the Battle of the Bulge, he and his company had been overrun. Even though badly wounded he was one of only 16 of 287 men in his unit to survive the entire ordeal. His treatment as a prisoner of the Germans during the last month of the war violated most of the Geneva Convention rules. He weighed about 60 pounds when he escaped, only to be captured by the Americans who thought he was just one more German posing as an American. Very lucky to be alive, he was finally recognized as an American and began his four months of recovery in European hospitals. When he eventually returned home to Galesville, he slept most of the first two days. Rested and having visited with his family, he decided to walk down to see the town. After stopping to visit with his old employer, he went next door to one of his old hangouts... There he was astonished to find German POWs drinking beer and having a good time. Army guards sat nearby with their rifles standing against a wall. Cram became incensed as memories of captivity and all his dead buddies swept over him. He rushed home and returned with his loaded 30/30 Winchester rifle. With rifle poised he pushed open the door and ordered all civilians to get out. Then he ordered the POWs and guards to line up and at gun point he marched them back to their prison camp. After a heated discussion with the camp commander the incident ended peacefully. But no more prisoners were allowed in downtown Galesville again.

–Betty Cowley, Stalag, Wisconsin

Not Shaving for Private Ryan

Art Johnson, Max Krueger, and Clarence "Duster" Downes of Racine, according to this 1940s postcard were the "Original Three Beards." They declared, "We have resolved not to shave for the duration - Since December 7th, 1941." This brave action, in conjunction with two atomic bombs, forced the Japanese to capitulate three and half years later.

HURLEY YOUTH CRAVES ACTION BUT WILL HELP

HURLEY - Before Pearl Harbor there was a little tavern in Hurley that was operated by a citizen named Joseph Romanowski. According to Romanowski, Hurley is a pretty tough little mining town in the northern part of the state... "Tough enough," says he, "to make Virginia City and Deadwood look like Pasadena during the Carnival of Roses." At any rate, there was enough excitement there to keep Joe contented. But when war broke out, the possibility of adventure was an irresistible attraction, so Joe joined the Army. Now, after eight months of service, Joe is bored. He hasn't seen a Jap or German yet. The only fight he has seen are the regularly scheduled boxing matches held at the Caribbean air base at which he is stationed. Of course he's had a certain amount of adventure in the tropics of the Central and South American countries where his job is to help so the pilots can wing in with their big bombers and pea shooters. Joe's ambition, he says, is to mix a "Mickey" for the Axis' big three of Hitler, Mussolini and Hirohito. Short of that, he'd like to slap a few Japs around just to keep in shape, but he'll do anything to help win the war. Two new stripes on his shirtsleeves proclaim Corporal Romanowski as a pretty good soldier, and while he has a brusk way about him, he really isn't tough. One also wonders from some of the things he says, if Hurley wouldn't be a nice quiet town in which to live.

–Milwaukee Telegram, 1943

War Prisoner — Discovered In Rural Tavern

An unattended German prisoner was taken into custody Friday night by a Federal Bureau of Investigation agent and Deputy Sheriff Leo Flarherty as he left the Solamita Tavern in Marblehead, the two reported to Sheriff Arnold Sook this morning. The FBI agent also reported the capture of the prisoner to his headquarters' in Milwaukee. At the prison camp at the fairgrounds, Second Lieutenant Walter F. Dempsey stated that no prisoner had actually escaped there. He said, however, that a mistake had been made in counting the men on one truck returning from their work. Sheriff Sook said that he was informed by the prison camp headquarters at the fairgrounds last night that one of the German prisoners had escaped. He immediately broadcast an alarm and assigned Deputy Flarherty to assist in the search. Police were notified of the escape and officers visited various places in the city looking for members of the guard unit to notify them to report back to their post immediately. Theaters also flashed notices on their screens notifying members of the guard unit to return to the fairgrounds. The reports spread rapidly through the city and in most cases were greatly exaggerated. Members of the guard unit who were off-duty at the time hurried back to the fairgrounds camp. Although no official statement was available from army sources, the prisoner picked up at Marblehead by the FBI and Deputy Flarherty is reported to have been a member of a crew which was working at a pea vinery in the vicinity. He apparently walked away and went to Marblehead. He was not at large more than an hour or two, Sheriff Sook said.

–Fond du Lac Commonwealth Reporter
July 22, 1944

Please Have Patience

Remember, December the Seventh, friend?
Well, to even the score we decided to send,
All of the help we could possibly spare,
To join in the scrap, it's our duty to share.

The girl known as Grace who waited on you,
Has taken her place in a factory crew;
And Don is a Doughboy, and our good friend Harry,
Walked out long ago, now is a sailor so merry,
There was Einar, Donald and Jack with whom all of you drank.

They're flyin', or marchin', or ridin' a tank;
We know you miss Ole who worked at the bar,
And Dara, the waitress, who followed him far.
Then there was Lorraine who lost her heart,
She is also out doing her part.

We know you won't mind when you hear our excuse,
Because all we can spare is in government use.
So please have some patience, be easy and free,
And that day that it's over,
THE DRINKS ARE ON ME!

Grim faced, alone, and weary of the world, Tedd Hagg of Sarona awaits the end of the war and a reunion with Einar, Lorraine, Ole and the others.

Maybe the folks in Cornucopia wanted to display this sextet to contest the old joke about "What do you call a good looking girl in Northern Wisconsin?"* Well, you can bet the home grown tomatoes on this Horn O' Plenty made the local yokels Horny O' Plenty.

The 1940s appeared to be a rainy decade in Bloomer, Moquah, and the rest of the state. On a cool September night, this group of female tavern patrons, possibly lubricated by several rounds of Duncan Spring Lager, are on the verge of dunkin' their bloomers. The result being the same wet and chilly fate to their monkeys, that befell Mary's, which was celebrated in drawing and verse at the Lakeview Tavern of Washburn.

Wisconsin Wet-Bars

Moquah Township, near Cornucopia, was the home of Koleski's Tavern. In 1947, during a torrential rainfall, the bar, which was on the edge of Fishermans' Creek, slid down the banks and floated down the swollen stream. The patrons had only moments to slam down their Bruenings, evacuate their bowels and then the building. The structure was later retrieved and placed on higher ground a few hundred feet away. Incidentally, any of the Cornucopia Cuties could have stopped in for a bottle of Coke, or maybe Uncle Fuzzy's Root Beer, but not the menfolk. "Nip," who owned and operated the bar, was from the old school and he would not sell nonalcoholic beverages to men. He died around 1949, a few weeks after achieving the Holy Grail of Cribbage, a perfect 27 hand.

CONTENTS 12 FLUID OZS.   INTERNAL REVENUE TAX PAID
STRONG
Duncan Spring
BEER
PERMIT NO. 9U-722-A UNION MADE
BLOOMER BREWERY, INC., BLOOMER, WIS., U. S. A.

*A Tourist

113

Eagle River ———————————————————————————●

"I am 85 years old and have memories of the dance halls back in the '30s. I loved to dance! When Prohibition began and until it ended in 1933 people just went to dance halls to dance. Most places had orchestras of four to eight musicians. They didn't use amplifiers. Some of the guys brought pocket flasks of moonshine and sold moonshine from their cars. Highway 70 ran west from Eagle River to the small town of St. Germain… Along this route were several dance halls or roadhouses: 'The Fly' owned by Frank Weirich, "The Spider" owned by Art DeNoyer and "Doc's Pill Box"… There was quite a community of Croations who settled in the Eagle River area in the early 1900's. They built themselves a hall where they gathered for dancing and dining. They had pig and lamb barbecues and served ethnic foods. They invited the public to these affairs. They had their own orchestra of stringed instruments and provided great music for dancing. They called themselves, "The Melody Strings."… They called their building "The Jug Hall" after their homeland, Yugoslavia… In the same area was Sam's Bar. It was owned by Sam Capich, also of Croatian decent. He sold beer for 5¢ a glass. Sam added a dance hall to his bar. My husband and his brother-in-law dug the basement by hand. They ran into hard-pan and had to use dynamite to get through. Sam was a little concerned, but the dynamite charges were small and only rattled the glasses on the shelves back of the bar a little. North past the small town of Conover, there was a roadhouse called "Barefoot Charlie's." Charlie's name was really Charles Haas, and although he dressed in buckskin clothing and went barefoot or wore moccasins, I don't think he had any Indian blood. He made moonshine and sold it right from his home. My family lived next to his place. We could see carloads of Indians drive in there and buy moonshine. Charlie had about four kids about the same age as the kids in my family and we played together a lot. When word came out that the Revenuer's were coming, Charlie would put his kids to work carrying bottles of moonshine down to the swamp and hiding them. After Prohibition was repealed, Charlie built a dance hall and bar. He decorated it with pieces of driftwood or stumps that resembled animals and carefully and cleverly arranged them. He had beer tapped out of a tree. He had a carousel out in his yard. Once a lady from the city, who had heard about his bare feet, came up north to see this colorful character. She was disappointed to see he had bare feet, not bear feet. She expected to see him walking around on feet that resembled a bear's.

–Evelyn Ayer

You wouldn't find a "row of fools on a row of stools" at Barefoot Charley's in Land O' Lakes. Maybe though, a "row of chumps on a row of stumps." The northwoods motif was carried to its extreme here in 1937.

Northern Beer...
"We Made It Good, You Wouldn't Drink It"

Before Les and I bought this place, Les was working at Billards Tavern downtown. The brewmaster from the Northern Brewery was a regular there ... Of course they had tap beer... they had Northern on tap... plus they had another beer on tap-Breunings... This guy came in and wanted a glass of beer. He said "Give me anything but Northern." Well, the brewmaster was sitting right there and turned around and looked at this guy and boy he got really angry! I don't know why that man said it but you know that happened a lot with anything local in those days. They stopped going for the home product... wouldn't even support the local brewery. Then my husband Les got a job at the brewery, too. I remember we were down in Milwaukee visiting my brother-in-law. He brought us to this huge new liquor store. We couldn't believe it when we saw a palate of Northern Beer priced at $1.99 a case. That was cheaper than we could buy it for wholesale at our bar. Even though it was a promotional thing they had to ship it down there. We came back and Les raised cain on it, you know. He said listen... if you want us to sell it the price has to change! When we bought this place out here [Les Bird's Tavern in South Superior] there was nothing... no business... we had to start from scratch. It was just a small little tavern—real run down. When we first came out here we put in a walk-in cooler. Very few taverns had walk-in coolers in those days... most just kept beer under the bar in a small cooler. Les decided that he would have a talk with Bob Rooney [owner of Northern Brewing Co. at the time]. Les said to Bob "Now I want a good price on this beer. I think I can sell a lot of Northern... and if you can sell it that cheap down there why can't you sell it to me for the same price! So they gave us a break and we passed that along to our customers. But we had a hard time convincing them to come around to it... but Les was still working at the brewery... and we were just starting out... this was in 1959. We got them to come around and we started buying 25 cases at a time... No other taverns bought that much... People thought we were crazy. "Oh you'll never sell all that...

Northern beer won't sell... not out here in South Superior." So the Northern Beer trucks pulled up. Well, the price was right! There was this same guy that would come in and order a bottle of Budweiser... well, he would take home a case of Northern! Oh, it wasn't because of the taste of the beer. It was good. It was because it was local that people would be embarrassed to buy it when they sat at the bar.

In those days the beer trucks would deliver to homes cases or pony kegs or if they were having a big party the full size kegs. The driver would tap it for them and get it ready for the party. He went to war in '42 and came back in '45... got the purple heart... never came home once... too hard, he said. He worked at the brewery delivering beer up until '49. One year for Christmas, Vic Nelson -he had those shorties named after him- had some silk ties made up for all the employees. The Northern Beer logo was painted on by some local artist. The guys weren't too happy. Some of them complained... That was the last time they got presents.

continued...

Joseph & Regina Hartel, Christmas 1956. Joe was the brewmaster for Northern and Eulberg.

We sure had some fun in the tap room there, though. It was just a little room they had the kegs in and a tub of hot water. We drank out of cans, like coffee cans. One pound coffee cans is what you drank out of there. No glasses or mugs. Well they had the hot water because the beer was so cold that you would get a headache! You'd hold the can in the hot water to warm it up! In later years they had what was called the 'Blue Room.' You could use that if you had a business and wanted to entertain. They furnished the room and the beer and didn't charge you a cent for it. Of course we'd tip the guy serving the beer. It would often be the brewmaster [Joe Hartel].

I remember Les telling about... well I wouldn't even mention names... it was one of our so called 'upper' citizens. He would stop down there with a carpenter and pay him with free beer that wasn't even his. The guy didn't know it was free. The bottling line didn't work that great either and they would sell the 'seconds' real cheap. I remember Les selling six-pack shorty bottles in a mesh bag for fifty cents. I think they were Vic's. I remember somebody was having a party and they ordered two kegs of Northern. This was later on and we didn't have Northern on tap. As it turned out these people only needed one keg of beer for their party.

The people at the bar would shake their head..."I won't drink that stuff - that stuff gives me a headache," belly aching about this or that. So anyway, we were stuck with that extra keg. So unbeknownst to anybody, Les thought "Well, hell, I'll put it on tap!" Well, the same guys that would never drink Northern was in here. They were drinking Schlitz. It was a lighter colored beer. Well, we ran out of it, so Les served 'em up Northerns and then they had another, and another. From then on we served them Northern and they thought it was Schlitz! We didn't have a Northern tap knob anymore. We never had one complaint, plus it was cheaper. Les was so pleased... you know he always had a soft spot for Northern. No one ever found out. Les and Walt bought the Palace Bar downtown before we moved out here. Well neither of 'em had any money or a credit rating so they went to Vic Nelson, who was also on the board of directors at the bank, and he co-signed for them. Vic was special!

–Nellie Bird, June 2000

Billard's Bar 1940: Les Bird, second from right... Bob Rooney, Northern Brewery Owner, third from right

116

Ladies, Watch Your Language

Carved in the bar was "Ladies, Please watch your language - There maybe a gentleman in our midst who might not understand youse!"...We had an all you can eat breakfast ham, bacon, pancakes, eggs, orange juice... one buck! We had Sunday regulars from Duluth... It was a rough life. You could say we never actually closed... The pulp cutters were still there at 5 in the morning... Kids were sleeping on the barstools in diapers and women were drinking just as hard as the men were... The FEX fraternity out of Superior... all them guys, they used to come down and have the paddle slapping... they would stay the whole weekend. Wild! Half the cops would be there whooping it up with them. When I die, pour a quart of whiskey on my grave. It's OK if you run it through your kidneys first!... Back a few years ago we would fish the lower end of Fox Creek. It was trout fishing opening weekend. I was walking down the stream and there was a commotion. Somebody was coming through the brush, sees me in the river and utters "Damn Tourists." Well I turned around and recognized the hat. Later on in the day in the Buckhorn Tavern, well, Bud Grant comes in with his maroon hat with the gold V on the front of it. It was

him in the woods and he didn't even recognize me... knew him from school. Sold the tavern to Ray Peterson. He left a light bulb on in the well. The whole place burnt in '66. They rebuilt it using cement bricks but it wasn't the same...

The above recollections are from Sharon and Joe Thayer, Jr. Sharon's mother owned the Halfway House in the late 1950s and early 1960s. This was the very same establishment featured in the newspaper account on page 51. We have no evidence of it, but this lumberjack honkytonk could also have served as a model for the peculiar northwoods-hillbilly hootenany, drawn by Norman Pettingill that is shown on the next page. Lumberjacks, hard-drinking women and kids in diapers are characters in both the recollections of Sharon as well as the artwork of Mr. Pettingill who lived only 10 miles away on Spider Lake.

The hard-drinking, hard-spanking, FEX fraternity of WSU

Bar Art

Northwoods Tavern

Halfway House in 1964

Norman Petingill
Northwoods Tavern, 1949
Pen and ink drawing
18-7/8 x 30
From the Permanent Collection of the John Michael Kohler Arts Center

Now if Professor Helene Stratman-Thomas would have traveled a bit farther northward in her search for folk artisans and discovered Mr. Pettingill, she certainly would have made a big intellectual fuss and hoo-ha over the Hieronymus Bosch of the swamps and jack pines. The illustrator, fur trapper, and theater owner created his pen and ink drawings from the 1930s through the early 1950s. Titles including Moron Gulch, Northwoods Tavern, Stew Mulligan's Hunting Lodge, Run, Shoot, Do Sumting— and Hack's Shacks appeared at first examination to be oddball caricatures of rural northwoods life. In consideration of Sharon Thayer's comments, instead of exaggeration perhaps these works had the realism of trompe l'oiel, maybe they were as unforgiving as a mugshot. With that in mind, the major accomplishment of Mr. Pettingill would not be in art, but in geography. With his representation of a northwoods populated by the gap toothed, jug-eared, in-bred and beetle-browed, Mr. Pettingill documented the previously unknown fact that the northern most point of the Ozarks was somewhere close to the Brule River.

Don't Drink and Drive, But If You Do... Drink Potosi

If you are a weekend wanderer and as tired of heavy traffic as I am, hop in your car and take this little trip... to the cool of Potosi, Wisc.

Potosi is nestled in a gulch above the Mississippi River. About 350 people call it home. Fifty of them work at the Potosi Brewing Company [1886-1972]. That's the home of "Good Old Potosi." You've heard of it.

The town, measuring over four miles long, but only 100 feet wide at its breadth, is located in the southwestern part of the state. Just about 130 meandering miles from Tomah and it's all good, uncongested road.

Last Friday I had my first opportunity to make a pilgrimage to the land of my favorite brew. It was a side trip from a more regular business type journey, I assure you, as I don't regularly make it a habit to visit with brewmasters in the middle of a work week.

I've been muttering "Good Old Potosi" during my relaxing hours for a number of years, and as we drive up the gulch into town, I was excited about touring the colorful and unique industry, built partially into the side of the towering rock walls. However, we arrived about an hour late and the tours had terminated at 3:30 in the afternoon. We were met at the office door by Bob Froehringer, a pleasant Dutchman who is one of the

company's sales representatives. As we talked outside the door I'm sure he could tell that I wasn't there to just talk. Probably because my parched lips and my periodic retorts, "Good Old Potosi!" We were invited into the hospitality inn next door.

Three generations of Schumacher Brewers in the hospitality room.

Thoroughly enjoying my frosty mug in the old-fashioned pub, we talked more comfortably about small town breweries and their much too evident disappearance from the American scene. Competition is keen and the small plant cannot match advertising campaigns and the huge manufacturing outputs of big outfits. As a promotional device, however, the little brewery like Potosi claims that it lets the stuff age in rock caves naturally and that it uses no chemical acting processes. I don't know if that makes much difference, but it was good enough to entice me to try another mug, and my-oh-my, it was good!

The Potosi Brewery "Rolling Bar" Circa 1940

continued... **119**

We then discussed Potosi as a community. The fronts of the houses in this little town come out from the rocky walls of the gulch, flush to the narrow sidewalks and streets. Its southern city limits is at the water lily-lined banks of the Mississippi, and the steady grade up through the town is very evident. You're out of quiet Potosi when you reach the high, farm land plateau, much different from where the town begins.

A number of years ago, the brewery threw annual sauerkraut feeds with free, cool refreshments as an added feature. The townspeople remember the feeds well, but "they are no more," many solemnly admit. The event sounded much like the old Fall Festivals that were held in Tomah for a number of years.

A Potosi picnic in the 1940s

Potosi is actually one of the last small breweries in the state. Many are being "bought up" by larger industries, but the employees of the southern Wisconsin firm speak optimistically about the next 50 and 75 years.

We said "bumps" to our host Mr. Froehringer, and he invited us back for a tour of the rustic plant and its in-the-rock aging areas at a later time... and during the tour hours-10:30 am - 3:30 pm.

I'll go back... maybe some of you will, too.

–*The Tomah Journal*
On the Write Side, August 4, 1963

The Potosi Hospitality Room

SEASON'S GREETING - HAN'S & BONNIE - MIKANA, WISCONSIN - PHONE 29F6

Alcholiday Time

The Alcholiday season has always been a special time of year to be in a Wisconsin tavern. A warm and brightly lit tavern, filled with customers the same, would be welcome respite on a cold and dark winter evening. In Mikana, Hans and Bonnie set a merry pace for their patrons with Hans pouring shots and Bonnie chug-a-lugging bottles of Breunig's.

WOMAN PRISONER HAS GIFT FOR BARTENDER

Mary Jones of Freeport, who was sent to the county jail from this city some time ago to serve fifteen days for drunkenness, was yesterday towed into the lockup at Janesville, an unhappy victim of the drink and morphine habit. Although the woman admitted she was without the wherewithal to pay her fare back to the Illinois city, she exhibited a phony diamond stud which she said was intended as a Christmas present for a handsome Janesville bartender with iron gray hair and promised if released to present the Yuletide offering to him and then secure enough money to pay her way back to the Sucker State.

–*Beloit Daily News, December 19, 1907*

For That Warm Sense
of
Well-Being
Drink **Calumet's**
Winter Brew Beer

***

A Healthful Drink for the Coldest Months of the Year

On Sale Now at Your Favorite Tavern

BREWED AND BOTTLED BY
Calumet Brewing Co., Inc.
CHILTON, WIS.

Season's Greetings
FROM
SNOOKIES TAVERN
The Place Where You Are Greeted
with the
BIGGEST SMILE IN TOWN
JUNG'S
Old Country Lager
and
BOCK BEER
as well as the choicest brands of liquors
are Personally served by SNOOKIE
You are always Welcome!
John Deppiesse, Prop.

Why That Smile, Santa?

By the looks of the line up of Badger breweries laying claims to Santa's patronage, he must have left his sleigh at the border and hitched it up to a beer wagon to be pulled by his favorite reindeer, Blitzen and Kreusened. Those probably weren't sleigh bells jingling over the dairy state, but empties of Marshfield family size quarts clanking together. Whether it was barhopping through Chilton to quaff a couple holiday brews, or tucking a case and a pony keg of Medford's finest under his arms, the jolly old elf made the most of his one night out a year.

OHIO LIQUOR BOARD BANS SANTA CLAUS

The Ohio board of liquor control, following similar action taken by boards in Michigan and Pennsylvania, has ruled that the picture of Santa Claus must not appear in advertising of liquor.

–*Beverage Retailer News*
November 1936

Wine Is A Mocker And Beer A Brawler ●

In the early part of the century, stick-in-the-muds, gloomy gus'es and other do-gooders began to spread the word on the evils of booze. Well, the squarehead population, eager to find a reason to brood or feel guilt about anything, lapped up this idea as if it were a bowl of hot oatmeal. It was not a unanimous feeling, though. This poem, inspired by the arrival of a Reverend Killjoy at a Scandinavian Christmastime Fiddling Holiday Hoedown somewhere in God's Country, is from the Trempealeau Historical Society. A notation found with the poem states:

"Later informed dance was at Aleckson's in Voss Cooley. They had intoxicating liquors at dances in those days. Reverend Hoxde went there to put a stop to it. Got into a bitter discussion with Haakon Grandberg."

Valley of Trempe'leaus' Christmas Ball

To a Christmas Ball many a youth did go,
In the beautiful Valley of Trempe'leau
Unbounded pleasure expecting to find,
As on warding exulting their way they did wind.

Merrily the strain of the fiddle did sound,
And cheerful and happy the voices around,
When, Lo and Behold! In walks the Priest,
More respected than others, but welcomed the least.

The older were struck with terror and shame,
And sought for their presence, sons and daughters, were to blame;
The youngsters who soon confirmed were to be,
And hither had come the frolic to see.

Some, in their flight, 'neath the bedstead did creep,
Others, in dismay, through the window did leap,
And for hours without in the cold did remain,
While Preacher within found his mission in vain.

Aye, behold us! (youth of this beautiful vale)
Whose amusements and pleasures our Priest would curtail,
As though the glee of our blossoming Prime
Were a soul staining Sin and a Crime.

Haakon Grandburg would have had a very festive time at the Blue Bird Tavern in the Phillips area about 1940, washing down his lefsa with Jul Glogg.

Was part of the discussion, Proverbs Chapter 20, verse 1: *Wine is a mocker and beer a brawler; whoever is led astray by them is not wise...* Was it countered by Chapter 31 V6: *Give beer to those who are perishing, wine to those in anguish; let them drink and forget their poverty and remember their misery no more...* or Ecclesiastes Chapter 3, or Timothy 1 Chapter 5 Verse 23: *No longer drink only water, but use a little wine for your stomach's sake and your frequent infirmities.*

Out Behind The Brewery

Beer, wine and spirits supposedly loosen the pens of writers and poets. Affecting both the great and the not-so-great, stimulating writers such as the usually pie-eyed Dylan Thomas or Edgar Allan Poe to uncountable numbers of lesser talents. It certainly could have worked for a cerebral laxative for whoever Mr. Hasty Peter was. His mental movement is shown below. Many bartenders owned copies of the poem and Arthur Janik, a Wisconsin saloon owner of the '30s and '40s thought highly enough of the effort to keep it in his personal papers, now held by the Wisconsin Historical Society Archives.

Good Ol' Potosi beer might have been a factor in the creation of the poem on the next page. It tells the tale of the Irish and the English carrying their long running feud from the British Isles all the way to the hard-drinking mining town of Potosi. It was written in the 1920s or early 1930s by a local high school student named John "Pappy" Doser. For years the brewery would stack its misfilled or mislabeled bottles behind the brewery. That resulted in a long standing tradition in Potosi of the local high schoolers, and younger, to make raids of the pile. The thirsty youngsters would then take their plunder high up in the hills behind the brewery for a Good Ol' Beer party, enjoying the view, the brew, and developing beer drinking skills they would utilize throughout their adult years in Potosi.

The Man Behind The Bar by Hasty Peter

You have read in song and story of the man behind the gun,
How he battled for "Old Glory" and the victories he won?
Oh the rattle of the battle was but music to his ears,
and we hail him as a hero and we welcome him with cheers,
We also sing the praises of the man behind the plow.
For we can't live without him-that's a fact we must allow,
But there's one whose praises I would sing and sing them near and far,
He's the Hero of all Heroes, is "The Man Behind the Bar."

Now the man behind the gun I vow has done some wondrous deeds,
And so had the man behind the plow who planted these wondrous seeds,
Each in his own peculiar way has served his county well,
But each expects to get his pay for what he has to sell.
The soldier gets his pension and the plowman gets his due
And neither ever knows or cares who pays the revenue.
But when this country needs the coin to carry on a war,
They always put a "war tax" on "The Man Behind the Bar."

He must pay the highest license, he must pay the highest rent,
He must settle with the agents though they don't take in a cent,
And when it comes to paying bills he's "Johnny on the Spot,"
He'll pay for what he sells you - whether you pay him or not.
Yet the preacher in the pulpit, and lecturer in the hall,
Will tell you that the churches are against him, one and all.
But when the church decides to hold a fair or bazaar,
They start in selling tickets to "The Man Behind the Bar."

And when you walk into his place he greets you with a smile,
Be you workman dressed in overalls or banker dressed in style;
Be you Irish, English, Dutch or French, it doesn't matter what,
He'll treat you as a gentleman, unless you prove you're not.
He must listen to all arguments that happen in his place,
And he shows no partiality for any creed or race.
The bunch outside can knock the "King" or "Kaiser" or the "Czar,"
But he has to be neutral, does "The Man Behind the Bar."

It matters not the aches and pains and hardships he endures,
He doesn't tell you his troubles, though you can always tell him yours,
And if the weather's hot or cold, or turns from rain to snow,
It's up to you to tell him so, he ain't suppose to know.
Should he sit down to read the news, some fool with half a jag
Pulls up a chair beside him and begins to chew the rag.
Though Job they say had patience, a more patient man by far
Than Job could ever to hope to be, is "The Man Behind the Bar."

He deserves a hero's medal for the many lives he's saved,
And upon the roll of honor his name should be engraved;
He deserves a lot of credit for the way he stands the strain,
And all the "bull" he has to swallow would drive most of us insane.
Yet the time will come when he must "shuffle off" the mortal world:
hang up his coat and apron, on this Earth no more to toil,
When St. Peter sees him coming he will leave the gates ajar
For he knows he's had his hell on earth, has "The Man Behind the Bar."

The Valley of the Drunken Men

The English, it seemed, had settled there first,
Dutch and Irish soon to follow;
Then the Irish set out to settle the Dutch,
"Twas a stormy little hollow"
Come as it would, in all mining towns,
The inevitable Saturday Night
The miners came in for a grub supply,
And a spree and free-for-all fight
They poured hard liquor down parched throats
And spit tobacco juice
Till smoldering feuds, well fanned with grog
Flamed---Then all hell broke loose

English chin felt Irish fist
And quick in turn was dealt
A solid blow with the table leg,
Opening an Irish pelt

The boom was on and lead was high
The miners were good spenders;
They save their dough for a week or so,
Then go on a reeling bender

So time went by with their spirits high
Until there came the day
When the mines had passed their prime
And they couldn't make them pay
Without a way to make their bread,
Many of the Miners left;
The little town then settled down
To die a lingering death
The shafts which once these miners worked
Now crumble in and sink.
But their old love still lingers on
Their love for all strong drink
Four hundred fifty humble souls
Still roam the narrow street,
Quite often looking glassy eyed,
And unsteady on their feet
The town is broke and no one has
A red cent to his name

With the natives it's just tradition
And has never been put to pen,
The legends of old Potosi,
The Valley of the Drunken Men

Ancient hills surround the hamlet
Scarce admitting the summer sun
Which tops the eastern crags at ten,
And sets again at one

The hey-day of the place has passed,
But still it lingers on
To see the day fade into night
And darkness into dawn

Time was when the red men
Called these hills their own,
Until the hardy pioneer
Came to make a home

"Thar's lead in them thar hills," they said
And rightly it was found;
Henceforth most the settlers
Dug a living in the ground
A motley crew were these hardshells
Men of might and brawn
Among them was the gaunt Jim Crow
And grizzly old St. John

But still somehow they will always have
Their beverage just the same

John Barleycorn passed long ago
Elsewhere thru the nation,
But in this little town he's still
Held high in veneration
The miners used to go to town
For bacon, beans and salt
But the grocery list now reads like this:
Sugar, yeast and malt
Then following a recipe
The brewers art they mock;
The stuff might be O.K. if aged,
But they drink it from a crock
And every fall when grapes are ripe
They fill their jugs and kegs
And before the wine is fit to drink,
They're down to bitter dregs
Every day they sip away
Always in a stupor
And no less than every two weeks
They go on a regular "Whooper"
It used to be that a young man
Using liquor was hard to find,
But "As the twig is bent," tis said,
"So the tree inclined"

"Tis an awful example," mothers say,
"For our young generation"
Who take their tonic just like chronic
'Tis their favorite recreation

Scarce a day goes by when someone is not
Having a glorious birthday,
Sometimes they last for days at a time,
Each succeeding day worse than the first day
And among their numbers are the men
Whose capacities knew no bounds
Who don't blink an eye when feeling dry
After drinking two dozen rounds

These are the men of older guard,
Guarding the town's dripping name
When the bartender says, "What's Yours?"
The answer is "Give me the Same"

And when a newcomer lands in town,
Be he ever so temperate and sober,
He soon learns their way and is lead astray,
His virtuous days are over
Loading some poor unsuspecting guy
Seems to be their chief delight:
"Have another," they beg, "Can't stand on one leg"
And he winds up going home tight
Liquor acts queer on some of these men,
And different effects are felt
Some come to blows when they get a wet nose
And the victor claims the belt

Some get owly and growl like dogs,
Some get really funny,
Others get numb and do not know
Shinola from wild honey
There are a few who can't stand much,
And are soon stretched out as if in death;
You can't tell it all on the veterans
Except for their odorous breath
But they are all jolly good fellows
From the veterans down to the beginners,
They have their one fault but I don't think you'd find
A better bunch of sinners
So pour me a potent one
While I put up the pen,
And let's drink a toast to the place we love most,
The Valley of the Drunken Men

–John "Pappy" Doser

125

LYIN' AND TIGERS AND BEARS

Through the decades the interior decorations of taverns have pretty much consisted of combinations of four different categories. Colorful beer and liquor advertising items, pictures of attractive females in various stages of undress, sports related paraphernalia, and nature displays. From the earliest times the latter has been the most popular and enduring, especially in the northern area of the state. Whether it was stuffed bears, mounted tiger muskies, or taxidermical tricks, there was rarely a tavern without at least one animal on display. You could view the biggest musky in the world at The Moccasin Bar in Hayward or the biggest display of Muskies at Frank Suick's Musky Bar in Antigo. Jack Kinzinger's Hunter's & Fisherman's Tavern in Lena and the Buckhorn of Spooner had huge collections that included bears, raccoons, foxes, badger, owls, bucks, does and fawns. The Buckhorn of Rice Lake featured shovel snakes, ripple dippers and dingbats all fabricated by the owner, Otto Rindlisbacher, who was an imaginative taxidermist. The Lake Venus Tavern in Monico (lower left) featured the biggest concoction of all with its "rhinelapus." Below, Jack Kinzinger proudly displays his silent menagerie which includes fox, bear, wolves, and at least five owls (to the gratitude of the area vermin). It is not noted how many passenger pigeons, great auks, or heath hens were included.

An audience of stuffed animals looked on as a slumbering saloon dog and thoroughly relaxed customer stage a lounging competition at Paul Shepreaux's Saloon in Stevens Point circa 1910.

Wisconsin Magazine Writes On Buckhorn Tavern Display ————————●

The "friendly" Buckhorn of Rice Lake had it all. At least two beers on tap (one, no doubt reserved for the local Breunig Brewery), dozens of stuffed animals, a tin ceiling, an extensive selection of pipes and tobacco, snuff, and a peanut machine.

An article entitled "The Friendly Buckhorn" appeared in the July edition of the Wisconsin Beverage News. Written by Otto Rindlisbacher in which the uniquely furnished local establishment is described so effectively that an editorial note accompanying the article states, "This sketch was prepared by Otto Rindlisbacher for use by Harry Coffey in an article. The editors found it so well done that they reprint it verbatim under Otto's byline."

Mr. Rindlisbacher tells of the numerous curios, relics and mounted wildlife specimens that adorn the interior of the Buckhorn, among them the 103-point buck shot near here a few years ago, the miniature mechanical replica of the famed "One Shot gang," and those rare "freaks" of nature, the Shovel Tailed Snake, the Wisconsin Dingbat and the Fur-herring, as well as innumerable other oddments.

The Buckhorn's collection of lumberjack musical instruments, reputed to be the world's largest, is also given considerable space in the article. It will be remembered that Mr. and Mrs. Otto Rindlisbacher and a company of performers journeyed to Washington, D.C., in both 1938 and 1940 where they played folk music on these instruments for the members of Congress. Recordings of their music have been preserved at Columbia University of Wisconsin and many other schools throughout the country, the article discloses.

–Rice Lake Chronicle, 1946

Dingbat

One Shot Gang

Other Wisconsin Creatures

Blood On The Tracks

Humiliated and heartbroken, a little black dog belonging to Hutchisons of 7 Manning on the Northside deliberately committed suicide yesterday by laying on the streetcar tracks in front of the store and allowing a car to run over him.

During the afternoon the dog was ordered out of Hutchison's Saloon, 620 Copeland Avenue, and given a kick on the way out. Not used to this kind of treatment, the animal seemed to take humiliation to heart and drooping his head, he sulked into the street and deliberately laid his head on a streetcar rail.

When the streetcar approached the dog, the motor man clanged the bell loudly but the dog refused to move. Witnesses say the little canine looked out the corners of his eyes at the approaching car and then closed his eyes and waited for the end. His head was completely severed from his body by the wheels of the streetcar. Those who witnessed the incident said it was a case of suicide, pure and simple.

–La Crosse Tribune, July 17, 1906

La Crosse Saloon with Dog circa 1906

Downtown La Crosse, street car tracks, circa 1925

Courtesy of U.W.- La Crosse, Murphy Library

130

Biggest Star From A Bar

Who was the biggest star that ever got his or her start in Wisconsin? The somewhat short list of names to consider would have to include Liberace, Fred MacMurray and Orson Welles. None of those would be the correct answer. Because the northwoods of Wisconsin was the origin of the biggest star in Hollywood of the 1960s. Being Gentle Ben, he was also the hairiest and smelliest. In the late 1950s, the bear cub who would become Gentle Ben was captured by Wisconsin teenager Jim Galarowicz, who gave him to Ivan Walter, the fellow pictured on the right. Ivan and his wife had a beer bar named the Ponderosa and a small game preserve outside of Langlade. The little cub was trained there by Ivan and eventually made his way to Hollywood to star on TV as "Gentle Ben." He later graced the cover of TV Guide as well as the menu for the Ponderosa.

So This Dog Walks Into A Bar...

Courtesy of Longbranch Saloon

Ronnie's Tavern of Minong

One afternoon a slightly grimy, tired looking dog slowly walks into a bar. The animal stands on his back feet, places his front paws on the bar and says to the bartender, "I am tired and weary; my butt is draggin'. Pour me a cold one." The bartender paused in astonishment at what he had just heard. He quickly collected his thoughts and realized this could be a moneymaking opportunity. He says to the dog, "Hey, how's about you and me teaming up. There's a traveling circus in town. I'll be your manager, I can get you a job there." "Ya right," said the dog. "Now just what would a traveling circus need a plumber for?"

So this deer walks into a country tavern and says, "I've just spent a hard day in the woods. Gimme a beer." "Sorry, nothing doing," says the bartender. "We don't serve deer in this bar." "Aw, c'mon", the deer replied, "Be a sport, I'm game."

One morning a fellow walked into a bar with a monkey on his shoulder. He ordered a glass of beer and sat down. The monkey then jumped from his shoulder and began an exploration of the tavern. Stopping at the end of the bar, he picked up a bottle cap, gave it a sniff, and swallowed it in one gulp. The bartender thought no harm done and watched as the little fellow continued on where he then paused by a cocktail glass, reached in and pulled out two olives which he devoured in an instant. Finally the little beast climbed aboard the pool table, grabbed the cue ball and opening wide, swallowed it in a single gulp. This made the bartender quite angry and he threw both of them out at once. A few weeks later both the man and his monkey returned. The bartender allowed them in, poured the man a beer, and kept a close eye on the monkey. It wasn't long before the monkey jumped from the man's shoulder, ran down the bar and grabbed a peanut. The monkey then partially bent over, lifted his tail and quickly inserted and withdrew the peanut in his backside, and then swallowed it hole. "Geeezz," said the bartender. "Did you see what he did, that is revolting." "Yeah, it is pretty rude," said the man. "He still eats everything in sight, but now he measures the diameter first."

Courtesy of Boettchers Tavern

Boettcher Deer Farm, Hayward area

Joe The Monkey ●

Most monkey bars are on playgrounds providing amusement for kids. In Saukville in the late 1940s adults had quite a few laughs at their own monkey bar, with a little monkey named "Joe" being the primate attraction. When WWII ended, Saukville native Pfc. Art Helm found himself in the far-off Philippines. (The globe behind the bar was used to keep track of the three Helm brothers.) Before departing, he paid 50¢ for a little spider monkey. He brought the monkey on the 20 day journey by troopship and train to his mother's tavern in Saukville. Some GIs on the ship were nice enough to give Joe a preview of his new habitat by letting him guzzle rum & cokes to his heart's content. The cocktailing, along with seasickness, left Joe spending the remainder of the trip draped over a pile of life jackets blowing bananas.

The Helm Family at Olga's Tavern. Joe the Monkey is with one of his adoptive uncles on the last stool.

He recovered and was a howl for all Saukvillians, commencing with his arrival at the train depot when he poked his head out of Art's jacket to the complete surprise of awaiting relatives. The late 1940s were as good as the tavern business ever got, and the good got better with the monkey-inspired business. It seemed as though everyone who was out for a night on the town, at least once during the evening, would stop into Olga's for some laughs watching the monkey shines. Occasionally the yolk would be on the barhoppers though. Joe worked cheap, a big treat for him would be an occasional hard boiled egg. Joe loved his eggs, but only the white portion. He would often eat the albumen and then bean the nearest gawking patron with the remainder before retreating to his cage in the basement.

Art with Joe behind the tavern

While Joe certainly was unusual, he wasn't unique. This ad for a Bonduel tavern from February 1934 shows there was at least one other tavern making money from monkeying around. There was no story or announcement in subsequent issues of the newspaper regarding the lucky winner of the event. Let's hope the little fellow was dressed warmly, the temperature that night around bar closing time was a nippy 14°.

A-1 and A-2

We've already mentioned Windy Jacob's Bar & Music Store. When one thinks of mutually enhancing twosomes, you might think of peanut butter and jelly, Laurel and Hardy, or bratwurst and sauerkraut. In Wisconsin you can add to the list: beer and cheese, beer and guns, and beer and cars.

It might not have been a good idea to ask the stern faced Walt, of Walt's Farmers and Woodsmens Bar of Park Falls, for a shot. With the arsenal behind him, he could have drawn a luger as easily as drawing a lager.

In Hillsboro a motorist had the option of getting lubricated at the same place their DeSoto did, Jim Holak's "Tavern and Garage." This stage curtain hung at the Yuba Opera House.

Normally one does not want their bartender to habitually "cut the cheese." This is not the case in Baumgartner's "Cheese Store and Tavern" of Monroe. As a matter of fact, it was encouraged. In the 1940s a patron could enjoy a glass of Golden Glow with a Limburger cheese sandwich, both locally produced.

BAR HUMOR

Snort Beer Through Your Nose

You can get a glass of beer, a cocktail, maybe a bit of lunch at a tavern. You can also buy some chips, a candy bar, or a pack of smokes. If you are in a place that has a display for pocket combs or nail clippers on the backbar, or a large jar of pig's knuckles or pickled eggs, you are in our kind of tavern. Two things you do not go into a tavern to obtain are knowledge or wisdom. As a matter of fact, if you do it right, you should walk out slightly more stupid than you walked in. It is about as easy to find a fool on top of a barstool as it is to find a candle on a birthday cake. Hence the threshold of what passes for wit and wisdom in a Wisconsin tavern has never been all that high, actually about the same as the book you are currently reading. For laughs, nothing such as a whoopie cushion for the barstools, or dribble glasses for the taps were required (they'd be redundant anyway). These humorous knick-knacks are far from snort-beer-thru-your-nose funny, more to the point, the value of these free jokes and cartoon trade stimulators from the 1930s and '40s were priced just about right.

Town Tavern shortly after it was built in 1933, and Mr. Sorlie showing off his new fishing rod.

135

BUCKHORN INN
Frog Legs — Steak — Chicken
Dancing Every Nite — Liquors
2 MILES from STILLWATER, MINN.
ON WIS. HI-WAY 35

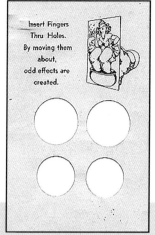

Insert Fingers
Thru Holes.
By moving them
about,
odd effects are
created.

The most fun you can
have with your hands
without washing them
afterwards.

*More finger fun!
Cover the ladies neck
and rotate 90°. A
completely different
scene is revealed.*

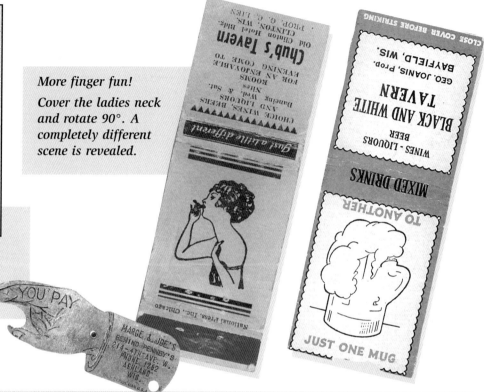

*The science behind the building of the pyramids or erecting the statues of
Easter Island are examples of lost technologies that have puzzled historians
for years. Well, here is another technology, nearly forgotten, that puzzled and
befuddled patrons of 1930s taverns. On the front of this handheld "pouring
sand novelty," the bartender pours the thirsty lady a mug of "Whiz Beer."
The sand pours into view in a clear plastic area from a reservoir hidden by
cardboard. Flip it over and one can graphically see the inevitable outcome
caused by the consumption of beer.*

License to jag!... James Bond had a license to kill, left is a license to swill. On a more sobering note is the 1949 court ordered personal prohibition imposed for the MVP of the Wisconsin Tavern League, the Otis T. Sprauge of the tiny town of Mt. Ida.

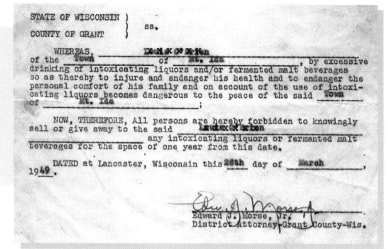

HOW TO LIVE ON $15 A WEEK

WHISKEY and BEER	$8.80
WIFE'S BEER	1.65
MEAT, FISH and GROCERIES	On Credit
RENT	Pay Next Week
Mid-Week WHISKEY	1.50
CIGARS	.20
LIFE INSURANCE (WIFE'S)	.50
MOVIES	.60
PINOCHLE CLUB	.50
COAL	Borrow Neighbors'
HOT TIP ON HORSES	.50
DOG FOOD	.60
SNUFF	.40
POKER GAME	1.40
TOTAL	$16.65

THIS MEANS GOING INTO DEBT
. . . . . SO CUT OUT THE WIFE'S BEER

Vee Get So Soon Dldt - Undt So Late Schmart
Better Vee Take One "At Little Bohemia"

137

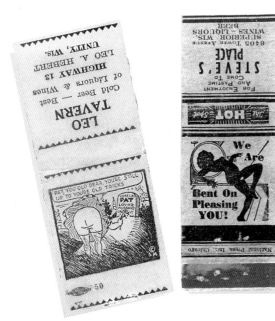

THE MIDGET

The Midget, popular tavern located just a mile north on Highway 51 at its intersection with County Trunk A, is the "home of gadgets." Fred Major, well known owner of the tavern, has a reputation for "springing jokes" on his patrons. An electrical contrivance that gives slight shocks to those seated at the bar; a fake cigar; pencils that mysteriously hang on walls with no visible means of support, and other tricks are used to amuse visitors. The tavern also has a dance hall, equipped with booths and an electric Victrola. Orchestras are also engaged at times to furnish music for dancing.

The Tomahawk Leader, 1935

So a hamburger walks in a bar and the bartender says, "I'm sorry, but we don't serve food here."

138

Fred Smith

One of Wisconsin's most original and prolific artists was tavern owner Fred Smith of Park Falls. The closest thing to the arts for most bartenders was drawing a beer and sculpting the head off with a foam scraper. Not so for Fred. "Nobody knows why I made them, not even me. This work just came to me naturally." Over a course of 15 years, next to his Rock Garden Tavern, Fred built the "Wisconsin Concrete Park," which consisted of over 200 different sculpted pieces formed out of cement, lumber, wire, broken glass, mirrors, beer and whiskey bottles, and other shiny or reflective doodads. The product was not airy, high-brow, modern art nonsense, but was as artistically accessible as an episode of the Honeymooners, yet as unusual as Chateau Mont-Redon at a Packer game. The creative process started at the age of 64 with a stone barbecue built to celebrate the victory of the 1948 Cleveland Indians in the World Series. What followed included Paul Bunyan's marble, Abe and Mary Todd Lincoln, the Lone Ranger, animals and simple working folk such as lumberjacks, farmers, and milk maids. In his words, "For all the American people everywhere, they need something like this." Amen, Fred, Amen.

"Here shows Chiann, the big beer drinker. He has been a cowboy in 17 different states. He has been a drinker all the while he was a cowboy. He found the famous Rhinelander Export Beer, which is the finest beer he ever drank in his life.

Only one beer! I bought a truckload of beer every time we went to Rhinelander. 200 cases every time."

-Fred Smith

Chiann the cowboy

Fred's tavern in later years

Norwegian Hell

In or near Stevens Point, sometime in the 1850s, there possibly was a tavern with the unlikely name of Norwegian Hell. No trace of the building remains, and its location is unknown. There are no photographs or drawings of the building, and its name appears only as a passing reference in "Stage Coach and Tavern Tales of the Old Northwest." The origin of the name is completely left to speculation. Were a Norwegian preacher's words of warning turned into an enticement by the calculating owner? Or did he just think that it would be a good name to go with the slogan "Drink Where Thor gets Hammered." What would Norwegian Hell be like anyway? For a true Norske, would it be staggering out of a howling storm and into a tavern, chilled and soaked through his union suit, and finding the bar with its beer gone flat, stacks of sardine tins but no church keys, green vegetables with the meals, and to further discover a party of passing Swedes had earlier consumed all of the lefsa and snoose? But worst of all, finding the pantry to be devoid of that Norwegian delicacy, embalmed cod, otherwise known as lutefisk. And after finding all of that, in this worst possible of Norwegian worlds, all the patrons of the bar would spend the evening talking about their feelings, instead of the latest Ole and Lena jokes:

One night at Norwegian Hell, Ole stumbled into the bar literally stinking drunk. He staggered over to a bar stool next to Lena, seated himself with some difficulty, and ordered a glass of Point. "Uff Da, Ole, Vat Stinks? Did you mess your pants?" an offended Lena asked. "Ya," said Ole, looking a little sheepish. "Vell, vy don't you go out back and clean yourself up?" "Ya, Lena, dats a gut idea, but I don't know if I'm done yet."

∙∙∙∙∙∙∙∙∙∙∙∙∙∙∙∙∙∙∙∙∙∙∙∙∙∙∙∙∙∙∙∙∙∙∙∙∙∙∙

Another night, Ole and Lena invited Sven to go out and have a few beers. Well, a few beers turned into a few pitchers, and about midnight Ole passed out, face down, in a puddle of beer on the bar. The bartender noticed a giggling Sven and Lena tiptoeing behind Ole and outside to the back of the building. The good bartender, concerned for his favorite customer, went out to investigate. Sure enough, by the time he found Ole's wagon, he could see Lena and Sven in the back going at it like a couple of teenagers. Outraged, he returned to the bar to rouse the sleeping

Ole. "Ole, you better get out to your wagon and see what is going on out there." Ole stumbled out and returned chuckling and shaking his head a few minutes later. "Ole, what are you laughing about. Did you see what I saw?" asked the bartender. "Ya," said Ole as he returned to his beer. "Oh, dat Sven, he is so drunk dat he tinks he is me."

∙∙∙∙∙∙∙∙∙∙∙∙∙∙∙∙∙∙∙∙∙∙∙∙∙∙∙∙∙∙∙∙∙∙∙∙∙∙∙

Sometime later, an obviously intoxicated Ole wandered into the nearly deserted bar and sat next to the only other patron. Ole said to him "Vell, vat you know?" "Vell, not too much, I'm youse sitting here drinking beer." "Hey," says Ole, "you sound like a Norske, are youse from Norway, too?" "Ya, I came over on da boat from Trondheim." "Ya don't say," said Ole. "I yam from Trondheim, too! Vell, vat de hell! Where about in Trondheim?" "Vell, I lived on a little fishing boat down in the harbor." This elicited a loud hoot from Ole who said "Vell golly, I better buy youse a beer den!" About this time one of the regulars came in and asked the bartender what was going on. The bartender replied, "Oh, not much, just Ole and his brother Sven are drinking again."

Bavarian Heaven

Outside of Sheboygan was "Bavarian Heaven," an establishment that had more mirthful connotations than the gloomy "Norwegian Hell" of their dour Nordic cousins. As with Norwegian Hell, very little remains of a factual basis regarding "Bavarian Heaven." This lack of a concrete record gives us the opportunity to surmise as to what a jolly, *Gemütlichkeit* - filled establishment Bavarian Heaven could have been. What comes to mind is rubenesque bar maids carrying platters of bratwurst and sausage and overflowing mugs of beer. A row of *Grossvatters* and *Grossmutters* snoozing in their rocking chairs - the long, low rays of the late afternoon sun glistening off drops of lager dripping from their mustaches. The saloon keeper delivering glasses of Weiss, Bock and Lager *schiess eims*. A jolly Umpah Band playing loudly enough to drown out the sound of sauerkraut induced flatulence being expelled by a crowd of Fred Mertz dopplegangers. Bavarian Heaven was one of the first in a long tradition of Germanic taverns throughout Wisconsin.

Interior of "Zum Golden Frosch," Fountain City, 1940s

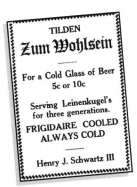

Here again is the ad from Rueckert's Tavern. Did you notice the unusual design? Sometimes the Germanic theme can be taken a little too far.

141

BREWERIANA

For over a century, tavern owners have had their establishments adorned both inside and out with colorful advertising items courtesy of their local breweries. The practice of the breweries distributing paraphernalia started in the late 1880s as advances in transportation, bottling methods and refrigeration allowed breweries to grow from small neighborhood industries to regional ones. As they distributed their products further and further from the home brewery, the beer makers could no longer rely on word-of-mouth to sell their product. Many saloons of the era accepted splendid backbars from the brewers. In turn the saloons would sell only their products. Items on a smaller scale have included porcelain signs, neons, lithographs, serving trays, clocks, lighted signs, and countless other promotional geegaws. The gang at Matt Udvoc's, probably somewhere in the Wisconsin northwoods, seemed to be pleased with their cardboard Pabst sign.

This turn-of-the-century lovely buxom, rosy cheeked gal in the full flower of youth, looking more like a milkmaid than a bar maid, pours a schooner and examines a product as pure as she. This advertising piece in all likelihood never saw the inside of a saloon. Eighty years after the demise of the Fred Miller Brewery, it was discovered at an auction in the Ashland area, in pristine condition, sharing a frame behind a portrait of George Washington. She was paired four score with another person of impeccable character.

143

Beer Art

POTOSI BREWERY'S OLD ADS BECOMING COLLECTORS' ITEMS

Everybody knows that beer is a work of art. Savored by artists and artisans alike. Now it appears the brewers have also created an art form in their advertising. Potosi Brewing Company, 111 years of age, has created several beer ads which have been recognized by collectors of Americana. One of them was selected for publication in the new book, "Brewed in America," a history of beer and ale in the United States, by Stanley Baron...

–Grant County Independent
April 25, 1963

Even the smallest of towns could hold some things that would interest breweriana collectors years later. On a cool spring day about 1950, the main street of Pine River sported such treasures as a porcelain Chief Oshkosh Sign, and porcelain with neon signs from Berlin Brewing and Blatz.

GIRL AND SERVING TRAY:
Americana of a bygone era is pictured in this old serving tray held by Shirley Gassen. The gents with the Uncle Sam beards are betting on a cock fight.

Through the ages the goat has been the traditional symbol of lechery as well as being closely associated with Bock Beer. This gentleman has gotten the goat as some sort of booby prize for a tavern related sport. Yesterday's junk is tomorrow's treasure and this Rhinelander Bock Beer poster would be a nifty addition to any breweriana collection.

144

It's The After Glow

Some things that are are seemingly obvious take a long time to be noticed. Humans had been drawing and painting for thousands of years before one day, somewhere in Europe in the 1400s, the idea of perspective was born. The game of football had been played for over 25 years before someone had the bright idea to pick up the ball and throw it, instead of kicking or running with it. In the late 1800s, breweries began to make major efforts to advertise and promote their product. From that time, and for the next 60 years, most of that publicizing was primarily endorsements to the taste or healthful qualities of the beverage, oddly avoiding its most important character, namely the euphoric, carefree feeling that results from drinking several glasses of brew. About 1940 or so, the advertising staff of Blumer's Brewery of Monroe began a campaign of stating that obvious fact about beer, "It's the after glow that makes golden glow taste and feel so good." They used the rhetorical tact for awhile, but the company went out of business for unrelated reasons. With its passing, also gone was refreshing honesty in that area of advertising. By the way, the verses to the right were not part of the accompanying advertisements but could have been. The first pays tribute to the miracle of alcohol, with a bottle of Golden Glow transforming a solitary and matronly gal from vacant to vivacious. A colorful attempt to win over lonely housewives from cooking sherry, their traditional and covert beverage of choice in the 1940s.

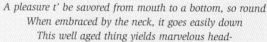

Widowed? Lonely? Is your husband lone-wolfing?
Does a long ago love, tug at your heartstrings?
Cold, lost and forgotten?... You have nothing to fear.
On Tap, in Can or Bottle, It's Amber Hued Cheer!
Get a Warm, Happy Feeling, from GOLDEN GLOW BEER!

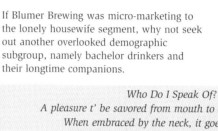

If Blumer Brewing was micro-marketing to the lonely housewife segment, why not seek out another overlooked demographic subgroup, namely bachelor drinkers and their longtime companions.

Who Do I Speak Of?
A pleasure t' be savored from mouth to a bottom, so round
When embraced by the neck, it goes easily down
This well aged thing yields marvelous head-
Whom or what do I speak, after what I have said?
Might it be my dapper companion that I hold so dear?
Don't be silly, dear reader, tis' my Golden Glow Beer!
A lager, if not fit for a King, then surely two Queens!

Far from the honesty of the Golden Glow approach, was the fantasy concocted by the folks at Marathon. Directed at Joe Schmoe Badger, sipping his beer in Central Wisconsin taverns, it pictures an unlikely scenario. While many, if not most, Wisconsin gals love their beer, it is unlikely they would be so good natured when calling to fetch their hubbies, and of course the typical Badgerette was, and is, of far sturdier stock than the delicate beauty pictured.

Relax on your barstool without a care or a worry-
finish your laughs and jokes with your pals, don't hurry
I don't want to nag, but when you're done with your fun...
Stick 6-packs of Marathon under your arms,
and stumble on home, to my negligeed charms.
And when you finally get home, a little weary and beery-
I'll do what I can to make you feel cheery.
Take off your shoes, rub your back, feeling better my Dearie?
I'll offer my amorous skills, as a pleasure to please ya-
After you're satisfied, I'll bake a piping hot pizza.

We owe a debt of gratitude to the Heileman Brewing Company of La Crosse for the very beautiful oil process, framed portrait of a Rembrandtesque group of beer drinking convivialists of the Middle Ages. As a work of art, the picture rates high, both in its warm coloring and the effective placing of its elements. A most delicate, yet highly appropriate boost for Old Style Lager in the old fashioned "Inn" sign, which can be seen through the oriel window of the private service room of the inn. The picture itself, a 30 by 36 inch gold framed masterpiece, carries no other advertising. The "Old Style Lager" sign shown on the outside of the inn has a legitimate place in the picture, regardless of what art school of thought may be applied in judging. It enhances, rather than detracts, from the artistic effect. We believe that subtle, artistic advertising of a product, especially in secondary media, is far more effective than blatant claims of superiority of product, smeared offensively over advertising displays, artistic or otherwise, as if often the case, not only in beverage advertising, but in pictorial advertising of many classes. Heileman's is to be congratulated on the artistic effectiveness of at least this one piece of its advertising. This artistic effectiveness is also predominant in Heileman's illustrated brochure, entitled "Heileman's Old Style Lager, Good Since 1850," a copy of which accompanied the picture, which latter occupies a place of honor in ye editor's sanctum.

–*Beverage Retailer News*
November 1, 1936

Where's Shorty?

"Where's Shorty?" was a question posed on matchbooks, calendars, cardboard signs and other items throughout the 1940s by the Rhinelander Brewing Company in promotion of its popular 7-ounce bottle. The beer was sold in taverns and liquor stores throughout Northern Wisconsin.

Photographic evidence reveals "Shorty" might have been about 200 miles south in the La Crosse area.

Eany, Meany, Miney, Mistletoe

We've already discussed Blumer Brewing and the unique approach they took to advertise their Golden Glow Beer. Here is another one-of-a-kind advertising idea that is in an entirely different category. Charley, of the Mistletoe Inn of Bradley, had a unique approach to business stimulation. He got a dog so big that the average patron would not be able to describe its size without taking the name of the Lord in vain. Charlie then gave the canine a distasteful name, and followed that up with at least two forms of advertising which featured the huge hound. There was this matchbook and postcard, let's hope that radio jingles and roadside billboards were kept to a minimum.

Three Lakes American Legion Bar sometime in the 1950s. In view, a beautiful Wurlitzer jukebox which was unlikely to host any Swastika records.

Unbelievably, there is some competition in regards to poor taste in business ideas for the state of Wisconsin. Around 1960, a small time Sauk Rapids entrepreneur of German descent started a new record company using a Swastika as the logo! Bear in mind this was only about 15 years after the end of World War II. A large portion of the product of the small record company went to fill jukeboxes in taverns, roller rinks and dancehalls. Vets of the big one probably pumped more fists into the jukes than they did nickels. (Except for maybe at Rueckert's Tavern in Bonduel). After the initial release, the name was changed to Cuca and the company had a successful 10 years or so releasing local artists and groups. The Cuca logo was first written in a fancy script, but in later days it inexplicably featured a sleeping Mexican peasant in a huge sombrero. Odd, I wonder if any Mexican marimba records were illustrated with fat white guys in crewcuts bowling?

The Germanic themed Cuca warehouse, Sauk Rapids

The Mystery of the Porcine Porcelain

From sometime in the 1930s until about 1946, a porcelain Golden Glow beer sign hung on a pole over the entrance to Junior's Bar in Stizer. However, by the late 1940s, Blumer Brewing was on the losing end of a battle with the big Milwaukee brewers and this sign was replaced by one from Schlitz, Blatz or Pabst.

It turned out to be quite a demotion. From the prominent position in the small town on the crest of a slight hill, and over the only bar in town, it had beckoned thirsty farmers and villagers for years. Its new location was not nearly as visible. For reasons not remembered, it was hauled a few miles out of town to adorn a pig shed on the back forty of a farmer's field. No longer did the sign hang over the comings and goings of the soused, but only the sows. Years later, probably in the 1970s, the pig shed, fences, sign, and porcine paraphernalia were bulldozed over and the sty was turned into additional acreage for corn. To this day the sign lies buried somewhere in that area.

Dog Under a Hot Tin Roof

The pooch that once lived in the doghouse behind Fairfield's Silverdome Bar had it made in the shade with his unique beer sign roof. These Pabst and Point Beer signs from the 1940s formed what was probably the largest canine held breweriana collection in the state of Wisconsin.

Danbury Mints

Myron Howland and the Mrs. proudly display an impressive collection of breweriana in their Danbury area tavern. A Leinenkugel's thermometer and beautiful reverse on glass clock, several Hamm's items and flawless conetop beer cans from Bruenings (background) and City Club (foreground).

149

Ancient Calendar

For some habitual over-indulgers, there is a saying, "One is too many, a dozen is not enough." When you are talking about exceptional breweriana, one was just right when the one was something as rare as the porcelain corner piece from Grand Rapids Brewing Company displayed on an otherwise unadorned establishment. The brewery was open between 1905 and 1920.

Memories of pioneer days are echoing through the old Klinkert residence at 2204 North 24th Street, Superior, as axes and crowbars knock out the aged timbers. Old papers tallowed with age and a calendar dated 1891 showed up in the attic as proof that its former owner, John Klinkert, pioneer brewer, built the house in 1890. But he built the house near Eighth and Catlin when he sold the Northern Brewery and established the Klinkert Brewing and Malting Company at 24th and Scranton. He moved his home with him, furniture, family, and all, intact. Drawn by a team of horses, Superior was but a young city then, it took two weeks to tow the high frame house to its present location. Though it was somewhat rough and tumble at times, the family lived in the house on its journey from one end of town to the other. Among old papers found in the home by George Ramstad and men who are razing the building are three checks drawn on the Northwestern National Bank of West Superior in 1898 by J.A. Klinkert, president of the firm, a legal document written in long hand and an ancient calendar.

Mrs. Bliss Robinson, 1710 North 21st Street, the former Lillian Klinkert, and the only survivor of the John Klinkerts, remembers well that two weeks on wheels. A high school student at the time, Mrs. Robinson recalls that when she came home from school the house would be a block further on and she never knew just where to find it. She remembers that most of the moving was done at night to avoid the street cars and low wires. Klinkert built the Klinkert Brewery at 24th and Scranton when he sold the Northern Brewery in 1890 and continued in the business until 1908 when he sold the land to the Northern Pacific Railway at their request. It is believed that the papers found in the attic were part of the office files which he stored in the attic of his home when he sold the brewery.

–*Superior Evening Telegram*
July 1955

The calendar mentioned in the above article is the only known item of breweriana from the long gone Klinkert Brewery. The calendar's whereabouts, 45 years after this article appeared in the local paper, is unknown.

Badger Boys & Gopher Girls

What is a lovely Minnesota girl doing hanging around Wisconsin taverns? Hasn't she heard the old joke about why Minnesota girls don't date Wisconsin boys? Actually, the circa 1935 cardboard cutie is peddling beer from the Gopher State's biggest brewery, Hamm's, to patrons of taverns in Hammond, Cameron and Osceola.

Courtesy of Doug Dahl

Freddy Rass's - Hammond

Osceola Historical Society

The Cascade - Osceola

Q. *Why don't Minnesota girls date Wisconsin boys?*

A. *Have you ever seen a gopher hole after a badger has been in it?*

Ma and Pa's Tavern - Cameron

151

Somewhere in rural Douglas County was the setting for this bucolic beer party attended by a bevy of hugging and beer slugging girls sometime in the late 1930s. When these Bobby-Soxers went to the "Malt Shop," they were probably referring to the tap room at the Northern Brewery. Interestingly, they are drinking bottles of Northern Blue Label Beer (although with the overt displays of affection it looks as though they might prefer Busch). Blue Label tin over cardboard signs and some backbar displays can be found today, but for reasons unknown, the bottle itself is extremely rare.

Frozen stiff Badger Boys enter the warm and snug Gopher Hole, also of rural Douglas County. About 1950, on a day colder than Bud Lang's butt.

This is the second Gopher Hole. The first one is up about two miles down the road on Oakdale and Minnesuing Road. Skids was put under it and it was pulled up the road. 24'x16' was about the size of it. It's a house now. A neighbor bought it from us for fifty bucks. They added on so they would have a bathroom. We opened the first Gopher Hole on May 11th, 1948. Too small, so we sold it on July 8th, 1956. We had the grand opening here. People say it had a dirt floor but it never did. This place was always packed on a Saturday night and there'd be people outside. One Saturday there was some people we didn't know and a scuffle started and it was so packed I couldn't get out from in back of the bar. My husband was trying to get their attention and he could not, so he took his .45 from under the bar and he got up on a bar stool and he aimed out the door right over their head. You want to know what a .45 sounds like in a small room? Like a cannon! Well, just like that, in two seconds flat, there wasn't a car in the yard and there was a couple of them down here at the curve. Another story they told about this place, that it had one door and two windows, we just pitched the beer cans out the back window. Not true either. There would be guys on their motorcycles and they would drive over to Amnicon Falls and they would ride up the falls on their Harleys. Afterward Tom Nollet would come over the hill standing on the seat of his motorcycle. Then they would ride the bikes right in here and do circles around the pool table and then drive out. One time, Big Woolly rolled a big light pole across the road and said, "Well, we wanted to get some more business out here." Then we had this doctor from Superior that would come in and he was drunk all the time. He'd come in and sweep everybody's beer off the bar. Boy, was he mean. When they had a dance in town, the guys would drop the girls off in town and then they would come out here. Then they would go back five minutes before the dance was over and pick up their girlfriends. "Goodbye to you and I might see you at one o'clock." We served Budweiser, Pabst, Miller, Schlitz, Eubling, Leinenkugel's, and of course Northern and Rex, Grain Belt, and Schmidt, too. Back in '53 when the big three went on strike, we had to scarf up any kind of beer we could get. And then Hamm's would say, "We can't keep up with everybody," so we couldn't get their beer either. Summertime people from Illinois came up here. "Well, that's strange, we can get all the Hamm's we want down there." They used that time during the strike to break into other people's territory. So we was high and dry! They lost all their customers around here. We haven't sold a can of Hamm's since then. Sold more Nordlager and Northern then. I don't know why they stopped making them. We carried a lot of different beers. Got most of our stuff from Zanuzoskis. You want another tall tale? Well, over there was some moose horns. One day there was three little old ladies. They saw those moose horns and wanted to know were they came from, so my husband, who was a teller of tall tales, tells these poor ladies that one day there was three grizzly bears crossing the road on their way to Michigan.

continued...

One of the ladies said, "Well, we didn't know there were horns on grizzly bears." Well, my husband says, "And I shot one and there's the horns." They believed the whole story. Another time he was over in Barnes and somebody gave him an old moth-eaten northern and he had that up there. So one day we touched it up and repainted it so it looked like a smelt and we told everyone it was the world's largest smelt… We had lots of old signs in here. Had two old Leinenkugel's mirrors. The nicest one we had was in the men's bathroom. I know who took it but I can't prove it. He handed it out the bathroom window to his buddy. Known him all my life, we called the cops, but never got it back. He still comes in. My customers say there was fights here all the time but I never see them. My husband had two pieces of equipment. One was a .45 and the other was a hickory cane hook handle and cut it off for a billy club more than a foot long. Well that scared the bejesus out of anyone who came in here. I kid you not! Louie Bannick was one of the biggest shyster sheriffs we ever had, besides Jenda. Crooked as could be. No bull! This was around '58 or so. Well, Eckbrock was sheriff for starters. He thought all the problems in the county were because of alcohol. We never knew when he

was going to show up. One day some kids were coming back from the Dairy Queen. There was a state trooper parked at the ball field and he started to chase these six kids in the car. They were speeding. So they gets to my place and come flying through the door and out the back into a hole we had dug for our septic tank. What a smell and what a fall! The state trooper comes in saying, "Who was driving that car?" Well, the rest was out in the woods. I'm quite sure the trooper got the license number. There was one door to this place and the Sheriff and Andy Baker and a couple of other cops would walk in and lock the door. Well, two would be inside checking ID's and the rest of 'em would be outside in the yard. They could never find anything wrong but a neighbor was here with two of her daughters, was sitting here having a beer and there was nothing they could do. But people kept complaining about that sheriff and the harassment. I was set up plenty of times by those guys but they never caught me! Another time some guy came in for a case of Leinenkugel's. Well, there was a couple of sixteen-year-olds outside waiting so I told my husband, "Do not sell a case of beer to those guys." So I'm coming back from the house just in time to see a case of Leinenkugel's going into the trunk of this car. Well, I

"In the picture, that's Bud Long and he had a well drilling outfit… and that's my husband Al inside the door. I believe that picture was taken in 1952. You know, I had ten kids of my own and a step child. I was sixteen when I got married and seventeen when Pat was born."

walked right up to 'em and grabbed that case of beer and right then a county squad pulled right behind the car! So you know what that was. Those kids are saying, "Give me back my three dollars" and I'm saying "Tough Luck" - it would have cost me five hundred.

There were a lot of instances like that. One time this kid come in, and I knew him, and he's got an ID - William Tung. So right behind him comes in two other guys so I check their ID's and both of theirs said William Tung, too. My son Patrick comes in the back door and says "Hey Maw, there's some kids out here giving out ID cards." I says to Bill, "So these guys is triplets and they all got your name?" To teach him a lesson, I call the police and I had one hell of a time getting the police out here. They want to catch somebody but don't care when I do. He ended up paying a fifty dollar fine. I said to Bill, "I'm only doing this to teach you a lesson, and this could have cost me a lot of money - even my license - and you don't have the right to do that to me." …Then there was the period of time in the summer when beer was being sold in Lake Nebagamon. Now that Glick Stite - we could never sell that 'cause you had to have a liquor license to sell it and we were just a beer bar. Well, there was three different places in Lake Nebagamon that were selling it outside at some summer festivals. They were selling that stuff to kids who couldn't get into the bars. Somebody knew the fuzz! There would even be all those cans outside my place. My gosh, there'd be teen dances in Nebagamon and there'd be five cops. So I finally got Jimmy the cop down here and I says, "These guys are selling beer out of the trunk of their car and I've called the cops four or five times. So Jimmy goes and calls the cops. So they finally came out and pinched the driver of the car and nobody else and there were three of them. Fifty dollars! I guess they were getting paid off by the sheriff... My husband named this place. He sat down and made a list. The Bee's Nest, The Hornet's Nest, The Squirrel's Cage. He wrote down about ten names. He picked it out of a hat, the Gopher Hole.

–Marti O'Brien

The Log Cabin Bar of El Paso ———●

A gasoline pump was installed in front of the station. Gasoline has remained a part of the business since it was opened. Beer and liquor were served at the bar until the 1940s when liquor was voted out of the township for a few years and only beer could be sold. Since then the Log Cabin has not applied for a liquor license, but has sold beer, both on tap and in the bottle.

From 1933 to 1937 the bar was owned by Cooney Bjornson and leased, first to Lewis Bowen, who was joined by his brother, Cricket Bowen. They were followed by Fred Raehsler, who also oiled horse harnesses in a dipping tank located in a corner of the bar. Cricket Bowen returned to operate the business, but it seemed no one made much of a profit in those first years.

In May 1937, Ernie Seifert, from Lost Creek, bought from Bjornson the business and a house located across the road. As part of the deal Ernie was asked to leave the Log Cabin Bar looking the way it was, for as long as Cooney was alive. Ernie kept his promise and changed the Log Cabin very little in the years afterwards.

The log house just off the road on what is now County Trunk G in El Paso, one of the landmarks of that section, is being taken down and the logs and timber will be used in erecting an oil station and tavern... Lewis Bowen will be the proprietor and the station will be called the Log Cabin Inn.

–Pierce County Herald July 22, 1933

continued...

155

There was an icehouse, approximately 24 x 30 feet long, located behind the bar. They put up their own ice, cutting large chunks from the millpond a quarter mile south on the river, filling the house during the winter with ice, which usually lasted until August.

The first year, in 1937, Lewis Bowen suggested that they have plenty of drinks on hand for the big 4th of July celebration, as there would be a huge crowd of people in El Paso. He suggested getting four barrels of beer along with 100 cases each of beer and pop. "It was probably the biggest day we ever had at the bar," said Ernie, "We almost made $500 that day alone." He had to make a special trip to Ellsworth to get extra beer, hauling 20 cases more in his car. "The bar was just packed with people. We opened up the east window and people were lining up from the outside to get their drinks. We had to hire extra help." James Young and Eddie Raehsler were tending bar. Lawrence Zimmer was minding the gas and oil; the womenfolk helped out inside and Ernie was getting the ice and taking care of the slot machines. "We had one 5¢ and one 10¢ machine and used to make out pretty well with all of them. Beer and pop were 5¢ a bottle then, liquor was 10¢ a shot, 50¢ a half-pint and $1 a bottle."

Ernie had not previously owned a tavern, but had some experience with patching and vulcanizing tubes working for his uncle in Ellsworth. Along with the bar business he soon began offering to do mechanical work on cars at the Log Cabin.

A pit was dug out a little northwest of the bar where they also did oil changes. This worked out until the insurance company thought it a hazard, so the mechanical work was discontinued. Ernie kept on with the tire and tube fixing business, even now patching a tire or tube occasionally.

During and shortly after World War II when good tires and rubber were scarce, tire fixing became a big part of the business. In those years everyone was having their tires repaired because it was quite hard to obtain new ones with lasting quality. One particular Memorial Day weekend, lasting three days, during World War II, Ernie recalled patching 66 tires. This added income helped the business through the war years. Rubber was not the only thing scarce. Beer companies cut a certain percent from the prewar monthly purchases. To make beer last a little longer, it was necessary for some owners to close their places at an earlier hour, or shut down a few days. Ernie recalled letting people drink for awhile, then shutting off the taps, let them drink for awhile and then do the same thing. That made the beer supply stretch a little farther and allowed him to remain open throughout the month. In 1938, the building was wired for electricity, which made the workload much easier as far as keeping the beverages cool. Refrigerators and coolers could be used. As far running water and plumbing, there has never been either at the bar. Ernie carries water from across the road for drinking and cleaning purposes. If one should find it necessary, the little path to "the bath" must still be followed for relief.

–*Pierce County Historical, Rick Foley*

> ...The largest crowd ever in Rush River Valley was at Fisherman's Rest the 4th of July Sunday. The day's entertainment of music, singing, tap dancing, and other amusement was carried out as advertised. The Farmer's Union kittenball team defeated the Camp Ellsworth CCC boys, 9 to 5, in a hard fought game. The large crowd taxed the many stands and Mr. Jones had to increase the number of helpers to take care of it. No accidents or mishaps of any kind marred the day's enjoyments for any of the visitors to the grounds...
>
> –*The Ellsworth Record, July 4, 1937*

"Hey Pal, How Far Is the Ol' Log Inn?

Loyal, about 1910. Look in the upper window of the unusual log cabin backbar display. In the upper window someone has placed the picture of a young female, presumably a soiled dove, smiling and beckoning any woodsmen at the bar to pay her a visit in her upstairs room.

Log Bar - Neenah	Log Cabin - La Crosse	Log House - Shorewood Terrace
Log Cabin - Bangor	Log Cabin - Madison	Log Hut - Tomahawk
Log Cabin - Baraboo	Log Cabin - Medford	Log Inn - Appleton
Log Cabin - Conover	Log Cabin - Middleton	Log Tavern - Burlington
Log Cabin - Danbury	Log Cabin - Northport	Log Tavern - Chippewa Falls
Log Cabin - Dorchester	Log Cabin - Potosi	Log Tavern - Kinney
Log Cabin - Delevan	Log Cabin - Salem	Log Tavern - Montello
Log Cabin - Hammond	Log Cabin - Sheboygan	Old Log Tavern - Fond du Lac
Log Cabin - Eagle Point	Log Cabin - South Range	Old Log Tavern - Fremont
Log Cabin - El Paso	Log Cabin - Stevens Point	Ye Olde Log Tavern - Bloomer
Log Cabin - Iron RIver	Log Cabin - Watertown	

What's In A Name?

Aw Comon Inn	Stevens Point	Stop Inn	East Bristol	
Buzz Inn	Green Bay	Stop Inn	La Crosse	
Cave Inn	Roberts	Stop Inn	Lily	
Curve Inn	Stensonville	Stop & Go Inn	Rosendale	
Dew Cum Inn	Reitsbrock	Stumble Inn	Waterloo	
Dew Drop Inn	Adams	Tumble Inn	Menasha	
Dew Drop Inn	Bagley	Wander Inn	Baraboo	
Dew Drop Inn	Dayton	Wander In	Chippewa Falls	
Dew Drop Inn	Fond du Lac	Wheel Inn	Eau Claire	
Dew Drop Inn	Granton	Wheel Inn	Fond du lac	
Dew Drop Inn	Hurley	Wheel Inn	Menasha	

Dew Drop Inn . . . . Janesville
Dew Drop Inn . . . . Superior
Dew Drop In Resort . . . . Rhinelander
Du Drop In . . . . Medford
Du Drop Inn . . . . Pigeon Falls
Du Kum Inn . . . . Jim Falls
Do-Dodge Inn . . . . Eau Claire
Done Inn . . . . Rockville
Don's Seldom Inn . . . . La Crosse
Drift Inn . . . . Merrimac
Duck In . . . . Shell Lake
Lloyds Never In . . . . Buena Vista
Miss Inn . . . . La Crosse
Peep-Inn . . . . Wausau
Pete's Walk-Inn . . . . Marinette
Roll Inn . . . . Chilton
Skip-Inn . . . . Stevens Point
Smile Inn . . . . Neenah
Step-In . . . . Manitowoc County

Club 2	Wisconsin Rapids
Club 9	Phillips
Club 10	Stevens Point
Club 11	Wausau
Club 12	Black River Falls
Club 12	Augusta

Club 13	Appleton
Club 14	La Crosse Area
Club 14	Mazomanie
Club 18	Mt. Horeb
Club 29	Marathon City
Club 35	Douglas County
Club 37	Eau Claire
Club 40	Colfax
Club 43	Shawano
Club 45	Clintonville
Club 47	Black Earth
Club 48	Rice Lake area
Club 53	La Crosse
Club 57	Thiensville
Club 64	Merrill
Club 70	Spooner
Club 73	Thorp
Club 77	Antigo
Club 83	North Lake
Club 95	Hixton
Club 98	Loyal
Club 107	Merrill
Club 2400	La Crosse
400 Club	Altoona
400 Club	Menomonie
400 Club	Neenah
515 Club	La Crosse
800 Club	La Crosse

You could hear the names Harmon Killebrew or Boog Powell and even if you knew only that they were baseball players, you could make a guess that they would be home run greats. Similarly in football, Bronko Nagurski sounds like a slashing, punishing runner. In a more literate sense, John Wayne would not have become John Wayne if he had stayed with his birth name of Marion Morrison. In the same vein, you can be reasonably sure that the taverns listed here would be places as comfortable to slip into as a pair of well worn shoes, where a joke could be heard, a pickled egg eaten, a foamy mug of beer savored and every conversation as predictable as night following day.

Rose's Brite Spot

Rose's Brite Spot - Fountain City

The Bean Hole - Hudson

Jim Holak's Tavern and Garage - Hillsboro

Sport's Tavern for Sports - Yuba

The Golden Frog - Fountain City

The Cherry Bowl Bar - Sturgeon Bay

Bavarian Heaven -Sheboygan

Uncle Gus's Bar - Wausau

Happyland - Superior

Rutabaga Tavern - Sheboygan Falls

Bean Sandwich - Durand

Keen Kutter Tavern - Cumberland

Crippen's Shebang - Eau Claire

Polish Hop - Agenda

Farmer's and Woodsmen's Bar - Park Falls

Home Sample Saloon - La Crosse

Ah-Ha Tavern - La Crosse

Polack Mary's - Stevens Point

The Hoople House - Marshfield

Laff-A-Lot Dance Hall - Stone Lake

Happy Jacks - North Seymour

Ding Dong Tavern - Boyd

Sunbeam Tavern - Chippewa Falls

Club Cigar - Superior

Olive's Zu Der Zee - Green Bay

Spit and Whistle - Prairie du Chien

Wishing Well Tap - Clintonville

Happy's Tavern - Evansville

Shady Glen Tavern - Hixton

High Life Tavern - Marinette

Happy Pines - Merrill

Happy's Tap - Merrill

Midget Bar - Merrill

Gesundheit Tavern - Merrill

Happy Hollow - Mosinee

Ed & Dot's Beer Bar - Norrie

Lyles's Beer Hut - Phillips

Jolly Farmer Bar - Randolph

Gusto Bar - Sheboygan

Hoovie's TicToc Tap - Tomahawk

Little Norway Bar - Wisconsin Dells

4-Ever Amber Bar - Hurley

Swing Club - Hurley

Club House Tavern - Laona

Fish Fry Tavern - Menasha

Cozy Nook - Jefferson

Wack's Tavern - Green River

Howie's Wonder Bar - Two Rivers

Hoo-Hoo Club - Oshkosh

Old Time Tavern - Gleason

What Goes In A Great Bar

The Moccasin Bar in Hayward had everything needed to satisfy the simple needs and wants of your basic Badger Barfly. What could go into this bar to improve it? Probably nothing short of a slightly tipsy Veronica Lake look-a-like with a fondness for playing Hank Williams on the jukebox and enough tokens in her purse to buy the house a round or two of Fitger's or Foxhead.

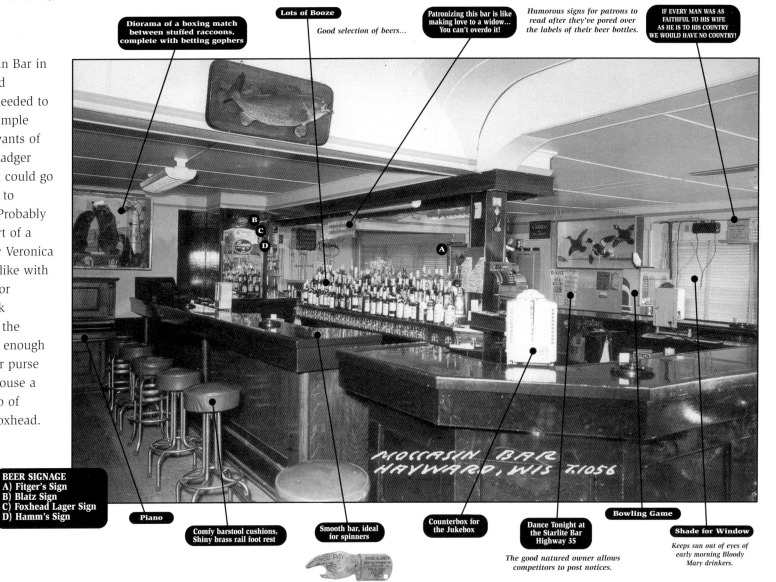

Diorama of a boxing match between stuffed raccoons, complete with betting gophers

Lots of Booze

Good selection of beers...

Patronizing this bar is like making love to a widow... You can't overdo it!

Humorous signs for patrons to read after they've pored over the labels of their beer bottles.

IF EVERY MAN WAS AS FAITHFUL TO HIS WIFE AS HE IS TO HIS COUNTRY WE WOULD HAVE NO COUNTRY!

BEER SIGNAGE
A) Fitger's Sign
B) Blatz Sign
C) Foxhead Lager Sign
D) Hamm's Sign

Piano

Comfy barstool cushions, Shiny brass rail foot rest

Smooth bar, ideal for spinners

Counterbox for the Jukebox

Dance Tonight at the Starlite Bar Highway 35

The good natured owner allows competitors to post notices.

Bowling Game

Shade for Window

Keeps sun out of eyes of early morning Bloody Mary drinkers.

160

Rose's Brite Spot, Fountain City

Beginning in 1946, Rose and Sandy Petrowski served cheer and Fountain Beer at the Brite Spot. The authors would like to recognize Rose for inspiring this book.

CLOSING TIME

Did you ever hear someone say when passing an old decrepit building, "If that building could talk, the stories it could tell." Take a look at this picture of the onetime Sylvia's Tavern, located on the shore of Lake Ellison at the end of a sand road in northern Wisconsin. Well, if this old building could talk, it would most likely slur its words, endlessly repeat unimportant points, and occasionally punctuate the conversation with saliva.

Sylvia's Tavern as it appeared a decade ago, and long after the last Blatz-sotted patron stumbled out.

At Rose's Brite Spot, after Sandy died, Rosie and her sister Lelah ran the business until 1992. They are both now deceased. When they operated the bar, it was frequented by locals from Blair, Ettrick and the surrounding area, and the patrons helped Rosie and Lelah tend bar at times. There was an outdoor bathroom, no indoor water, and if you wanted ice in your drinks, it was chipped off a block with an ice pick. The Brite Spot is now a private residence, presumably with running water.

The El Paso Cabin Bar never did install indoor plumbing, it closed in 1989 and Ernie passed away soon after. The building is now used as a seasonal bait shop.

A close examination of the photo of the deer in the tavern at Boettcher's Deer Farm, shows the instability of the brewing industry as well as the seemingly unchanging nature of the candy bar market. All of the beers on tap or advertised in the picture are either out of business or are orphan brands, existing in name only and brewed by other companies. On the other hand, every brand of candy in view is still readily available today.

The original Carnival Club in Hurley was destroyed by a fire years ago. A nightclub has recently opened there, using the same name, and also featuring dancing girls. Hurley had vice related scandals all the way up to 1980. That year, a county judge was removed from office and sent to prison for lying to a grand jury and obstructing justice in regards to sex related charges. Tawdry behavior at that time, by the late 1990s it would be presidential.

Charlie's Mistletoe is still in business, but completely remodeled and under a different name. The great dog is buried behind the building by the shore of the lake. Charlie himself is probably buried somewhere in town.

The Buckhorn of Rice Lake is long gone. Otto Rinslbacher died sometime in the 1970s. His unusual collection was dispersed to several museums and historical groups and the building itself has been leveled. The Buckhorn of Spooner remains in business and is one of the great taverns of Wisconsin.

Fightin' Fifield, the former Fisticuffs Capital of Wisconsin, once had 27 saloons, it now has just one. Two log cabin style taverns, dating from the 1930s or earlier, were torn down in the summer of 2002.

Besides being a musician, Boyd Skuldt was an auctioneer and an inventor too. In 1960, he patented a collapsible canvas tent trailer and founded a company that built and sold them throughout the Midwest. He still plays the guitar, but the rest of his one-man orchestra is in storage.

In Watertown, the saloon at 121 West Main, which was run by one William Beisner, in later years became the Streamline Bar and after that it went by the inelegant name of "The Feedbag." The address is now occupied by a portion of the Watertown Daily Times.

In Chilton in the summer of 1942, the 29-year-old Melchior Bloomer stood trial on a charge of first degree manslaughter in the death of the 76-year-old Chief of Police Steffes. He was acquitted. He stayed in business and lived in Chilton until the late 1960s or 1970s. There is now a bowling alley at the site of the tavern. If you are in the area, absolutely make it a point to stop at the Calumet Brew Pub in Chilton.

There is still lots of shooting going in and about the vicinity of the Halfway House, but nowadays it is by deer hunters shooting whitetails on the outside and wild turkey on the inside. The Barnes area saloon in which hard-drinking Farmer Nelson took a bullet for taking an interest in the bartender's wife, is still in business after 80 + years. It is in a new building, however, the original log building burnt in the 1960s.

In 1945, Ralph Capone, brother of Al, bought Billy's Bar. Ralph was a member of several civic organizations in town and by every account was a well regarded citizen. But, the citizens of Mercer knew him by his behavior there and not in Chicago. The bar and hotel have since been replaced by a parking lot.

Mike Healy, who owned the Walter's Brewery in 1987, really was ahead of his time. In addition to brewing the fine old standby Walter's, "The Beer That Was Beer," Mike turned out several craft brews, including the fondly remembered Eau Claire All Malt (one of the first beers in recent times to declare that it was compliant with the Rheinheitsgebot - Bavarian Purity Law). He also reestablished the tradition of the outdoor beer garden in Eau

Claire. The new Walter's Park was at the same location where one had been in the 1880s. It was a bucolic setting with trees, picnic tables, and live music. On a summer afternoon or evening, it was a perfect place to enjoy a glass of suds. The park was closed by the city after too many crabby neighbors complained about the patrons having a good time. It is now fenced-in and neglected.

Ah, to sit down to play cards in a saloon in a town called "Pokerville" in turn-of-the-century Wisconsin! "Uh, bartender, how about a fresh deck and a mug of Old Regulator, please." Unfortunately, Pokerville cashed in its chips long ago. The village featured several saloons, one of which featured a "Tenpin Alley" for an early version of bowling. By the 1930s, all that was left was an abandoned building or two. Its location was about one mile from the present day town of Blue Mound.

The Moccasin Bar of Hayward is still operating under the same name. Several record breaking muskies are on display as well as a large assortment of taxidermical oddities. Among the curiosities to be viewed today are the boxing animals that appear in the photo on page 160. It is well worth a stop to see. The foot rail is gone, as are the piano, counterbox, and the availability of Fitger's, Foxhead and Blatz.

In Fountain City, the Golden Frog is also still going strong, or as the locals say, "Business is hopping." The Monarch is still "the place for a good time around the billiard tables, or with cards, or just with a glass of refreshing beer."

Do try the Fountain Brew, brewed to the original recipe by the Viking Brewing Company and served only at the Monarch. It was named one of the "100 Great Wisconsin Taverns" by Dennis Broyer in his 1999 book. We agree. Another product of the Fountain Brewing Company still lives on as well. They had a brand called Fountain Club in the late 1950s. When the brewmaster moved on to Heileman's in La Crosse, supposedly he tinkered with the recipe a smidgen and the result was the very popular, long selling Heileman's Special Export.

On the subject of the Great Existing Taverns of Wisconsin, and we had hoped you'd ask, here is a 12-pack plus of the authors' favorite taverns, in alphabetical order, based on a complicated formula involving beer selection, availability of pickled eggs, presence of dogs, jukebox selection, congeniality, original furnishings, etc.: The Anchor in Superior, Baumgertner's in Monroe, The Buckhorn in Spooner, The Casino in La Crosse, the Cave Inn in Roberts, D and D's in Yuba, Joe's in Fountain City, Judy's in Iron River, Ken and Dee's in Wilson, the Harmony Bar in Madison, the Kurth Brewery Bar in Columbus, Leo and Leona's in Newburg Corners, The Longhorn in Minong, The Missouri Tavern in Springfield Corners, The Nine Mile Club near Oxbo, Rolland's Brew Pub of Chilton, The Twin Ports Brewing Company of Superior. Posthumous honors are extended to both Sylvia's in Barnes and Rose's Brite Spot near Fountain City. The three saddest words of poetry or prose are those little words, "this tavern closed."

The Gopher Hole is still in business, but like a real Gopher Hole, it is not open in the winter. Stop by for one anytime between April and October.

No trace of Mary Hogan's Tavern outside of Plainfield remains if the directions that appeared in the newspaper article were correct. However, there is an abandoned tavern on the same road in the opposite direction, but the authors did not want to look like creeps by asking the locals about it. Hite Snow's tavern is also long gone, presumably bulldozed over during the widening of the highway. Cad's Tavern has been completely modernized and operates under a different name. One of the few identifiable remnants is a metal sign post that once held a porcelain "Cad's Tavern" sign. Nowadays they serve a very tasty fish fry on Friday nights.

The location of Trixie's in Minocqua is now occupied by B.J.'s Sport Shop. We are not sure if B and J are the owners' initials or a tribute to the previous business on the site.

The kegged beer that was attempted to be tapped at the Osceola temperance meeting could very well have been the product of Veit Geiger's brewery at nearby Osceola Mills (changed to Osceola in 1897), which operated from the late 1870s to sometime in the 1880s. This was the same brewery that was written about in the 1933 article on page 96. Today, virtually no trace of the building exists.

Farmington Center was immediately south of Osceola in Polk County.

Stills and moonshine did not die out with Prohibition. An Arcadia couple recently told the story of when they moved into the area in the early 1980s, they would stop from time to time at a local rural tavern. While the wife, who drank beer or wine had no problems, the husband, who liked to have a cocktail, would behave very strangely after only having a drink or two, including one time in which he drove into the ditch on the way home. The place was later raided by the sheriff and other authorities and a local farmer was arrested for supplying very high-octane moonshine to the joint. In other words, using the moonshine as an alcoholic base would yield a mixed drink with 3 or 4 times the potency of a normal one.

It is not unusual for dives to end up in some type of water, and the feral saloon outside of Nelson, mentioned in the Teasdale Report, was not an exception. Absolutely no trace remains of the river bottom roadhouse; the approximate area where it was located is today backwater swamp. A few miles downstream are the more substantial remains of the Castle Rock Brewery. The limestone foundation sits a hundred or so feet into the woods north of Highway 35 and about 2 or 3 miles south of Fountain City. Stop at the Midway Bar for beer or cocktail and afterwards look for a gravel road leading up the hillside a couple hundred feet south of their parking lot. You should be able to see the remains just beyond a No Trespassing sign.

Jockey's Tavern in Waupun had banjos plunking and cocktail glasses tinkling until about 1968 or so. The building at 300 East Main underwent several transformations from department store to supper club to its present state as a Chinese restaurant.

Happily, in Lena, the extraordinary Hunter's and Fisherman's Tavern remains in business with the extensive collection of taxidermy still on display.

In Wauzeka, Oscar no longer provides a congenial evening, but his tavern is still open, complete with the 30 foot bar. It was one of the last taverns in Wisconsin to offer the use of spittoons to the patrons, with several available along the bar until late in the 1950s.

JFK's stop in Spooner helped in the primary where he defeated Hubert Humphrey. In the general election, Richard Nixon carried Spooner 768 to 560.

Nips of Moquah is now "Esther's," and males can now purchase and consume soft drinks there. They even sell O'Doul's and similar products, for crying out loud! On a positive note, it remains a member of the prestigious "Outdoor Biffie" club.

The old mill in Denmark that housed Hendricksen's Tavern still houses a tavern. Although the structure is nearly 100 years removed from the milling industry, during a recent remodeling they found small piles of grain on and about the joists and undersides of the flooring.

The Frank Liddlefeld who was murdered in Stacey's Saloon in Rhinelander was in all likelihood the husband of the Widow Liddlefeld mentioned in the Teasdale report. Her secretive sideline apparently allowed her to keep her residence in the nice neighborhood for a few years, but by 1920, she was no longer listed in the city phone book. Also, seeing as she wished to keep her activities a secret, we thought it best to do the same - her and her husband's names are the only pseudonyms in this book.

The Midget, "Home of Gadgets" and funnyman bartender Fred Majors, remains in business outside of Tomahawk. Fred and his gags and gadgets are long gone. Let's hope, as you are reading this, he is in Heaven's Tap Room sliding a whoopie cushion on the barstool of Hilma Willa or offering Uncle Ab an exploding cigar.

In Minong, what was Ronnie's Tavern is now the Longhorn and is remarkably unchanged. It is well worth a stop, presumably dogs are still welcome.

In tiny Pine River, the taverns that displayed the Berliner and Chief Oshkosh porcelain beer signs are both gone. One of the buildings sat vacant for a long time before collapsing about 15 years ago. No one remembers what happened to the other building. For the remaining tavern, Saturday nights are slow and there is a 8:00 p.m. closing time. The busy days are Sundays with polka bands playing every afternoon.

Ma Gordon's Tavern was moved several years after her death in 1972. It continued to operate at the new location for awhile and was then converted into a private residence. The whereabouts, or existence of, her reed organ is unknown. However, the sounds of her voice and the instrument possibly live on. Besides recording Ma, the late Professor Stratham-Thomas recorded dozens of other folk songs, instrumentals, recitations and related musical treasures. She went to nearly every corner of Wisconsin throughout the 1940s in search of old time musicians of the era. The tapes made on these trips, including Ma's 1941 session, were given to the Library of Congress. According to Folk Songs Out of Wisconsin, the professor possessed "the personal characteristics that make a good collector: warmth, self-confidence, and a touch of humility… dealing with plain, often reticent people in out-of-the-way places… success or failure hinged on the ability to meet lumberjacks, fiddlers, and rural housewives on their own terms, openly and sympathetically." Hmmm… after that endorsement, I would say she put away her share of Schoens and pretzels after all.

Ed Bauer, the "World's Largest Tavern Owner," at one time tipped the scales at a bit over 800 pounds, or the equivalent of over 4 - 16 gallon kegs of beer. He had a brother who was heavy as well, but not at the world class proportions of Ed. Supposedly, they both were big players in the Campbellsport area liquor industry, during and after Prohibition. The never-married Ed passed away around 1960. His former tavern is still in business as the Amber Inn.

The Loafers Lodge is now Fred and Jerry's. Glenn Hope left the tavern business and became a well respected antiques dealer. Sadly, he was killed in a car accident in the late 1990s while returning home from an out of town antiques show.

Where the Port Washington Brewery once stood is now occupied by a condominium. What became of the wonderful beer machine at the brewery is a mystery.

Uncle Ab's smoke and gambling-filled establishment in Mineral Point, which was built in the 1830s, was later connected to several other buildings in the 1860s, and became the Walker House. That business operated until 1900. Afterwards it spent quite a while as a boarding house. Some locals say it was haunted by Ed Chaffee, who was hung for murder in Mineral Point in 1842. It is doubtful, but repeated just the same, that he rode to the gallows astride his own coffin while swigging a bottle of beer. Ed was also quite a jokester, for his last meal he supposedly requested "a slice of the heart" of the judge who presided at his trial. (It was denied.) The building was refurbished in the 1980s but has been sitting idle for several years. It is worth a trip to see the building, though, There is a great brewpub, the Brewery Creek Inn, a short distance away, and Mineral Point is one of the most picturesque towns in Wisconsin.

At one time, if names mean anything, Merrill just possibly could have been one of the greatest towns in Wisconsin to go for an evening of pleasurable bar hopping. In the 1950s the town boasted the highest Wisconcentration of taverns per capita in the state, besting the claims from Eau Claire, Oliver, Cudahy, La Crosse and Superior. What with the Happy Tap, the Midget Bar, the Gesundheit Tavern, Buttsy and Evie's, and the Happy Pine, how could you miss? They are almost all gone now. The exception is the Gesundheit Tavern, which is still in business at the same location, just as it has been since 1874. A nice place to stop for one when you're in town. Buttsy & Evie's was moved across the highway about twenty years ago and remains in business as the Hub Inn. No doodlesucker music there nowadays, just a poorly stocked CD jukebox.

The Blue Heron outside of Hayward is still open as a supper club and bar. Alas, if modern day Sad Sacks at the Blue Heron want to commiserate over "He'll Have to Go," they will need to bring a Walkman with them because there is no longer a jukebox on the site. Nobody remembers what happened to the splendid Wurlitzer 24. However, if you go west, near the Minnesota border, there exists a Machu Picchu-like site of post-war Americana. A small tavern that sits by a gravel county road looks from the outside to be a typical country bar. But in a corner on the inside is one tiny little area that time has forgotten. In that corner sits one of the rarest jukeboxes ever

made, a chrome-laden Philbin Maestro dating from the early 1950s. The box is still stocked with Hank Williams and Ricky Nelson 78s, ready to play for a nickel. Not only that, but on the wall behind the juke is a Regal Supreme Beer Mirror, advertising the product of a brewery that went out of business about 1953. The important point is that this is not some kind of retro-themed decoration - it is not a recently manufactured setting. It is a very small area that has stayed the same for about a half a century. You can think sentimentally of this tiny time resistant area being the lone remnant of a simpler era, or you can look at it as a place that the owners just never got around to changing. But however you think of it, let's just keep its existence a secret between you and us and don't let any big time collector creep in on it.

Olga's Tavern, the former home of Joe the Monkey, is now the Sportsmen's Inn. As for Joe, while many monkeys spent their lives in servitude to an organ grinder, he got to do his own organ grinding. Joe had been resident of Olga's for about 4 years when the Milwaukee Zoo called saying they had heard of Joe and requested his stud services. They had a lonely lady monkey at the zoo who needed companionship. Joe left for the big city to what seemed would be an enjoyable retirement for the little fellow. However, after 6 months, the zookeepers called to say Joe was in bad shape. They did not know whether he picked up some kind of illness in his new environment or he was just plain spent from the unceasing

demands of the monkess. Art immediately went to see Joe and was instantly recognized by his little friend. By that point, Joe was partially paralyzed and had to struggle to greet Art. There was little that could be done, but Art was able to be with Joe during his final hours. Later in the 1970s, Art was elected and reelected Sheriff of Ozaukee County and served in that position for 12 years.

In Danbury, Howland's Resort is long gone. Those nice conetops sitting on the bar no doubt hit the trash can a few minutes after Myron and the photographer emptied them.

In Beaver Dam, the Eagle Buffet and Schrader's have been gone for many, many years. The Hotel Beaver was razed in the late 1990s. It has been over 30 years since the last bullhead dinner was served by the late Ma & Pa Jones. Pa was the self-proclaimed "World's Fastest Bullhead Skinner." There are no recognized successors for this title, and the bullheads sleep easier in the depths of Beaver Dam Lake. As for Windy, he died in 1967. Today what was his tavern is doing just fine. Now known as Maly's Bus Stop, you can enjoy an excellent Friday night fish fry as you view murals dating from the 1930s to the 1970s. Another Beaver Dam musician with ties to a Beaver Dam saloon ended up very famous. Actor, saxophone player, and genuine Hollywood nice guy Fred MacMurray grew up in Beaver Dam. His grandfather was the owner of Martin's Saloon.

In the Stevens Point section of the Teasdale report, the detective curiously mentions a "can

167

of beer." According to the "Beer Can Collectors of America," beer cans were not introduced until about 1933. Perhaps he is referring to some type of metal mug. Of the people identified in the report: the conniving Gullen sisters, Harvey Wade, Fred Sanders, Stella Sieps and the bartenders, only Fred Sanders appeared in the 1914 Stevens Point City Directory. The randy Fred Sanders was a painter who lived at 545 Water Street.

In Superior, Alex O'Kash quit bartending and became a beat cop for several years before taking an upper level position with the state of Wisconsin. Recently, he published three very interesting books of his reminiscence of the 1940s and 1950s. The Blue Moon was leveled years ago. Several members of the family now run Molly's which is on of the most interesting bars in Wisconsin and worth a visit. The pictures of Silver Boots Mona were part of an unusual discovery. Herman's Pool Hall stood vacant for many years after the owner's death in the late 1960s or early 1970s. When the ramshackle building was being torn down, an envelope containing about 25 black and white photos was found hidden behind the backbar. The photos were mostly of his consort, Silver Boots Mona in various poses with various people. The TipTop Bar, which was shown in one of the photos, was next to the pool hall and was also leveled. The last time anyone in Superior saw Mona was in the mid-1970s. Of the saloons mentioned in the Teasdale report and along Third Street,

almost all are gone, many of the addresses are vacant lots. Although, some things don't change. The building, which 80 years ago housed the Naughtous Saloon and Hazel Long's "neatly furnished" sporting house, is today home to two bars, one of which caters to the hard drinking, newest generation of Superior saloon patrons, the other features some very common "exotic" dancers.

The Potosi Brewery called it quits on December 31, 1972 and the buildings soon fell in to disrepair. Happily, today the brewery is going a restoration which will include a microbrewery, restaurant and hopefully a national breweriana museum. The former taproom is still in use as a tavern. You can see more about the project at www.potosibrewery.com.

In Oshkosh, when the Teasdale detective's self censored description of Pueppkes as a "real H---hole, a very tough class frequents this place," he must have meant a heck hole. In a circa 1913 photo of the saloon, not used in this book, a sign on the wall near an elegant backbar offers buttermilk by the glass, for gosh darn sakes.

Ruekert's Tavern in Bonduel is still in business. The establishment is now called the 3rd Generation in honor of the third generation of Ruekert's operating the place. They no longer give away monkeys or decorate their ads with swastikas. Incidentally, the use of the swastikas was really quite harmless at the time. You might know, the swastika is a very old design. Until

World War II and it's close association with the Nazis, swastikas were considered symbols of good luck.

You can be the jury in the Cad Bates murder. There have been two books written about the incident. A very fine account by District Attorney John Potter entitled "The Tangled Web" was published by the Waubesa Press a few years back. The daughter-in-law of Ed Kaneski wrote "Please Pass the Roses," which defended her late father-in-law. What was indefensible is the fact that in his sworn testimony during the trial, on the night of the murder, Ed said that he ordered "a bottle of beer," instead of opting for a delicious glass of Point Special which Cad had on tap.

Outside of Park Falls, with bottle raised after 50 summers and 50 winters, Chiann the Cowboy still stands; always wishing and hoping for one last delicious drop of his beloved Rhinelander Export. The Rhinelander Brewery did not last as long as its cement-headed fan, the taps were turned off in 1967. Happily, Fred Smith's concrete creations are still on display very near to where they were created. Although Fred passed away in 1976, the collection is being tended to by "The Friends of Fred Smith" and the Price County Forestry Department, after being given to them by the Kohler Foundation. The Rock Garden Tavern is still in business as well, under a new name with no connection to the collection next door. While, thankfully, Fred's sculpture artistry can still be enjoyed today, unfortunately, his talents as a musician exist only as a memory to a handful of Park Falls old-timers. Inside the modestly decorated tavern Fred would occasionally treat his customers to Boyd Skuldt-like musical performances: singing and shouting with sleigh bells tied to his knees while playing a fiddle or mandolin, dancing on the tavern floor or leaping onto the tables. What transpired inside might have been as astonishing a sight as the festive, but immobile, statuary he left behind.

In the early 1980s, the Hoople House was locked and abandoned. Taped to the inside window of the front door was a note, handwritten in pencil, asking, "Please don't knock... everyone is sick." The interior of the empty bar was illuminated only by the light of a neon sign for Figi's Certified Beer. Today the building is completely gone and replaced by a mobile home.

A 1958 photo of Tibbie's of Indian Ford shows the giant Old Style Grenadier absent; he perhaps had marched northward for a date with the Miller Maiden.

Barefoot Charlie's, outside of Land O' Lakes, survived (without Charlie) until well into the 1980s when it burned. To that point it had remained largely intact, including the stump barstools and the beer dispensing tree. All that was left, as of the summer of 2000, was a stone fireplace and crumbling chimney that were surrounded by the encroaching northwoods.

History is a study of changes, and fact and fiction of Americana includes spectacular falls, losses, and regrettable transformations. Changes of stature from the tremendous into the lamentable, in the manner of Jay Gatsby, with dreams unachieved, floating lifeless in his swimming pool, the mutation of vinyl records to compact discs, interleague play, the mass appeal of light beer, from as vast an entity as the vanished herds of free roaming buffalo to a rusted and broken beer clock in an abandoned brewery. You can ponder those changes, all forever, none for better, and realize that is what history is made of. As Ruth Popper said in the closing moments of the Last Picture Show, "Sonny, you shouldna come here. I'm around that corner now, you've ruined it and your needing it won't make it come back." Then also consider the misfortune and plight of Ervin Ressie's Gingerbread Tavern. The aged, beached river boat, where wooden floors had warped with age, and booths and walls were darkened to rich hues by scores of scores of pipes and cigars, where hunters and fishermen exchanged tales, and inebriates occasionally traded punches, where money could be spent in a jukebox, for a pickled pig's foot or a glass of Peerless Amber, that great tavern operated until 1985. To that splendid part of Wisconsin history, the fates did not show the same mercy that was extended to Barefoot Charlie's or The Carnival Club. In a pitiful metamorphosis, the building as of 2003, was an incense filled shop featuring crafts, crystals and new age CDs.

Thanks To... (maybe some hokey beer toast here) ———————•

Evelyn Ayer

Baraboo Historical Society

James Bennett

Berlin Historical Society

Angie Bronson

Buckhorn Tavern in Spooner

Nellie Bird

Phillip Braithwaite

Tim Callies

Darlene Chaney

Eldbjorg Tobin and the
Chippewa Valley Museum

Harry Ellsworth Cole

Jim Coole

Betty Cowley

Scott Cross and the Oshkosh
Public Museum

Doug Dahl of the Doll House in
Hammond

Chuckles Davis

Cindy Douglas and the Saukville
Historical Society

Cecelia Dwyer

Elcora Cigar Company

Dolly Ferrell and the Eagle River
Historical Society

Ron Finstead

Greg Frey

Carol Fure and the Burnett
County Historical Society

the Family of Bessie Gordon

Amy Galarowicz

Tom Geise

Annette Griswold and the
Milwaukee Journal Sentinel

Louise Guggisberg

Dick & Regina Hartel

Kay Haen and Dennis Schartner
of the Institute Saloon

Mike Healey

Susan Hilliard of the Pheasant Inn

Bill Hefnieder

Art & Jean Helm

Shirley Hess and the Hartford
Historical Society

Nita Hope

Bob Jackson

William Jaenning and the
Watertown Historical Society

Marj Kammueller and The
Fountain City Area Historical
Society

James Keuhl of the Pleasant View

Lori and John of the Monarch
Tavern in Fountain City

Darlene Metlzer of the Prescott
Area Historical Society

John Mogenson

Sandy Moen

Buttsy Mosser & Family

Molly and Oscar Muench

Shawn Naggy

The New London Historical
Society

Marti O'Brien

the Osceola Sun

Alex O'Kash

Lucien Orsoni

Mike Paulus

Arden Peterson

John Pickar

Terry Post

The Prentice Historical Society

Ervin Ressie and family

Bob Schuster

Marvon Shay

Barry Singer

Boyd Skuldt

Marvin Shay

The helpful employees
at the Spooner Advocate

Steven Stenslie

Stevens Point Journal

Kathy Stuart of the
Cascade bar in Osceola

Robert Swanson

Jenny Terry

Sharon Thayer

Sandy Thorsen & Family

The Tomah Journal

John Turk

Allan Vannatta and the Potosi
Brewery Foundation

Walt Vogel and the Two Rivers
Historical Society

George Waxwing

Doug White

The Wisconsin Historical Society

The Wisconsin State Journal

The Wisconsin Tavern League

William Zimmer and the Neenah
Historical Society

The Public Libraries of
Rhinelander, Somerset, Superior
and Waupun

The Area Research Centers in
Green Bay, Menomonie, La Crosse
and Stevens Point

Acknowledgments ━━━━━━━━━━━━━━━━━━━━●

1. Badger Breweries
   by Wayne Kroll

2. **Stagecoach and Tavern Tales of the Old Northwest**
   Harry Ellsworth Cole
   Southern Illinois University Press
   P.O. Box 3697, Carbondale, IL 62902-3697

3. Wisconsin Death Trip... Michael Lesy
   Anchor Books Doubleday... 1973
   666 Fifth Avenue, NY, NY 10103

4. **Yuba - A Story of a Wisconsin Czech Community**
   Hynek Printing
   175 North Congress Street
   Richlind Center, WI 53581
   Phillip Braithwaite
   4996 Tower Line Road, Marshall, WI 53559
   608-655-3700
   -or-
   Gorman Braihwaite
   804 Hillsborough Ave.,
   Hillsboro, WI 54634

5. Wisconsin Magazine of History Winter 1965-1966
   (Teasdale story)

6. **Gangster Holidays "The Lore and Legends of the**
   Bad Guys"
   Tom Holatz
   North Star Press of St. Cloud, Inc. 1989
   P.O. Box 451,
   St. Cloud, MN 56302

7. **Hurley - Still No Angel**
   Lewis C. Reimann 1954
   Northwoods Publishers
   1725 Landsdowne Road, Ann Arbor, MI

8. Breweries of Wisconsin
   Jerry Apps
   University of Wisconsin Press 1992
   114 North Murray Street
   Madison, WI 53715

9. True Tales of La Crosse
   Copyright 1994 by Douglas Connell
   P.O. Box 2372
   La Crosse, WI 54602

10. The American Sketch Book : A Collection of
    Historical Incidents With Descriptions of
    Corresponding Localities
    Edited By Bella French
    Sketch Book Company 1874-75
    La Crosse, WI Publishers

11. **No Direction Home: The Life and Music of Bob**
    Dylan
    Robert Shelton
    Beech Tree Books
    105 Madison Avenue, NY 10016

12. **The Lumberjack Queens**
    J.C. Ryan
    St. Louis County Historical Society 634.9 r955l

13. The Art of Fred Smith: The Wisconsin Concrete
    Park
    Lisa Stone & Jim Zanzi
    Published by Price County Forestry Department
    and Friends of Fred Smith Weber and Sons, Inc.
    Park Falls, WI

14. Liberace: An American Boy
    Darden Asbury Pyron
    University of Chicago Press 2000

15. Folk Songs Out of Wisconsin
    Edited by Harry B. Peters
    The State Historical Society of Wisconsin 1977

16. The Tangled Web
    John M. Potter
    Waubesa Press
    ISBN 1-878569-13-9

17. Please Pass the Roses
    Colleen Kohler Kanieski

18. "STALAG WISCONSIN: Inside WW II Prisoner-of-
    War Camps" Published by Betty Cowley

19. William Culbert interview extracts
    Joanne Flemming interview June 29, 1986
    Chippewa Valley Museum

20. Berlin's Memories in 1976

21. Stratford Centennial Book

22. "A History of Prescott, Wisconsin"
    by Dorothy Eaton Ahlgren and Mary Cotter Beeler
    copyright 1996 by the Prescott Area Historical
    Society.

Newspapers

Bar Closes But Memories Continue
Steven Point Journal
May 1, 1982
Nick Schultz

On the Write Side
John Kenny
Tomah Journal and Monitor-Herald
August 1, 1963

(note: BOLD means quoted directly, not-bold used as general reference)

Bill Moen is a graduate of Concordia College of St. Paul. In his career, he has worked as a Technical Recruiter, a Vocational Counselor and as a Mechanical Designer, but one of his favorite positions was one of his earliest when he checked IDs and took cover charge in a Duluth nightclub. He has previously written articles and record reviews for Midwest Wine and Spirits and Kicks Magazine. His first memory of a Wisconsin Tavern was being given the Bum's Rush at age 10, after wandering into the Cherry Bowl Bar in Sturgeon Bay and attempting to purchase a bottle of Orange Crush. He and his wife Sandra, and their two boys live in the Twin Cites.

Doug Davis was born in Germany but has been a Wisconsin resident most of his adult life. He has been a Social Worker for a non-profit organization for 15 years. Doug has written articles for Lake Superior Magazine and the American Breweriana Association. Doug plays and sings in the Huckleberries who have burned it down in dozens of northern Wisconsin backwoods taverns for over 25 years. Doug also enjoys kayaking, collecting 78s and breweriana from Wisconsin. His partner Louise and two children, Amanda and Alexander, live in Superior.

We'd love to do a Volume II, or better yet, "Another Round of Badger Bars and Tavern Tales." If you would like to contribute interesting photos, stories, or items of note, please let us know. Contact us at badgerbars@taverntales.net

If you are interested, there are two fine organizations for collectors of breweriana: the American Breweriana Association and the National Association Breweriana Advertising. Their websites are: www.americanbreweriana.org and www.nababrew.org